Wow foi

When I was asked to write a moving book, I was and still am honored, for I had recently read Bishop Blake's books, which pleasantly and richly impacted me spiritually and educationally. After having read this book, I am extremely pleased to announce to the world that "Bishop Blake has done it again."

Once I started reading this book, I found it difficult to stop, for the more I read, the more I wanted to read. This book is written in a way that makes it an enjoyable read, especially in light of the subject matter. Further, this book is written in a way that both a person with a fifth grade education and a person with a PhD can easily navigate and understand what is being said and taught. This is not an easy task.

I sincerely appreciate Bishop Blake for writing this book.

Attorney David Walker, P.A.
Law Offices, Stuart, Florida

From rags to riches—spiritual foundation or pipe dream? Is the pursuit of wealth a carnal desire? In *My Wealthy Place*, Pastor Cornelius Blake sheds light on this heartrending matter. We should be constantly working on self-improvement. He reminds us that were are not by ourselves in this quest no matter the reason or your current or past condition. Pastor Cornelius started life in what most would consider dire circumstances and climbed higher through faith!

My Wealthy Place shows us that we each have the power to use our abilities to secure and enjoy God's bounty as we faithfully use our God-given talents to acquire wealth. Enjoy your pursuit of wealth knowing that God is always with you. This book gives you the tools you will need.

Eula R. Clarke
Attorney at Law, Stuart City Commissioner

Unfortunately, we live in a get rich society; even more unfortunate is the fact that this spirit has made its way into the church. It was for that reason I had some initial reservation about what I thought was yet another book on how Christians can name it and claim it. I was wrong about this one.

Bishop Cornelius Blake has done his homework and research: this book has a solid, biblical basis for the arguments he makes about acquiring wealth. I am looking forward to putting into practice the biblical principles that are jam-packed in this book.

Mr. Shamus Gordon

The CANDLE Project, President and CEO

My Wealthy Place is a book full of exhilarating knowledge about God's thoughts and principles regarding wealth. I was completely enthralled while reading its pages. Once you begin to read its pages, it will captivate your attention, educate you, and motivate you to reach higher heights than you ever dreamed possible. Moreover, if you follow its principles, it will position you to receive all that God has in store and planned for you (Jeremiah 29:11)

Dr. Donna Mills

S. Lucie County School Board Member

My daily goal is to help people become properly protected, debt free, and financially independent. *My Wealthy Place* is full of ways to accomplish those things. Read it, apply is principles, share it with others, and most important, give God all the glory for your journey.

Rod L. Gaskin

Financial Coach

My Wealthy Place is a clear and compelling read. It posits that sound biblical teaching on money is the catalyst for change and transformation when it comes to economic empowerment. The lived experience of the author is proof that the practical application of the principles contained in Scripture can move anyone from a mind-set of scarcity to experience abundance.

Bishop Delroy Powell
National Leader for New Testament Assembly, England

My Wealthy Place takes you to a destination most people spend a lifetime searching to find. It causes you to question your individual gifts and talents in such a way that draws you closer to the source, the Creator. Bishop Blake's teaching has done spiritually what most bankers attempt to do financially, that is, get people thinking, talking, and acting on how to acquire, grow, and retain wealth. The central message that God gives every person the ability to generate wealth is the key to unlock His supernatural generosity and what was intended for humanity collectively and individually. This book compels you to reevaluate what you think you know about talent and treasure and to reconnect to the one true source of all things valuable.

Natasha Fernander-Johnson
Banker

I am so honored that God allowed me to meet Bishop Cornelius Blake. He is a man of great revelation and truth. Everyone who reads and applies the perpetual principles in this book will definitely experience their wealthy place!

Dr. Shannon C. Cook
Cochairman, The Power2Prosper

Many people live paycheck to paycheck and figure they cannot save; however, everyone can save. It just takes discipline. The most important advice that I can recommend is to start saving early, make a budget, and stick to it. Interesting fact: 55 percent of millionaires develop and live on a budget.

My Wealthy Place provides practical advice so everyone can create the future they desire, not a future someone else designs for them. Let's all use the gifts and talents we were blessed with to achieve financial wealth and prosperity.

Dawn Bloomfield
Banker

∾

My Wealthy Place
Psalm 66:12

MY WEALTHY PLACE

How to Go From Being Broke to Being Blessed

Cornelius Blake

WESTBOW
PRESS®
A DIVISION OF THOMAS NELSON
& ZONDERVAN

This book is a work of non-fiction. Unless otherwise noted, the author and the publisher make no explicit guarantees as to the accuracy of the information contained in this book and in some cases, names of people and places have been altered to protect their privacy.

WestBow Press books may be ordered through booksellers or by contacting:

WestBow Press
A Division of Thomas Nelson & Zondervan
1663 Liberty Drive
Bloomington, IN 47403
www.westbowpress.com
1 (866) 928-1240

Because of the dynamic nature of the Internet, any web addresses or links contained in this book may have changed since publication and may no longer be valid. The views expressed in this work are solely those of the author and do not necessarily reflect the views of the publisher, and the publisher hereby disclaims any responsibility for them.

Any people depicted in stock imagery provided by Thinkstock are models, and such images are being used for illustrative purposes only.
Certain stock imagery © Thinkstock.

ISBN: 978-1-5127-4788-1 (sc)
ISBN: 978-1-5127-4789-8 (hc)
ISBN: 978-1-5127-4787-4 (e)

Library of Congress Control Number: 2016910715

Print information available on the last page.

WestBow Press rev. date: 08/30/2016

~

Thou hast caused men to ride over our heads; we went through fire and through water: but thou broughtest us out into a wealthy place.

—Psalm 66:12 KJV

~

Foreword

Don't fear, little flock. Your Father wants to share his kingdom with you.
—Luke 12:32 ERV

Reverend Cornelius Blake has written this book in a brilliant, balanced approach at understanding how to manage money before it manages you. His background lends itself to understanding the right approach to money management. Born in Jamaica from meager means, he has become a student of how to manage little until it evolves into more.

Through family and faith in God, he was able to relocate to England and during that time educate himself in various areas of money management and life skills.

His quote, "Unlike geese, who can fly in only one direction (north or south) due to their genetic coding or instinct, you can fly east, west, north, or south for a better life." He explains that opportunity is no longer just local but global.

Having lived in various parts of the world, he has a broader understanding of how money works in different environments and different stages of life. Bishop Blake has opened our eyes so we don't have to go just one direction; there are many paths to follow that can bring success to our lives.

This book is less financial analysis and more the understanding that geographical boundaries can and should be removed.

Cornelius is a powerful ordained bishop in the Church of God and has a wealth of knowledge in dealing with people through his daily encounters with his parishioners.

Because of his abilities to communicate from the pulpit, his skills have allowed him to be not only skilled in that area but also put his experiences in book form to help those who need a broader understanding of money management. This explains the popularity and appeal this book will have to any reader.

This book explains the challenge to your wealthy place. Through this book, you are reminded the only thing between you and your wealth is how you think.

Bishop Blake, thank you for bringing balance biblically and financially into our lives.

Bishop (Dr.) Keith L. Ivester
Administrative Bishop
Church of God Florida

Dr. Cornelius Blake is one of the most qualified people, I believe, in the Christian world and is able to bring this truth to believers and non-believers at the same time. As the subjects of Wealth and Prosperity seem to be major topics of readers throughout the world today it is very necessary for them to be dealt with on a Biblical, easy-to-read, Revelation basis. I highly recommend "My Wealthy Place' as a fresh insight and dynamic way to deal with Prayer, Faith, Dreams, and the Abundant Life!

Dr. H. Michael Chitwood
CEO & President
Chitwood & Chitwood, PC
General Overseer
International Congress of Churches & Ministers

This Book Belongs to:

_____

Given by:

_____

Date:

_____

Occasion:

_____

Contents

Foreword ix

Dedication xvii

For Starters   The Truth about Money xix

Section I 1

1   The Acquisition of Wealth—A Worthy and
    Biblical Ambition 3

2   The Golden Rules Governing the
    Acquisition of Wealth 13

3   Five Distinctive Ways to Acquire Wealth 31

4   Developing a Wealthy Biblical Mind-Set 40

Section II 51

5   Tapping into Your Wealth-Creating Abilities 53

6   Use What God Has Given You to Create Wealth 77

7   Identifying Your Wealth-Creating Abilities 95

Section III 109

8   Wiping Out the Number-One Enemy of
    Wealth Creation 111

Section IV 131

9   *Forbes'* Wealthiest People of the Ancient World 133
10   Thoughts On Wealth In The Life Of Jesus 160

Section V 173

11   Thoughts on Work and Wealth 175
12   Working for Yourself vs. Working for Others 187
13   Creating Multiple Income Streams 195
14   Climbing the Wealth Ladder 207
15   Promotion to Your Wealthy Place
     by the Anointing 238

Section VII 265

16   What to Do with the Wealth God Gave You 267
17   Honoring God with Your Wealth—
     The Premise of Tithing 284
18   Honoring God with Your Wealth—
     The Practice of Tithing 303
19   Honoring God with Your Wealth—
     The Principle of Blessing 315

Section VIII 329

20   If It's Going to Be, It's Up to Me! 331

For Afters   Nobody Listens to Poor People 359
Acknowledgement 363
About the Author 365
Other Books by Bishop Cornelius Blake 367
Notes 369

Dedication

I dedicate this book to people who have allowed me the sacred honor of serving them as their pastor. The friends and families of all nations. I wish for all of you purpose, productivity, prestige, power, and prosperity in every segment of your life.

Second, I dedicate this book to my mentors, pastors, and life-long friends Pastor Errol Sampson, Bishop Owen Reid, Pastor Paulus Taylor, Bishop Winston Freckleton, and Pastor Junior Demetrius. Gentlemen, thanks for your mentorship and enduring friendship for all these years. I wish you wealth in every area of your life.

Key Text

Thou hast caused men to ride over our heads; we went through fire and through water: but thou broughtest us out into a wealthy *place*.

Psalm 66:12 (KJV)

For Starters

The Truth about Money

Bread is made for laughter, and wine gladdens
life, and money answers everything.
—Ecclesiastes 10:19 ESV

Two important subjects most people don't like talking about are sex and money, but almost everyone wants lots of both. I hope you get my sense of humor. Let's get serious. You can tell from this opening icebreaker that this book will address a serious subject matter—money.

Money, Not Really a Necessary Luxury

Our lives are dominated by money. Can you think of a day when you didn't think about money? We all spend most of our time earning, saving, thinking about, spending, investing, and worrying about money and how we're going to do without it.

We all have to deal with money every day just to survive not to mention to succeed. We need money just to keep our head above water. We need money to pay the rent or mortgage, pay the car loan, put food on the table, and put clothes on our backs. Whether we like to talk about it or not, we have to deal with money or money-related issues every day. So what's the problem?

Money answereth all things. (Ecclesiastes 10:19)

The Concept of Money

Money is just a concept; we can't see or feel it unless we have a gold bar in our hands. The concept of money is fluid enough to have spawned so many slang expressions—bread, bucks, cabbage, cash, change, chips, currency, dough, green, jack, kale, legal tender, long green, loot, lucre, needful (love this one), scratch, shekels, and many more. Whatever term you use, money is powerful and necessary. If you noticed, I didn't refer to it as a necessary evil; I'll explain that later.

We can reckon our wealth by adding up all we own in all forms. It comes with enormous baggage, and most people believe that to want it or have it is bad. But how can we call something evil that we use daily for our necessities? That attitude scares money away from us.

Money is not a frivolous matter or simply a concept but a spiritual matter, and it's more spiritual than you can imagine. We cannot be mature followers of Jesus Christ without settling the issue of money in our lives.

Money Is God's Gracious Gift to You

Our loving and gracious God has given His children three precious gifts: time, talent, and treasure. Yes, treasure. He's put some money into your hands. According to the Bible, we received money for three purposes.

Purpose 1: Money as a Spiritual Test

How you handle money has spiritual and eternal implications. Jesus spoke more about the subject of money than He did about any other subject. Money was given to us as a test of our characters, values, priorities, maturity, responsibility, and faithfulness to our heavenly Father. Yes, money is a test of all kinds of things.

According to the Scriptures, the way we handle money has a direct relation to God and to a large degree will determine if we can be trusted with spiritual wealth. Consider the parable of the unjust steward.

> Whoever is faithful in small matters will be faithful in large ones; whoever is dishonest in small matters will be dishonest in large ones. If, then, you have not been faithful in handling worldly wealth, how can you be trusted with true wealth? (Luke 16:10–11 GNB)

Purpose 2: Money as a Tool

God also gives us money as a tool; that's a pretty cool definition because without money, we cannot function. It's not a treasure to be hoarded but to be used to accomplish His work.

> Tell them to use their money to do good. They should be rich in good works and should give generously to those in need, always being ready to share with others whatever God has given them. (1 Timothy 6:18 NLT)

Purpose 3: Money as a Testimonial

Third, God gives us money as testimony to His bounty. He wants to bless us with wealth that can be seen by unchurched folks, friends, families, colleagues, associates, neighbors, and so on as evidence of His blessing on our lives.

> Lord, you have hidden away many wonderful things for your followers. You have done so many good things for those who trust in you. You have blessed them so that all the world can see. (Psalm 31:19 ERV)

The Almighty's Original Intent

God never intended us to be controlled by financial intuitions; rather, He wanted us to control those institutions. He never intended His children to be borrowers but lenders.

> And the LORD shall make thee the head, and not the tail; and thou shalt be above only, and thou shalt not be beneath; if that thou hearken unto the commandments of the LORD thy God, which I command thee this day, to observe and to do them. (Deuteronomy 28:13 KJV)

Never Say, "It's Just a Dollar"

In light of the Lord's teaching on the right use of earthly possessions in regard to the prospect of rewards in the world to come, here are two insights to keep in mind as you read this book. First, take care how you spend every dollar. Never say, *"It's just a dollar!"* It's never the amount that determines your reward but what you do with whatever you have. Try not to waste any dollar. If you cannot manage a dollar, perhaps you won't be able to manage ten or a hundred or a thousand dollars. Your money management always starts with a dollar. Second, treat money as your best friend, a trusted companion who wants to help you fulfill your dreams.

Since money is God's gift to us, it's neither good nor bad; it depends on whose hands it is in. If money is in the hands of an evil person, it will take on the characteristic of evil. Money in the hand of a righteous person will be righteous.

Anybody Can Make Money

What's exciting about money is that it cannot tell who's handling it. Anybody can make money regardless of race, sex, or creed. Money isn't prejudiced even if the world is and even if the playing field is not level for everyone. The social and economic system is structured to favor certain classes and races, but my dear friend, money doesn't discriminate.

Money is there for the taking by anyone who has the right attitude toward it; a balloon of any color will rise; what's important is its content. It's not what you look like that will carry you to your wealthy place, it's what's in you that will do that.

Only you can make your life better; no one will be handing a better life or money to you, and it can be challenging to acquire wealth, but it's certainly possible.

Purpose of the Book

I want to challenge your perceptions of money if you think it's bad; I want to provoke some strong emotions in you about wealth. I hope this book will motivate you. You might have talents, but you might lack the motivation to use them to acquire wealth. I hope you'll be inspired by this book to develop and set in motion your wealth plan. Thomas Carlyle said, "The best effect of any book is that it excites the reader to activity." *(Thinkexist.com)* This book is a starting point for anyone wishing to take control of his or her finances and go from being broke to being blessed.

I challenge you not to settle for less than you can earn. God gave us the power (an important word here) to prosper, so let's go to the wealthy place!

Cornelius Blake

Section I

My Wealthy Place
Psalm 66:12

Chapter 1

The Acquisition of Wealth—A Worthy and Biblical Ambition

*You shall remember the LORD your God, for it is he who
gives you power to get wealth that he may confirm his covenant
that he swore to your fathers, as it is this day.*
—Deuteronomy 8:18 ESV

Wealth—An Emotionally Charged Word

The word *wealth* invokes many mental pictures and emotions in us all; one of my purposes for writing this book was to provoke in my readers a strong desire to acquire wealth.

People are indeed getting wealthier. According to recent *Forbes* reports, there are more millionaires today than at any other time. But wealth means different things to different people, so it's important to define what it means. Some people think of wealth in terms of possessions while others think of things that are truly important and lasting such as faith, family, and friends. Many people will choose both. I asked a number of people, "What does it mean to be wealthy?" I was amazed at the variety of responses.

Many Shades of Wealth

To some, wealth means not having to worry about price tags. To others, it means there's food on the table, a roof over their heads, and clothes on their backs. Others

Key Phrase

To be wealthy, we must first think wealthy. To have success, we must first think success. We have to develop a positive wealth or money consciousness.

think wealth means having enough that they don't have to beg. Still others think of wealth as the freedom to do whatever they wish. And some think of wealth as having millions of dollars.

> You shall remember the lord your God, for it is he who gives you power to get wealth that he may confirm his covenant that he swore to your fathers, as it is this day. (Deuteronomy 8:18 ESV)

We could read this as,

> But you shall remember Jehovah your God, for it is He who gives you the power to acquire much money or property; riches; large possessions of money, goods, or land; great abundance of worldly goods; affluence; opulence, valuable products, or contents.

I think of wealth as enough to do want, live where I want, drive what I want, see what I wish to see, go where I wish to go, and, most important, bless my generation, my church, my community, and my nation.

A Negative Mind-Set about Money

People's differences are expressed in many ways. Some like big houses while others prefer small homes. Some people like big cars while others like small cars. Some people like swimming while others love skiing. Some people like lots of nice things, but others couldn't care less about them. Some people love to stay home while others love

Poverty doesn't keep you humble—poverty humiliates you!

to travel. Some people are frightened by progress while others love it.

Some of these differences don't matter, but one difference that does is this: the vast majority believe it isn't possible to become wealthy and won't even try to gain wealth. They feel uncomfortable talking about money; they harbor negative attitudes about money and the pursuit of wealth. Why wouldn't everyone aspire to be wealthy? Beats me! But I must confess I was a member of that tribe for years; I considered *money* a dirty word.

Our Formative Years

I can trace my negative attitude toward money to my childhood programming. Many of us can trace our opinions about wealth to the wrong information we received about God and wealth during our formative years.

I grew up in Jamaica with my grandparents, who were poor but hardworking people. I was told I'd been born in a small mud and grass hut. In the early sixties, when I was nine months old, my parents immigrated to Great Britain for economic reasons, leaving me in the care of my grandparents. I never met my parents until I was in my late teens. My childhood days were extremely hard, as were my teenage years.

My grandmother was blind, and my grandfather worked the field to make sure food was on the table. When he became ill, I continued to work the field and took care of them. For many months, I missed out on school to labor with him.

After my grandfather's death, we would have gone without food many nights if loving neighbors hadn't had pity on us. I loved my grandparents, who were two of the most God-fearing, loving people to grace this spinning planet, but I'm not sure if they helped or hindered me as far as my

Key Phrase

Many of us can trace our opinions about wealth to the wrong information we received about God and wealth during our formative years.

attitude about acquiring wealth was concerned.

I was programmed to think that it didn't matter how hard I worked, that work would never make me rich because it wasn't God's will. My grandparents had taken a vow of poverty; they proudly purported, "Poverty will keep you humble." But thank God I have long purged my mind of that doctrine because it isn't true. Poverty doesn't keep you humble—poverty humiliates you!

There's nothing humbling about having my home or car repossessed or my children kicked out of private school because I can't afford it. There's nothing humbling about not being able to afford health care or food. There's nothing humbling about being broke, disgusted, and busted.

Bad Influence

Others who reinforced my negative view of money included educators, relatives, friends, and, worst of all, religious leaders. They taught me bad concepts about money that I carried around for almost two decades. The secular world as well plants seeds in the minds of people that all churches and preachers are just after their money. This is such a hypocritical statement because every institution, company, billboard, commercial, restaurant, mall, outlet, business, and so on is geared toward one thing only: getting your money. The church provides a service to people and has a right to be funded just as any other institution does, but unfortunately, it has demonized money.

The Church's Demonization of Money

The church has traditionally compared the pursuit of wealth with idolatry, and that's affected Christians' attitude toward it. This demon is still very much alive, but we'll cast him out in Jesus' name.

According to the traditional teaching, the poorer you are, the holier you are; it's unnecessary to mention that if you're rich, you're ungodly. On the other extreme, many wealthy folks believe that being wealthy is a sign of God's special favor and that being poor is a sign of God's displeasure. Neither of these philosophies is healthy.

Carefully examine the following Scriptures. Many preachers have used them to spread the poverty message and to reinforce the self-defeating thinking that money is evil. These beliefs are rooted in the misapplication of the following Scriptures. A brief rebuttal follows each quotation.

The Poverty Message Propagation Texts

> There was a rich man who was clothed in purple and fine linen and who feasted sumptuously every day. And at his gate was laid a poor man named Lazarus, covered with sores, who desired to be fed with what fell from the rich man's table. Moreover, even the dogs came and licked his sores. The poor man died and was carried by the angels to Abraham's side. The rich man also died and was buried, and in Hades, being in torment, he lifted up his eyes and saw Abraham far off and Lazarus at his side. (Luke 16:19–23 ESV)

The Rebuttal

The poor man went to heaven and the rich man went to hell; this suggests rich folks won't be going heaven. But that wasn't the point

Jesus was making; He was simply talking about human destinies, not wealth. Let us consider some more texts.

> But those who desire to be rich fall into temptation, into a snare, into many senseless and harmful desires that plunge people into ruin and destruction. (1 Timothy 6:9 ESV)

> Then Jesus said to his followers, "The truth is, it will be very hard for a rich person to enter God's kingdom. Yes, I tell you, it is easier for a camel to go through the eye of a needle than for a rich person to enter God's kingdom." (Matthew 19:23–24 ERV)

> No servant can serve two masters, for either he will hate the one and love the other, or he will be devoted to the one and despise the other. You cannot serve God and money. (Luke 16:13 ESV)

> And he lifted up his eyes on his disciples, and said: "Blessed are you who are poor, for yours is the kingdom of God." (Luke 6: 20 ESV)

> Jesus, seeing that he had become sad, said, "How difficult it is for those who have wealth to enter the kingdom of God!" (Luke 18:24 ESV)

The Rebuttal

Note that Jesus didn't say it was impossible for rich folks to go to heaven; He said it was difficult. I believe poverty as well as riches can be obstacles to salvation and discipleship.

Other passages also talk about the dangers of wealthy but not against possessing it.

But those who
desire to be rich
fall into temptation,
into a snare, into
many senseless and
harmful desires that
plunge people into

Key Phrase

God has given us the power to acquire wealth;
why would He be against something He
authorized us to have? It doesn't add up.

ruin and destruction. For the love of money is a root
of all kinds of evils. It is through this craving that
some have wandered away from the faith and pierced
themselves with many pangs. But as for you, O man of
God, flee these things. Pursue righteousness, godliness,
faith, love, steadfastness, gentleness. (1 Timothy 6:9–
11 ESV)

The Rebuttal

Folks often misquoted this verse by saying, "Money is the root of
all evil." Pay close attention to the text: "The love of money is a root of
all kinds of evils"; it's the love of money, not money itself, that is a, not
the, root of all kinds of evils. Two big differences. It means there is more
than one root of evils—anger and the desire for power are two others.

I was taught, "There's not enough money for everybody, and God
didn't create everyone to be rich." The problem here is how do we
know whom God wants to be rich and who He wants to be poor?
There's no way of knowing. The first time I heard this concept, I
naturally concluded that God hadn't ordained me to become rich. I
was somewhat bright, handsome, and hardworking, but things weren't
working out for me, so perhaps they were right, I thought.

The gospel I was brought up on taught that true wealth consisted
only of faith, happiness, love, freedom from things of the world,
self-denial, and following Jesus. The church of Jesus Christ must
make its mind up about money. It cannot keep preaching against

money when every Sunday it's begging people to give money to further the gospel.

Final Word

When we read these Scriptures in isolation, we'll likely conclude that God is against wealth. But we must study the Bible as a whole, not just choose a verse here and there to justify our negative thinking about money.

We have to conclude that the overwhelming teaching of the Bible is that God is not against His children possessing wealth. The question then is, should Christians desire to get rich? Of course! According to Deuteronomy 8:18, the pursuit of wealth is a worthy and legitimate biblical ambition. God has given us the power to acquire wealth; why would He be against something He authorized us to have? It doesn't add up.

My advice to you is to earn as much money as you can by following the rules; you'll have no problem with God. Stay focused on Jesus Christ and His Word; your perspective is all that matters. We'll talk about these rules governing wealth in the next chapter.

My Personal Wealth Notes

My Wealthy Place

Psalm 66:12

Chapter 2

The Golden Rules Governing the Acquisition of Wealth

Beware lest you say in your heart, "My power and the
might of my hand have gotten me this wealth."
—Deuteronomy 8:17 ESV

The wealth of the earth is God's gift to us. We must acknowledge that God is the proprietor of everything. When it comes to money, many think, *I acquired it, so it's mine.* But that's wrong. It all belongs to the Lord, who entrusted it to us; we have no rightful ownership of our possessions.

> The silver is mine, and the gold is mine, declares the LORD of hosts. (Haggai 2:8 ESV)

> Yours, O LORD, is the greatness and the power and the glory and the victory and the majesty, for all that is in the heavens and in the earth is yours. Yours is the kingdom, O LORD, and you are exalted as head above all. Both riches and honor come from you, and you rule over all. In your hand are power and might, and in your hand it is to make great and to give strength to all. (1 Chronicles 29:11–12 ESV)

The second golden rule governing the acquisition of wealth is that if God blesses you with riches, you must decide to serve God, not gold. God doesn't care what you have as long as you don't put it before Him; this includes your spouse, car, house, children, and so on. God is opposed to your being controlled by money and serving it rather than making it serve you.

God created the wealth of the earth for Adam and Eve, but He created them for Himself. What He was saying was, "You can have all the wealth of the earth as long as I have you."

In God We Trust—A Subtle Reminder

We all hold tightly to our money when we put our trust in it, and we hang onto it loosely when we trust in God. We read on our money, *"In God We Trust."* We should be grateful for this reminder from our government. I believe when this phrase appeared on coins in the 1860s and on bills in the 1950s that it was inspired Holy Spirit. This profound statement on the US money constantly remind us of the need to put God first; He is the source of our blessings.

Consider God's instructions to His children in Deuteronomy 8. *Deuteronomy* means the "second law." This book contains Moses' farewell pep talk to the Israelites in which he reviewed and renewed God's covenant with them for the sake of the new generation. They had come to the end of their forty years of wandering and were getting ready to enter the land of Canaan, their wealthy place. He wanted to instruct the people how to behave there. Joshua was a transitional leader charged with leading the people into the wealthy place. The application here is this: we have to become *"blessable"* before God can bless us; we have to be able to handle wealth.

The main reason God doesn't give some of us money is that He knows some of us aren't mature enough to handle it. Some of us would forget about God in times of prosperity, times when we tend to forget about the importance of peace, love, knowledge of God, the presence of the Holy Spirit, integrity, humility, character, patience, joy, and so on. When the clock strikes midnight and the carriage turns into a pumpkin, we wouldn't have the inner wealth to see us through.

Deuteronomy was written to help Israel avoid this pitfall. The spiritual lesson here is the principle of wealth readiness—God won't give us more than we can handle. We've seen what happens to some people who win millions in the lottery but aren't prepared to handle it. Please carry these thoughts in your mind as you read the instructions given to Israel in particular and to us in general. Please underline the following key words: *remember, forget, beware,* and *bless.*

> All the commandments which I command you this day shall you be careful to do, that you may live and multiply and go in and possess the land which Jehovah swore to your fathers.

Reasons for God's Testings

> And you shall remember all the way which Jehovah your God led you these forty years in the wilderness in order to humble you, to prove you, to know what is in your heart, whether you would keep His commandments or not. And He humbled you and allowed you to hunger, and then He fed you with manna, which you did not know, neither did your fathers know it, so that He might make you know that man shall not live by bread alone, but by every word that comes out of the mouth of Jehovah man shall live.

> Your clothing did not wear out on you, nor did your foot swell, these forty years. And you have known with your heart that, as a man chastens his son, so Jehovah your God chastens you. And you shall keep

the commandments of Jehovah your God, to walk in His ways and to fear Him.

Description of the Wealthy Place

For Jehovah your God brings you into a good land, a land of brooks of water, of fountains and depths that spring out of valleys and hills, a land of wheat and barley and vines and fig trees and pomegranates, a land of olive oil and honey, a land in which you shall eat bread without want.

You shall not lack any thing in it. It is a land whose stones are iron, and out of whose hills you may dig copper. And you shall eat and be satisfied, then you shall bless Jehovah your God for the good land which He has given you.

Warnings of Backsliding in Prosperity

Beware that you do not forget Jehovah your God, in not keeping His commandments, and His judgments, and His statutes, which I command you today, lest when you have eaten and are full and have built good houses and lived in them.

And when your herds and your flocks multiply, and your silver and your gold is multiplied, and all that you have is multiplied, then your heart might be lifted up, and you might forget Jehovah your God who brought you forth out of the land of Egypt, from the house of slaves.

The Process

He led you through the great and terrible wilderness, with fiery serpents and scorpions and thirsty ground, where there was no water, who brought you forth water out of the rock of flint, who fed you in the wilderness with manna which your fathers did not know, so that He might humble you.

And so that He might prove you, to do you good in your latter end, and so that you might not say in your heart, My power and the might of my hand has gotten me this wealth. But you shall remember Jehovah your God, for it is He who gives you power to get wealth, so that He may confirm His covenant which He has sworn to your fathers, as it is today. (Deuteronomy 8:1–18 MKKV)

Sight

Sight is the second rule governing the acquisition of wealth. The above passages contain valuable wisdom or rules about the acquisition of wealth for all of us to obey as we stand poised to step into our wealthy place. God gave His children a graphic description of their wealthy place because the prerequisite for stepping into it relies on sight; we must see it before we can possess it. I like the Kings James rendering of the word for *sight*—"behold"; that sounds more divine. God often said, "Behold, I have set before thee ..." This is consistent with His dealings with us. When God is getting ready to bless us, He generally gives us a vision of what He wants to do in our lives. He never allows anyone to possess new territory without first giving that person a vision of it. So God first gave the people a vision of their wealthy place. Let's dive into it.

- **A Land of Great Outward Pleasantness** (vv. 7–9): The land they were about to enter was fertile, well-watered, picturesque, and fruitful.

17

- **A Land of Exhaustless Plenty** (vv. 9–10): "They shall eat bread without scarceness." They would have large herds and flocks, much silver and gold, and homes filled with good things.

- **A Land of Great Natural Advantages** (v. 10): They would have wood, water, metals, fertile soil, good pasturage, and blessings of every kind. God gave them the wealth of the earth for their pleasure.

What Does Your Wealthy Place Look Like?

What is God showing you? What would you like Him to accomplish in your life? Take a few moments to write down what He's showing you right now. Like a camera, let your heart capture it—click! Think it and ink it. He will give you the ability to accomplish whatever He shows you.

Let's consider a few other biblical examples of sight and apply them to our lives. First, Abram was great a beholder.

> The LORD said to Abram, after Lot had separated from him, "Lift up your eyes and look from the place where you are, northward and southward and eastward and westward, for all the land that you see I will give to you and to your offspring forever. I will make your offspring as the dust of the earth, so that if one can count the dust of the earth, your offspring also can be counted. Arise, walk through the length and the breadth of the land, for I will give it to you." So Abram moved his tent and came and settled by the oaks of Mamre, which are at Hebron, and there he built an altar to the LORD. (Genesis 13:14–18 ESV)

The Lord told Abraham to behold all that was around him; He didn't want him to miss anything; He wanted Abraham to understand that

Key Phrase

The spiritual lesson here is the principle of wealth readiness—God won't give us more than we can handle.

opportunities to create wealth were everywhere.

Be Globally Minded

Be globally minded! Today, you don't need to leave your home to create wealth if you have access to the Internet. Access to technology is available to almost everyone; people even in the remotest parts of the world are creating wealth thanks to the Internet. You too can develop a global business from your hut, garage, dinner table, or even prison cell.

We face global, not just local competition today. The Internet has erased then concept of distance and has made it possible for us to compete on the world stage. Everything we need to become successful, powerful, and prosperous is within our reach. As we speak, a health seminar, a wealth seminar, a start-up business seminar, a publishing seminar, and a job fair are going on somewhere. But they won't come looking for you—you must look for them.

> Seek and you will find; knock and it will be opened for you. (Matthew 7:7 LEB)

If you seek, not just need, you will find. God is challenging you to look from where you are to where you want to go. There are opportunities all around you; you don't have to miss out due to geographical biases.

Looking vs. Seeing

Two people can look at the same thing and see it differently. One will discard it as a problem while the other will see it as a possibility. One will see failure while the other will see fortune. Consider this story. A footwear businessman send two of his sales staff into a foreign land to conduct a feasibility study. They both learned people there didn't wear shoes. They both wrote to their boss. The first one wrote,

Key Phrase

When God is getting ready to bless us, He generally gives us a vision of what He wants to do in our lives.

> Dear Sir,
>
> I am writing to let you know we both arrived safely, the weather is lovely, and the people are very friendly. However, I noticed they do not wear shoes, so please do not send any shoes. I will be taking the next available flight back home.
>
> Yours sincerely,
> John Brown

The second wrote,

> Dear Sir,
>
> I am writing to let you know that we both reach safely, the weather is lovely, and the people are very friendly.
>
> I am so excited to inform you that the locals do not wear shoes here. Please send thousands of shoes; we have a great opportunity to expand our business. I look forward to receiving the first shipment as soon as possible.
>
> Yours sincerely,
> James Brown

One salesperson was blind to the opportunity while the other saw opportunity. Incredible! The world is full of people who see only what is visible to the naked eye; they should learn to see with their minds.

We assume problems are problems, not opportunities, and we let them pass us by. They may never come again. We shouldn't expect opportunities to always be nicely wrapped. Many people never become wealthy because they aren't trained to spot opportunities right in front of their eyes.

The way to recognize global and local opportunities is to look for problems to solve. I guarantee there are plenty of them around, and people will pay big bucks for solutions.

Second, God told Abram,

> All the land that you see I will give to you and your offspring forever. (Genesis 13:15 NIV)

As I mentioned above, there's a difference between looking and seeing. To look means to direct your eyes in a particular direction. To see is to imagine the possibility in what you see. Don't miss this. God told Abraham to look, but only what he saw would He give him. To see it is to have it. If you can't see it, you can't have it. I wish we could all become wealthy by simply looking and seeing. These are just the first steps toward becoming wealthy.

Third, God showed him how wealthy he would become.

> I will make your offspring like the dust of the earth, so that if anyone could count the dust, then your offspring could be counted. (Genesis 13:16 NIV)

This is promise of the future. If we can see the promise, in most cases, we will be willing to pay the price. Unless these first two steps are translated into what Abraham did next, nothing will be accomplished.

Key Phrase

The only way to create a good financial future for yourself and those depending on you requires labor; without that one ingredient, you won't realize your dreams and visions.

Fourth, God told Abram to work the land.

> Go, walk through the length and breadth of the land,
> for I am giving it to you. (Genesis 13:17 NIV)

If you want to enter your wealthy place, you have to get up off your blessed assurance and do something! You cannot just sit idly by waiting to get wealthy by providential intervention, accident, or chance; you have to take practical steps. Many people have inherited great wealth, and others have won the lottery, but the odds are against that. Most people want to be wealthy but with little or no pain.

Do not miss the fifth point: Abraham acted immediately to the divine instruction. The Abraham principle applies to you as well.

> Abram moved his tent and came and settled by the oaks
> of Mamre, which are at Hebron, and there he built an
> altar to the LORD. (Genesis 13:18 ESV)

He moved his tent—he took action! Yeah, that's the catch. Allow me to reinforce a couple of points here. First, there are no babies without labor. The only way to create a good financial future for yourself and those depending on you requires labor; without that one ingredient, you won't realize your dreams and visions. To become wealthy, you'll have to move your tent.

The Secret World of Spies

Consider God's instruction to Moses.

> Choose one of the leaders from each of the twelve tribes and send them as spies to explore the land of Canaan, which I am giving to the Israelites. (Numbers 13:1–2 GNB)

Joshua, Moses' successor, commissioned two spies to check out the Promised Land, the wealthy place.

> Then Joshua sent two spies from the camp at Acacia with orders to go and secretly explore the land of Canaan, especially the city of Jericho. When they came to the city, they went to spend the night in the house of a prostitute named Rahab. (Joshua 2:1 GNB)

The intent for sending out these spies was to make an impression on the people. Seeing is believing, and if God could get them to see their wealthy place, perhaps they could seize it.

A Prophetic Prediction

Nothing happens by chance; perhaps you've been wandering in the wilderness of poverty for most of your life and God has allowed you to pick up this book to give you the instructions and motivation you need to move to your wealthy place. I'm convinced this could be your Deuteronomy season and God is getting you ready for it. But first, quit doing what's not working! If you have been taking the classes, reading the books, feeding on the ideas, studying wealth, looking for opportunities, and brainstorming ideas, if you've found a mentor who has accomplished what you'd like to accomplish, these are signs your transition to the wealthy place is nigh.

Keep on looking! Behold the opportunities, possibilities, promises, and the payoff! Opportunities are everywhere, and possibilities are endless especially in America. But let us dive into another word that we discover in the text.

"Beware!"

The first word we talked about, *sight,* translated as "behold," a positive word, whereas, the second word, *beware,* is a negative word, a word of caution. The divine injunction to remember is,

> Beware that you do not forget Jehovah your God, in not keeping His commandments, and His judgments, and His statutes, which I command you today. (Deuteronomy 8:11 MJKV)

You Don't Understand—His Name Was Judas!

If Judas, the greatest villain of all times, was with us today, his message to us would be the same: "Beware of what you become in pursuit of wealth." Judas betrayed Christ for thirty pieces of silver. I believe Judas must have been a man of great integrity; otherwise, he wouldn't have been entrusted with such a high office of a treasurer. Just imagine what it feels like to be sold out by your trusted friend in the name of money. The narrative is so fascinating to read. This is Hollywood material.

> Then one of the twelve followers went to talk to the leading priests. This was the follower named Judas Iscariot. He said, "I will hand Jesus over to you. What will you pay me for doing this?" The priests gave him 30 silver coins. After that Judas waited for the best time to hand Jesus over to them. (Matthew 26:14–16 ERV)

24

In those days, thirty pieces of silver was the equivalent to about 113 days' wages for a common laborer, quite a sizeable piece of fortune. According to the story, while Jesus and the other disciples were praying in the garden of Gethsemane,

> Judas, one of the twelve apostles came there. He had a big crowd of people with him, all carrying swords and clubs. They had been sent from the leading priests and the older leaders of the people. Judas planned to do something to show them which one was Jesus. He said, "The one I kiss will be Jesus. Arrest him." So he went to Jesus and said, "Hello, Teacher!" Then Judas kissed him. Jesus answered, "Friend, do the thing you came to do." Then the men came and grabbed Jesus and arrested him. (Matthew 26:47–49 ERV)

Judas had the courage to watch from a distance. Again, I cannot argue this better than the Bible does.

> Judas saw that they had decided to kill Jesus. He was the one who had handed him over. When he saw what happened, he was very sorry for what he had done. So he took the 30 silver coins back to the priests and the older leaders. Judas said, "I sinned. I handed over to you an innocent man to be killed." The Jewish leaders answered, "We don't care! That's a problem for you, not us." (Matthew 27:3–4 ERV)

I'm not sure what Judas thought. Perhaps he believed the Master would simply escape as He often had, and Judas would still have the money. When he saw things didn't work out that way, he had regrets for betraying his Friend for the love of money. He wasn't unhappy with the money, he was unhappy with whom he had become.

He pleaded with the leaders to take back the money, but they retorted, "That's your problem, Judas. You should have thought about it before. We got our man and you got what you wanted!"

Key Phrase

The way that you spend your money says a lot about your personal philosophy, your attitude, and your values.

Having no further recourse, Judas threw the money on the floor. He realized he had become a double crosser. He hanged his worthless self. What a sad story. The worst kind of unhappiness is to be unhappy with yourself.

To this day, Judas is telling us from the grave, "Don't sell out your virtue and values and soul for money. Beware! I paid too big of a price!" In 1 Timothy 6:10–11, the author warned us that we should not love money to the extent that we give up our faith to get it. That's not a profitable exchange!

Imagine all the things that you could achieve or acquire—cars, mansions, spouse, wealth, you name it. Put them all together and they're nothing compared to your soul.

> For what shall it profit a man if he shall gain the whole world and lose his own soul? Or what shall a man give in exchange for his soul? (Mark 8:36–37 MKJV)

Bless!

The word speaks to the proper response to wealth. According to *Vine's Expository Dictionary of Old and New Testament Words,* the word *bless* means "to praise, to celebrate with praise, of that which is addressed to God, acknowledging His goodness and blessings." This is the way to behave when blessings, abundance, and prosperity are flowing your way.

> When you have eaten and are full, then you shall bless
> the Lord your God for the good land which He has
> given. (Deuteronomy 8:10 NKJV)

We bless the Lord even before we eat. It's easy to become
complacent and cynical when we're in our wealthy place. God doesn't
care what we have or how much we have as long as we remember
where He brought us from and where we are now. A failure to bless
God will release a wave of curses on your life even if you have entered
your wealthy place.

Is It God's Will for Everyone to Be Wealthy?

In the previous chapter, we determined it was God's will for
Christian to prosper. But does He want everyone to prosper? I say yes.
The question, however, is whether everyone will become wealthy. No.

Is it God's will for all people to be saved? Yes. Will all be saved?
No. Gaining wealth and salvation depends largely on many factors such
as personal choice, belief system, and wrong opinions you hold about
God and wealth.

Based on Scripture, we can conclude that wealth is God's gift to
us to enjoy and use for His glory. The wealthiest man who ever lived
supports this philosophy wrote,

> Here is what I have found out: the best thing we can
> do is eat and drink and enjoy what we have worked for
> during the short life that God has given us; this is our
> fate. If God gives us wealth and property and lets us
> enjoy them, we should be grateful and enjoy what we
> have worked for. It is a gift from God. (Ecclesiastes
> 5:18–19 GNB)

Achieving wealth also depends on your relationship with Him,
your level of maturity, assignment, anointing, willingness to work hard,

willingness to let God remain the center of your life, and obeying the rules governing money. Scripture tells us to see wealth as a friend, not a foe, and to never forget we are divine creations connected to God, who has granted us all the potential to achieve wealth.

> I can do all this through him who gives me strength.
> (Philippians 4:13 NIV)

Many of us don't fathom the awesomeness of our relationship with our Creator. When we are in a relationship with Him, He knows our capacity and abilities, and anything is possible for us in the kingdom. We can be as creative as our Creator is and apply ourselves to the Word of God; supernatural blessings will be released into our lives. Read this aloud: "I can accomplish anything that I apply myself to because I know that I am connected to the Divine source."

Final Word

Dr. Paul Franklin Crouch Sr. wrote, "One of the biggest lies the devil has dumped on you and me-in fact, on the whole church and body of Christ—is 'Christians should be poor.' Poverty produces piety and holiness and humility, and on and on the lie goes!" *Ask Me for Anything, Dr. Paul Franklin Crouch, Sr. Publisher: Trinity Christian Center of Santa Ana, Inc. (2015), page 39.*

I call on you to reject that mind-set. Decide to have God's best for yourself so you can bless your family, church, colleagues, company, community, constituency, and country. On your journey to your wealthy place, don't forget the divine order governing the acquisition of wealth.

> Seek the kingdom of God, and all these things shall
> be added to you. Do not fear, little flock, for it is your
> Father's good pleasure to give you the kingdom. (Luke
> 12:31–32 MKJV)

My Personal Wealth Notes

My Wealthy Place

Psalm 66:12

Chapter 3

Five Distinctive Ways to Acquire Wealth

Wealth you get by dishonesty will do you no good, but honesty can save your life.
—Proverbs 10:2 GNB

People do crazy and wicked things to become wealthy, and this is especially the case in the business world, where money laundering, white-collar crime, scams, and insider trading take place. Don't be a part of any of that. Before we dive into five ways to acquire wealth, let us examine six ways not to.

First, many people become wealthy by deceiving their customers.

> You say to yourselves, "We can hardly wait for the holy days to be over so that we can sell our grain. When will the Sabbath end, so that we can start selling again? Then we can overcharge, use false measures, and fix the scales to cheat our customers. We can sell worthless wheat at a high price. We'll find someone poor who can't pay his debts, not even the price of a pair of sandals, and we'll buy him as a slave." (Amos 8:5–6 GNB)

Second, others become wealthy by defrauding their employees.

> Masters, be fair and just in the way you treat your slaves. Remember that you too have a Master in heaven. (Colossians 4:1 GNB)

Third, some people acquire wealth by delaying payments.

> Do not rob or take advantage of anyone. Do not hold back the wages of someone you have hired, not even for one night. (Leviticus 19:13 GNB)

Fourth, others acquire wealth by defaulting on loans.

> The wicked borrow and never pay back, but good people are generous with their gifts. (Psalm 37:21 GNB)

Fifth, many people acquire wealth by deceiving the government.

> That is also why you pay taxes, because the authorities are working for God when they fulfill their duties. Pay, then, what you owe them; pay them your personal and property taxes, and show respect and honor for them all. (Romans 13:6–7 GNB)

Sixth, and worst of all, many people acquire wealth by defrauding the Lord.

> I ask you, is it right for a person to cheat God? Of course not, yet you are cheating me. "How?" you ask. In the matter of tithes and offerings. (Malachi 3:8 GNB)

And there are more ways. Some win the lottery, others discover fortunes, and others inherit wealth. But the vast majority have to stay up late and rise early to work on their dreams until they succeed. And they do so honestly, as they should.

> Wealth you get by dishonesty will do you no good, but honesty can save your life. (Proverbs 10:2 GNB)

> Whosoever walks in integrity walks securely, but he who makes his ways crooked will be found out. (Proverbs 10:9 ESV)

> Dishonest gain will never last. So why take the risk? (Proverbs 21:6 LB)

From time to time, we all have to deal with integrity issues such as the temptation to add a little more to our expense reports or telling small lies. We shouldn't! We should adhere to the above Scriptures and give evidence of our integrity, honesty, and ethics. In my way of thinking, we can build wealth in five ways. Let's go over them.

Building Wealth with Your Mind

The first distinctive way to acquire wealth is with your mind. I'll elaborate on the power of the mind in the next chapter, so in the meantime, please hold on to this truth: You possess the most powerful wealthy generating apparatus the world has ever known...the human mind. "Your mind is money." It takes just one good idea to change your life. My daughter, Othnielle, posted the following on her blog: *"The best product you own was once somebody's idea on a piece of paper"* (asprinkleofsass. wordpress.com). It's been said that each year, we all get at least three good ideas that if we acted on would change our financial future. Sadly, only a few act on their ideas.

But here's what's interesting—nobody has a monopoly on your ideas. Harvey S. Firestone, founder of the Firestone Tire and Rubber Company, said, "If you have ideas, you have the main asset you need, and there isn't any limit to what *you* can do with your business and your life. Ideas are any man's greatest asset."

One of the ways to create wealth is to use your mental acuity to negotiate deals. Wealth is a consequence of your smart thinking coupled with hard work.

An Opportunity of a Lifetime

Check out what Jesus said here.

Key Phrase

Being financially intelligent simply means having several financial options or strategies to acquire wealth and the ability to maximize them for your benefit and His glory.

The kingdom of heaven is like treasure hidden in a field. When a man found it, he hid it again, and then in his joy went and sold all he had and bought that field. (Matthew 13:44 NIV)

A poor man stumbled upon a once-in-life-time opportunity and took advantage of it. According to ancient laws regulating riches in those days, if a workman discovered treasure on someone else's property, it would be the property of the owner of the field. He became the owner of the field so he could claim the treasure. He used his God-given mind to change his life.

Has anything ever lit your fire that much? Has an opportunity ever turned you on so much that you were willing to risk everything to take advantage of it? Do you realize how much your life could change if you became excited about an opportunity like that?

This man knew he had found something special, and he wisely hid it again. We can talk about our good ideas with a mentor, but we shouldn't broadcast them over CNN until the time is right. That way, we preserve what we have uncovered and aren't subject to the naysayers.

Write down some life-changing ideas you've had and act on them! Be creative with the mind the Creator has given you. Your mind is money, and you can market your services and build your own brand. People will pay you big money to do their thinking for them.

Building Wealth with Your Muscles

The second distinctive way to acquire wealth is with your muscles—hard work. God told Adam,

> Through painful toil you will eat food from it all the days of your life … By the sweat of your brow you will eat your food until you return to the ground, since from it you were taken; for dust you are and to dust you will return. (Genesis 3:17b, 19 NIV)

Key Phrase

If you have ideas, you have the main asset you need, and there isn't any limit to what you can do with your business and your life. Ideas are any man's greatest asset.

—*Harvey S. Firestone*

Many people make money by physical labor, the only way they know, but their muscles will eventually fail them. Take my advice—explore other ways to earn money. If you have skills such as knitting, sewing, furniture making, and so on, that's good, but skills alone are no good by themselves; you have to market them. Get whatever help you need to do so.

Building Wealth with Your Mouth

If you're good at speaking, consider a career in motivational speaking. Are you good at giving instructions? Why not become an advisor in your area of expertise? Are you funny? Why not consider a career as a comedian? Good at singing? Get on *American Idol, America's Got Talent, Britain's Got Talent*, or *Sunday's Best*.

I read a great story about a young woman in *Essence* magazine who made her first million by creating "You Blog for Fun/Gossip Site." That's cool. If you're good at gossiping, why not get paid for it?

God has given us mouths, and some of us have the gift of gab. If that's the case with you, why not use it to make money?

Building Wealth with Wealth Itself

According to Scripture, you can earn money with money itself.

> A very important man was preparing to go to a country far away to be made a king. Then he planned to return home and rule his people. So he called ten of his servants together. He gave a bag of money to each servant. He said, "Do business with this money until I come back."
>
> But the man was made king. When he came home, he said, "Call those servants who have my money. I want to know how much more money they earned with it."
>
> The first servant came and said, "Sir, I earned ten bags of money with the one bag you gave me."
>
> The second servant said, "Sir, with your one bag of money I earned five bags." (Luke 19:13, 15, 16, 18 ERV)

Money can indeed make money. Set a portion of your income aside for sowing purposes. We'll elaborate on this later, but for now, talk with your banker about putting your money to work. Educate yourself on the concept of compound interest. Money is like a seed, and if you eat all your seed, you won't have a harvest.

Building Wealth through Miracles

Yes, you can earn money by miracles, the power of God. Money miracles still happen. Recently, a California couple stumbled on a pot of ancient gold right in their backyard worth more than $10 million, and such windfalls have happened to others as well going way back.

On April 16 over two thousand years ago, Jesus and His disciples' taxes were due and they didn't have any money. That's how I know it was April 16. Should Jesus have paid taxes? I'll answer that in my next book!

Jesus sent Peter to catch a fish, look in its mouth, and find some "miracle money." Peter did just that and found enough to pay the taxes for them all.

> After Jesus and his disciples arrived in Capernaum, the collectors of the two-drachma temple tax came to Peter and asked, "Doesn't your teacher pay the temple tax?" "Yes, he does," he replied. When Peter came into the house, Jesus was the first to speak. "What do you think, Simon?" he asked. "From whom do the kings of the earth collect duty and taxes—from their own children or from others?" "From others," Peter answered. "Then the children are exempt," Jesus said to him. "But so that we may not cause offense, go to the lake and throw out your line. Take the first fish you catch; open its mouth and you will find a four-drachma coin. Take it and give it to them for my tax and yours." (Matthew 17:24–27 NIV)

There's no record of that happening before or after this, so don't wait around for any miracle money. On the other hand, don't count yourself out either. If you're connected with the Miracle Worker, you stand a good chance of stumbling across some miracle money one of these days. Therefore, live your life with a miracle mentality.

Final Word

Our heavenly Father has endowed us with minds, muscles, mouths, some money (doesn't matter how much), and occasional money miracles. Being financially intelligent simply means having several financial options or strategies to acquire wealth and the ability to maximize them for your benefit and His glory.

My Personal Wealth Notes

My Wealthy Place

Psalm 66:12

Chapter 4

Developing a Wealthy Biblical Mind-Set

Do not conform yourselves to the standards of this world, but let God transform
you inwardly by a complete change of your mind. Then you will be able to
know the will of God what is good and is pleasing to him and is perfect.
—Romans 12:2 GNB

In the previous chapters, we dealt with negative mind-sets toward money, the golden rules governing the acquiring of wealth, and five ways to acquire wealth. In this chapter, I write about developing a biblical mind-set toward money.

If you want to break the cycle of debt and go from being broke to the blessed life, start thinking about wealth in ways you've never thought of it before. Write down all your negative attitudes toward the acquisition of money and articulate your contempt against this stinking thinking. Consciously choose a new biblical mind-set and allow the Word of God to purge all your limiting beliefs about money.

Metamorphosis of the Mind

God's desire for you is to think differently and live differently from the world.

> Do not conform to the patterns of this world, but be
> ye transformed by the renewing of your mind? Do

not miss this—then you will be able to test and approve what God's will is—His good pleasing and perfect will. (Romans 12:2 ESV)

Key Phrase

Maybe you have all the skills and talents you need to become a smashing money success, but perhaps the way you were programmed to think about money is sabotaging your future.

Some argue, "It doesn't matter what you believe about wealth and life in general," but that's not true. What you believe makes all the difference in the world because what you believe determines how you behave. That's correct—acquiring wealth begins with your thinking; your mind is your most important money-making asset. It's from the mind-set to action. Your mind is money; to achieve financial success, you must first become successful in the mind. Thinking wealthy is the centerpiece or the chief cornerstone, or better still, the foundation on which wealth is erected. Our success or failure begins with our minds, and especially when it comes to money, the way we think is everything.

Maybe you have all the skills and talents you need to become a smashing money success, but perhaps the way you were programmed to think about money is sabotaging your future. If you don't believe you should have money, guess what? You never will. But if you upgrade your thinking, you'll give yourself a better chance to become wealthy.

Playing Mind Games

I should write "minds" because we have a conscious mind and a subconscious mind. That is mind-boggling. Let's discuss the mind.

The Conscious Mind

Your conscious mind is a masterpiece that controls the most technical, complex, complicated, and largest chemical plant in the whole world, your body. I know; that's mind-blowing. Your body is regulated by your subconscious mind. When you retire tonight, you won't consciously think of how you'll keep the blood flowing and your organs working. How does that work? Your subconscious mind sends signals to the right nerves and muscles without a conscious thought on your part.

Key Phrase

When we learn to think differently, we will begin to live differently, and as we learn to think God's way about wealth, we will begin to live God's way.

The Subconscious Mind

The subconscious mind is very powerful and dominant and will very often override your conscious mind. Let's say that consciously, you want to be wealthy. But if you've acquired a subconscious seed of another persuasion that money is bad and having truckloads of it is ungodly, chances are you'll never become wealthy; your subconscious mind will overrule your conscious mind. That's why you have to take control of your mind—subconscious as well as conscious—with the Word of God.

The Master Supplanter

I know who is responsible for negative subconscious thoughts about wealth—the devil, the master supplanter, the deceiver. But you can expel that demon in Jesus' name if you consciously develop a new mind, the mind of Christ, about wealth, which is well documented in His Word. Studying His Word will rid your subconscious of negative thoughts about money and allow you to achieve prosperity.

When we learn to think differently, we will begin to live differently, and as we learn to think God's way about wealth, we will begin to live God's way.

Key Phrase

If you've acquired a subconscious seed of another persuasion that money is bad and having truckloads of it is ungodly, chances are you'll never become wealthy.

A New Mind

Highly successful and wealthy people approach life and wealth from perspectives different from those of most people. A poverty-programed mentality will usually produce poor results. To do well in life, we must first learn to think well. To be wealthy, we must first think wealthy. To have success, we must first think success. We have to develop a positive wealth or money consciousness. The multimillionaire and president of Peak Potentials Training, T. Harv Eker, argued, "There is secret psychology to money. Most people don't know about it. That's why most people never become financially successful. A lack of money is not the problem; it is merely a symptom of what's going on inside you."[1]

I'm not suggesting you'll automatically become wealthy by simply thinking about it; the vast majority of us have gone past that concept a long time ago. But perhaps the way some people think about life, wealth, and money could be holding them back.

My Mental Metamorphosis

I used to think most poor people were poor because of their circumstances, but I changed my mind when my mentor told me wealth was a matter of desire, decision, discipline, determination, and most important, a mental metamorphosis. That concept smote my consciousness and gave me a new biblical mind-set about money.

I completed a twelve-week course on biblical economics; I read every book on wealth I could lay my hands on and fed on their ideas like mental bread. I also read over a thousand Scripture verses on wealth and soaked them up like a sponge. I was

Key Phrase

Listen, the lack of money (LOM) or wealthy is the root of all my problem.

astounded at how this process changed my life.

The first thing I noticed after I began to think the thoughts of Christ was that my speech, body, and plans automatically adapted to my new way of thinking.

> For as (man) he thinketh within himself, so is he. (Proverbs 23:7 ASV)

My friend, I dare you to try it. If you do, you'll start behaving the way you're thinking. My new mind took me to the next level of living. I'm now thinking in a way that keeps me looking for new opportunities and possibilities. Go through this process daily—spin your own cocoon. Once you've made this transformation, you'll never want to go back to the old way of thinking. Instead of saying, "It's impossible to get rich," you'll say, "It may be tough to become wealthy, but it's possible especially in America. What the heck! I'll die trying."

How to Foster a Biblical Mind-Set

The way to build a biblical mind-set is to constantly fill your mind with the Word of God. I challenge you to create a new biblical mind-set by declaring these biblical affirmations.

> He will love you and bless you, so that you will increase in number and have many children; he will bless your fields, so that you will have grain, wine, and olive oil; and he will bless you by giving you many cattle and sheep. He will give you all these blessings in the land

that he promised your ancestors he would give to you. No people in the world will be as richly blessed as you. (Deuteronomy 7:13–14 GNB)

Wisdom and knowledge are granted to you. I will also give you riches, possessions, and honor, such as none of the kings had who were before you, and none after you shall have the like. (2 Chronicles 1:12 ESV)

I have riches and honor to give, prosperity and success. What you get from me is better than the finest gold, better than the purest silver. I walk the way of righteousness; I follow the paths of justice, giving wealth to those who love me, filling their houses with treasures. (Proverbs 8:18–21 GNB)

The blessing of the LORD brings wealth, without painful toil for it. (Proverbs 10:22 NIV)

Always remember what is written in that book of law. Speak about that book and study it day and night. Then you can be sure to obey what is written there. If you do this, you will be wise and successful in everything you do. (Joshua 1:8 ERV)

Let them shout for joy, and be glad, that favour my righteous cause: yea, let them say continually, Let the LORD be magnified, which hath pleasure in the prosperity of his servant. (Psalm 35:27 NKJV)

Delight thyself also in the LORD; and he shall give thee the desires of thine heart. Commit thy way unto the LORD; trust also in him; and he shall bring it to pass. (Psalm 37:4–5)

Blessed be the Lord, who daily loadeth us with benefits, even the God of our salvation. Selah. (Psalm 68:19 KJV)

Praise ye the LORD. Blessed is the man that feareth the LORD that delighteth greatly in his commandments. His seed shall be mighty upon earth: the generation of the upright shall be blessed. Wealth and riches shall be in his house: and his righteousness endureth forever. (Psalm 112:1–3 KJV)

I will enjoy blessing them. With all my heart and soul I will faithfully plant them in this land. (Jerimiah 32:41 GW)

I alone know the plans I have for you, plans to bring you prosperity and not disaster, plans to bring about the future you hope for. (Jeremiah 29:11 GNB)

Blessed is the one who does not walk in step with the wicked or stand in the way that sinners take or sit in the company of mockers, but whose delight is in the law of the LORD, and who meditates on his law day and night. That person is like a tree planted by streams of water, which yields its fruit in season and whose leaf does not wither—whatever they do prospers. (Psalm 1:1–3 NIV)

The thief comes only to steal and kill and destroy; I have come that they may have life, and have it to the full. (John 10:10 NIV)

And God is able to bless you abundantly, so that in all things at all times, having all that you need, you will abound in every good work. As it is written: "They have freely scattered their gifts to the poor; their righteousness endures forever." Now he who supplies seed to the sower and bread for food will also supply and increase your store of seed and will enlarge the harvest of your righteousness. You will be enriched in every way so that you can be generous on every occasion, and through us your generosity will result in thanksgiving to God lasts forever. (2 Corinthians 9:8–11 NIV)

Here are some biblical affirmations that will help to transform how you see, feel, and think about wealth and determine your present and your future. The way to get rid of the negative mind-set is to replace it with a new one. Read these aloud.

- Money is God's gift to me to be used for His glory.
- Possessing money will not make me less godly.
- Money does not discriminate.
- Money is necessary just for my day-to-day survival.
- Money is my friend, not my foe.
- Money is not the root of evil.
- Money is the root of great vacations.
- Money is the root of freedom from the constant demands of creditors.
- Money is the root of good health.
- Money is the root of great opportunity.
- Money is the root of influence.
- Money is the root of prestige and possibilities.
- Money is the root of benevolence and excitement.
- Money is the root of living where I want to live.
- Money is the root of buying what I want to buy.
- Money is the root of great education for my children and grandchildren.
- Money is the root of building a financial wall around my family.
- Money is the root of blessing myself.
- Money is the root of blessing my community.
- Money is the root of blessing my church.
- Money is the root of blessing my country.

Final Word

Listen, the lack of money (LOM) or wealth is the root of all my problem. Wealth is your spiritual heritage. Your heavenly Father has a covenant of abundance and prosperity with you; He wants you to be prosperous, healthy, and successful. But the principle of spiritual readiness teaches us that God won't give us more than we can mentally handle. The mind can achieve what it can conceive and believe. This is why your mind needs to line up with what God says about you.

> And the LORD said, "...and this they begin to do: and now nothing will be restrained from them, which they have imagined to do." (Genesis 11:6 KJV)

You don't need to worry about getting wealthy and then succumbing to all the worries, sorrows, heartache, and pain so often associated with wealth, for the Bible says,

> The blessing of the LORD makes rich, and he adds no sorrow with it. (Proverbs 10:22 ESV)

My Personal Wealthy Place Notes

Section II

My Wealthy Place
Psalm 66:12

Chapter 5

Tapping into Your Wealth-Creating Abilities

You shall remember the LORD your God, for it is he who
gives you power to get wealth that he may confirm his covenant
that he swore to your fathers, as it is this day.
—Deuteronomy 8:18 ERS

Stop!

L et me caution you before you get engrossed in this chapter because you'll be mentally challenged with my take on spiritual gifts and their connection with the acquisition of wealth.

The key word in the above passage from Deuteronomy is *power.* It didn't say God gives you wealth because God doesn't directly gives wealth to anyone; rather, He gives wealth indirectly by giving you the power or ability to acquire wealth. Big difference.

Interestingly, the word *power* in Deuteronomy 8:18 and Acts 1:8, where Jesus told His followers they would receive power to be witnesses, means the same.

> But you will receive power when the Holy Spirit has come upon you, and you will be my witnesses in Jerusalem and in all Judea and Samaria, and to the end of the earth. (Acts 1:8 ESV)

Here's another important verse in which *power* was used.

> And Jesus came and spake unto them, saying, all power is given unto me in heaven and in earth. Go ye therefore, and teach all nations, baptizing them in the name of the Father, and of the Son, and of the Holy Ghost: Teaching them to observe all things whatsoever I have commanded you: and, lo, I am with you always, even unto the end of the world. Amen. (Matthew 28:18–20 KJV)

The power God the Father gave God the Son was to be used by Jesus' followers to make disciples. The power to achieve wealth was the same power that raised Jesus from the dead.

> You will also know the unlimited greatness of his power as it works with might and strength for us, the believers. He worked with that same power in Christ when he brought him back to life and gave him the highest position in heaven. (Ephesians 1:19–20 GW)

This was the same power that made the apostle Paul a minister of the gospel.

> Whereof I was made a minister, according to the gift of the grace of God given unto me by the effectual working of his power. (Ephesians 3:7 KJV)

Everything that we need for life was given to us by the same power.

> According as His divine power has given to us all things that pertain to life and godliness, through the knowledge of Him who has called us to glory and virtue. (2 Peter 1:3 MKJV)

Jesus said,

> Behold, I give unto you power to tread on serpents and
> scorpions, and over all the power of the enemy: and
> nothing shall by any means hurt you. (Luke 10:19 KJV)

My friends, the power to achieve wealth, the power to witness, the power that raised Jesus from the dead, the power to become a minister of the gospel, the gift of salvation, the gift of faith, the gift of the Holy Spirit, the gift of eternal life, the power to live a victorious life and to prosper all come from the same source—God.

The Five Dimensions of God's Power

Let me summarize: In my study of my favorite book, the Bible, I discovered that the *'power'* of God as it relates to your life is employed in at least *five* ways and is made available to us through the gospel. They are as follows:

First: you receive divine *'power'* unto salvation: Salvation not only means deliverance from sin, but also deliverance from sickness and poverty. Salvation mark your initiation into the kingdom where everything is possible.

> For I am not ashamed of the gospel, for it is the power
> of God for salvation to everyone who believes, to the
> Jew first and also to the Greek. (Romans 1:16 ESV)

Second: *you receive divine 'power' unto stabilization:* The word means to be steady and stable during your time during times of uncertainty.

> Let us give glory to God! He is able to make you stand firm in your faith, according to the Good News. I preach about Jesus Christ and according to the revelation of the secret truth which was hidden for long ages in the past.(Romans 16:25 GNB)

Third: *you receive divine 'power' unto* **preservation:** The word mean safekeeping. God's power is able to keep you safe during your earthly pilgrimage.

> They are for you, who through faith are kept safe by God's power for the salvation which is ready to be revealed at the end of time. (I Peter 1:5 GNB)

Fourth: *you receive divine 'power'* **unto presentation:** The final goal of God's power is to hand you over to your Heavenly Father. In essence, this is complete and final restoration of everything that Adam has lost through sin to you.

> Now to him who is able to keep you from stumbling and to present you blameless before the presence of his glory with great joy, to the only God, our Savior, through Jesus Christ our Lord, be glory, majesty, dominion, and authority, before all time and now and forever. Amen (Jude 1:24-25 ESV)

Fifth: *you receive divine 'power'* **to procure prosperity:** Whilst you are here on earth, God wants you to be prosperous and wealthy, hence, He has provided you with the power to acquire wealth live out the abundant life.

> Beware lest you say in your heart, 'My power and the might of my hand have gotten me this wealth.'

You shall remember the LORD your God, for it is he who gives you power to get wealth, that he may confirm his covenant that he swore to your fathers, as it is this day. (Deuteronomy 8:17-18 ESV)

God, the Ultimate Giver

There are different kinds of spiritual gifts, but the same Spirit gives them. There are different ways of serving, but the same Lord is served. There are different abilities to perform service, but the same God gives ability to all for their particular service. The Spirit's presence is shown in some way in each person for the good of all. The Spirit gives one person a message full of wisdom, while to another person the same Spirit gives a message full of knowledge. One and the same Spirit gives faith to one person, while to another person he gives the power to heal.

The Spirit gives one person the power to work miracles; to another, the gift of speaking God's message; and to yet another, the ability to tell the difference between gifts that come from the Spirit and those that do not. To one person he gives the ability to speak in strange tongues, and to another he gives the ability to explain what is said. But it is one and the same Spirit who does all this; as he wishes, he gives a different gift to each person. (1 Corinthians 12:4–11 GNB)

Here's a list of spiritual abilities I want you to ponder.

- **The Gift of Preaching** is the ability to publicly communicate God's Word in inspired ways that convict unbelievers while challenging and building up believers.

- **The Gift of Evangelism** is the ability to communicate the good news of Jesus Christ to the unsaved and to lead them to respond with faith.

- **The Gift of Apostleship** is the ability to plant new churches and oversee their development.

- **The Gift of Teaching** is the ability to educate the people of God by clearly explaining and applying the Scriptures (and any literature) in a way that provokes learning.

- **The Gift of Encouragement** is the ability to inspire and motivate the people of God to act on scriptural principles particularly when they're discouraged and unstable in their faith.

- **The Gift of Wisdom** is the ability to fathom God's wisdom in life's situations and communicate it in a way people will understand.

- **The Gift of Intercession** is the ability to intercede for the needs of others, persevere in prayer, and not become discouraged until the answer comes.

- **The Gift of Pastoring** is the ability to care for the spiritual needs of people in spiritual growth.

- **The Gift of Music** is the God-given ability to play musical instruments to celebrate His presence.

The Universality of the Anointing

Plant this seed in the matrix of your spiritual womb: all the abilities listed above, including the ability to get wealth in Deuteronomy 8:18, are God-given abilities and functions of the same anointing. It is often believed that the only function of the anointing is to operate from a church pulpit. That's a mistake.

Folks also tend to think that the ability to acquire wealth and the impartation to preach come from different sources and almost infer that the power to get wealth comes from a magical or mystical origin. Not at all. According to the text, the ability to acquire wealth is a gift of the Holy Spirit or God just as are pastoring and teaching.

Your Divine Right to Prosper

Our omnipotent God has given you the power—the right, strength, privilege, authority and most important, the dignity—to acquire wealth. This power is sinful only when it's used for sinful reasons. God gave special gifts to people not just for ministry gifts but also for construction, carpentry, making fine jewelry, and so on.

> And Jehovah spake unto Moses, saying, See, I have called by name Bezalel the son of Uri, the son of Hur, of the tribe of Judah: And I have filled him with the Spirit of God, in wisdom, and in understanding, and in knowledge, and in all manner of workmanship, to devise skillful works, to work in gold, and in silver, and in brass, and in cutting of stones for setting, and in carving of wood, to work in all manner of workmanship. (Exodus 31:1–5 ERV)

Got Talent

One of my favorite TV shows is *America's Got Talent*. It brought back to American culture the concept of a variety show. It's a celebration of the American spirit

that features singers, dancers, comedians, contortionists, impressionists, jugglers, magicians, and other performers vying for a chance to win American's hearts and $1 million. Every time I watch this program, I'm blown away. Whenever I see how incredibly talented people are, I'm reminded God made us that way.

Discover Yourself

I've been pastoring for many years, and one of the most common excuses I've heard people give for their lack of success is, "I just don't have any skills or abilities to offer. I'm just not good at anything." They're wrong. The problem is that the majority of people never take the time to discover, develop, and deploy their talents for the glory of God. God gives the ability to *all* to perform their particular services. According to the psalmist, He has been equipping us all for success long before we were born.

> You created every part of me; you put me together in my mother's womb. I praise you because you are to be feared; all you do is strange and wonderful. I know it with all my heart. When my bones were being formed, carefully put together in my mother's womb, when I was growing there in secret, you knew that I was there You saw me before I was born. The days allotted to me had all been recorded in your book, before any of them ever began. (Psalm 139:13–16 GNB)

Read aloud what the above passage says about you. With that fact firmly embedded in your mind, understand that you're a

Key Phrase

The ability to acquire wealth is a gift of the Holy Spirit or God just as are pastoring and teaching.

creative genius; God created you with abilities and talents, so there's no logical reason why you shouldn't be a smashing success. Check out the following facts and misconceptions that folks entertain about abilities.

Facts about Abilities

- You were born with skills and abilities. Many people think that all talents, skills, and abilities have to be learned in the classroom and by experience. But I believe that when folks say, "She just seems to have a natural ability to sing" or "He's a natural performer," they're correct!

- Many people possess certain God-given abilities they use without being aware of them. At this moment, you're probably utilizing skills and talents you're not conscious of. That's because they come so naturally to you that you don't even realize it. I encourage you to consciously identify your skills and abilities.

- You probably have more than one natural ability, talent, or skill. University studies have confirmed that the average person possesses between 500 and 700 skills or abilities and that a vast number of these skills were inborn. Some of the basic skills were learned at home, in the street, in the classroom, or somewhere else.

- Your skills, talents, and abilities are transferable from one environment to another. You can deploy them in a secular environment and a Christian environment alike, so don't limit yourself. Know who you are, know what you have, and know whom you have.

Wisdom from the Parables of Investments

If you're still in doubt about your wealth-creating abilities, ponder the parable of the talents and glean some valuable lessons from it.

> Once there was a man who was about to leave home on a trip; he called his servants and put them in charge of his property. He gave to each one according to his ability: to one he gave five thousand gold coins, to another he gave two thousand, and to another he gave one thousand. Then he left on his trip.
>
> The servant who had received five thousand coins went at once and invested his money and earned another five thousand. In the same way the servant who had received two thousand coins earned another two thousand.
>
> But the servant who had received one thousand coins went off, dug a hole in the ground, and hid his master's money. After a long time the master of those servants came back and settled accounts with them. The servant who had received five thousand coins came in and handed over the other five thousand. "You gave me five thousand coins, sir," he said. "Look! Here are another five thousand that I have earned."
>
> "Well done, you good and faithful servant!" said his master. "You have been faithful in managing small amounts, so I will put you in charge of large amounts. Come on in and share my happiness!"

Then the servant who had been given two thousand coins came in and said, "You gave me two thousand coins, sir. Look! Here are another two thousand that I have earned." "Well done, you good and faithful servant!" said his master. "You have been faithful in managing small amounts, so I will put you in charge of large amounts. Come on in and share my happiness!"

Then the servant who had received one thousand coins came in and said, "Sir, I know you are a hard man; you reap harvests where you did not plant, and you gather crops where you did not scatter seed. I was afraid, so I went off and hid your money in the ground. Look! Here is what belongs to you." "You bad and lazy servant!" his master said. "You knew, did you, that I reap harvests where I did not plant, and gather crops where I did not scatter seed? Well, then, you should have deposited my money in the bank, and I would have received it all back with interest when I returned. Now, take the money away from him and give it to the one who has ten thousand coins.

For to every person who has something, even more will be given, and he will have more than enough; but the person who has nothing, even the little that he has will be taken away from him. As for this useless servant— throw him outside in the darkness; there he will cry and gnash his teeth." (Matthew 24:14–30 GNB)

The Anatomy of the Parable

Many theologians believe this parable is about money or financial intelligence since the word *talent*, used in some translations, means "money" in Greek. Some believe it refers to the gifts of the Holy Spirit, while others link it to the call of God and the anointing. And some believe the parable illustrates diligence or faithfulness in view of the second coming of Jesus Christ. All these are possibilities.

Many believe it refers to our natural skills and abilities, and this is perhaps so. Finally, some refer to it as the story of investment, and they could be right. But I think this parable is about our personal responsibility to use whatever God has entrusted us with whether it's time, talents, or treasure. For the purpose of our discussion, I want to talk about it in terms of our talents.

Whatever your personal view regarding this parable, here are five life-changing truths or principles to consider. Let the lessons that follow from this parable inspire and motivate you to put your desire for wealth goals in high gear.

Key Phrase

God created you with abilities and talents, so there's no logical reason why you shouldn't be a smashing success.

Principle of Possession

God is the CEO of our talents, which include our time and treasure. We don't own anything; everything we have belongs to God, who lends it to us. The story tells us, "The servants were entrusted with their master's property." We didn't choose our talent or talents, God did. They are ours to use, manage, and enjoy. When we die, our talents will go to someone else.

Difference in the Proportions

The talents differed greatly in this parable; one servant got five, another two, and the third just one. Many people ask, "Why the difference?" Others say, "Life isn't fair. Why is God partial?" Let me break this to you gently. Even kids know life is unfair. Socially and economically, the odds of getting wealthy are stacked against certain racial groups. But don't forget that if you work hard, you can still succeed. Though we're all equal in God's eyes, we don't possess equal giftedness.

Key Phrase

Given the same set of opportunities coupled with difficulties, some people will earn more than others by virtue of their efforts.

Different by Design

We all have different talents because we're all different; we're entrusted according to our abilities and capabilities. God made us all; He knows what each of us is capable of and has endowed us accordingly: "He gave to each according to his ability." Some people have more talents than others, and some have fewer; some people have more opportunities, and others have fewer.

Here's what really matters. Everybody in the story received a talent; we all received something to work with. We all have at least one talent, skill, gift, anointing, or natural ability to use for His glory and to enrich our lives. What really matters is not what we have but what we have done with it. Whether you were allocated one or two talents, are you working with them? If you work them, they will work for you.

You-Niquely Talented

God has uniquely endowed you to fulfill a specific function, so don't be surprised if He entrusts you with great responsibility or wealth to establish His kingdom on earth. If God has given you the ability to earn a hundred thousand and you're making only fifty thousand, you're living below your potential. Don't limit yourself!

God doesn't demand those who receive two talents to make ten, but He does expects them to make full use of the seed money or talent they have received. Everyone is to work according to his or her capability. Let's look at a similar parable.

The Parable of the Pound

Key Phrase

A nobleman went into a far country to receive for himself a kingdom and then return. Calling ten of his servants, he gave them ten minas, and said to them, "Engage in business until I come." (Luke 19:12–13 ESV)

Whether you were allocated one or two talents, are you working with them? If you work them, they will work for you.

Many people refer to this parable and the previous parable as twin parables. In this one, the man gave his servants the same amount of money to put to work. Many Bible teachers believe that he did this not to teach them how to make money but to test their capabilities and responsibility. However, we all have to agree the nobleman used money here to test them. The Greek word *pragmateuomai* means to do business, to trade for gain, to use money to make money. This is the only place that it is used in the New Testament.

But why the same amounts? The answer is in the results: the talents and the pounds represent the opportunity given us to use or not use; it's that simple. Given the same set of opportunities coupled with difficulties, some people will earn more than others by virtue of their efforts.

Principle of Productivity or Utilization

It's wrong not to put to use the gifts and talents God has entrusted to us; we must not bury, hoard, waste, or store them. They must be invested in the kingdom so God will receive maximum return for His investment in you.

What Makes God Upset?

Let's talk about the third fellow, who upset his master. God is upset when we fail to use the gifts or talents He invested in us. The master had strong words for the one who had buried his talent. He was trying to make the point that he had expected a return on his investment. Could you be doing same thing with your talents? That's intolerable.

Key Phrase

We all have at least one talent, skill, gift, anointing, or natural ability to use for His glory and to enrich our lives. What really matters is not what we have but what we have done with it.

> Take the one bag of money from that servant and give it to the servant who has ten bags. (Matthew 25:28 ERV)

What you don't use, you'll certainly lose. Whether God has blessed you with one, two, or five talents, use that for His glory. If you don't use it, you are no longer entitled to it. It's better to attempt to do something and fail than attempt to do nothing with your talents. Yes my friend, the universe's CEO is upset when we don't at least try to do something noble, magnificent, worthy, and remarkable with the talents He has entrusted to us.

Principle of Accountability

You have the freedom to do whatever you choose with your talents, but one day, you'll have to explain to God whatever you have or haven't done with them.

> After a long time the master came home. He asked the servants what they did with his (talent) money. (Matthew 25:19 ESV)

"Good question," you say. No! It's the all-important question when it comes to your talents.

Exams and Audits

Do those two words scare you? They scare me especially when I'm not prepared. I've never been audited by the IRS, but I heard it's not a friendly process. Have you thought about being audited by God one day? That will be a life audit.

Key Phrase

It's wrong not to put to use the gifts and talents God has entrusted to us; we must not bury, hoard, waste, or store them.

> So each of us will have to explain to God about the things we do. (Romans 14:12 ERV)

That's sobering. God already has all your information, so you won't be able to hide anything from Him. If you dare say, "I can't remember where I hid that talent," God will say, "Allow me to remind you exactly what you did with that talent." His final exam will consist of a major question: "What did you do with the gifts and talents you were given?" Fortunately, you know this question is coming on the exam and you have time to prepare to give a good answer. You'll be audited one day, so start preparing for that now!

I Was Afraid

The guy who buried his talents said,

> I was "afraid," so I went off and hid your money in the ground. Look! (Matthew 25:25 GNB)

You might cringe at this guy's reasons for not putting his talents or skills to work, but isn't fear the main reason folks don't use their talents? If fear isn't dealt with, it can paralyze you and ruin your chance of a better future. The fear of failure is real; it's something we learn. The fear of losing is real for rich and poor alike. Fear normally disguises itself by posing as caution or timidity. Fear will cause you to scale back and bury your talent. Don't allow your fear to kill you. Conquer it before it conquers you. It's that simple.

Do you think the other two servants in the parables who doubled their money weren't fearful? I don't think so. You cannot be legitimately courageous without some element of fear. Courage simply means going ahead despite your fear. The fear of losing paralyzed the fellow who buried his talent. What was the big difference between him and the others? For them, the desire to become wealthy was more powerful than their fear of losing what they had. Fear kept the first generation of Israel out of its wealthy place; all except Joshua and Caleb died in the wilderness.

Key Phrase

You have the freedom to do whatever you choose with your talents, but one day, you'll have to explain to God whatever you have or haven't done with them.

> None of the men who have seen my glory and my signs that I did in Egypt and in the wilderness, and yet have put me to the test these ten times and have not obeyed my voice, shall see the land that I swore to give to their fathers. And none of those who despised me shall see it. But my servant Caleb, because he has a different spirit and has followed me fully, I will bring into the land into which he went, and his descendants shall possess it. (Numbers 14:22–24 ESV)

This applies to you as well; fear will keep you from your wealthy place. What's keeping you from using your God-given talents? What's your excuse?

Excuses, Excuses

Here are some of the most common excuses I've heard people give for not living their financial dreams of becoming wealthy.

- I'm not smart enough
- I don't have the education.
- I'm not good enough or have the personality.
- It's too difficult.
- It'll take too long.
- It's too much hassle.
- I'm not deserving enough.
- It's not in my nature.
- I'm not the right color, race, or class.
- It's never happened in my family.
- The system won't allow me.
- I'm too young.
- I'm too old.
- God doesn't want me to be wealthy.
- Others are more talented than me.

Let me fill you in on a secret: Whenever God blesses you with a talent, the devil will always try to attach some fear to it to keep you from using it. What you fear most is often a revelation of what you have a natural talent for.

If you want to be successful, do whatever you're afraid of doing; refuse to play it safe. Tap into those wealth-creating talents and abilities the CEO of the universe has invested in you. You might just succeed. Here's a life verse the Holy Spirit laid on my heart.

> So begin planting early in the morning, and don't stop working until evening. You don't know what might make you rich. Maybe everything you do will be successful. (Ecclesiastes 11:6 ERV)

I bet you were inspired by that verse. Here's another revelation I want to plant in your spirit. I wondered why there were only three servants in one version of that parable, and the Spirit revealed this to me: the three servants represent the three options we have in life: we can squander our lives, we

Key Phrase

Whenever God blesses you with a talent, the devil will always try to attach some fear to it to keep you from using it.

can spend them, or we can sow them. I sincerely hope we all choose the third option.

You Can Be Only You

Consider the excuse, "Others are more talented than me." Couple that with the guy who buried his talent. Often, the people who consider themselves to be the least talented are likely to do nothing with them. This excuse takes many forms: "There are better (writers, investors, salespeople, artists—this list goes on and on) than me, so I won't (write, invest, sell, paint, and so on)."

Forgive me if I say, "That's dumb!" Just because there are people with more talent than you isn't a good reason not to use your God-given talent. One question that won't be on your final exam with God is, "Why weren't you like so and so?" One question that will be on that exam is, "Why didn't you use the talent I gave you?" Mark this: you can only be you, and for that matter, you can do something in a way that only you can do, so stop comparing yourself with other people. Don't take my word for it.

> Don't compare yourself with others. Each of you must take responsibility for doing the creative best you can with your life. (Galatians 6:4–5 MSG)

Fifth and Final: The Principle of Promotion

The master commended and promoted the two servants who doubled his investments.

71

Well done, you good and faithful servant!' said his master. 'You have been faithful in managing small amounts, so I will put you in charge of large amounts. Come on in and share my happiness! (Matthew 25:21 GNB)

Key Phrase

One question that won't be on your final exam with God is, "Why weren't you like so and so?"

There's a life principle here: God is constantly assessing performance and dishing out rewards for now and will do so for eternity. Poor management of your talents will disqualify you from your next dimension of wealth, equally proper management of them will promote you to your next dimension of wealth.

In the parable of the minas in Luke 19:16–19, one servant was given ten cities and the others were given five. Did you get that? God will reward you in heaven, but here's what's really cool—He will reward you on earth if you use your talents. He's particularly paying attention to how you handle the little things. As the text says, if you're faithful in managing the small amounts or taking advantage of the small opportunities, God will entrust you with more and more, your circles will widen, your talents will increase, and your opportunities will be more plentiful and greater, believe me.

I dare you to tap into your God-given abilities that will propel you to the next level of wealth as long as you're faithful in managing the little things. I'm saddened by the fact that too many people are sitting back and waiting for big opportunities and are missing out on the small opportunities every day that could lead to the big opportunities.

A Real Shot at Success

Those who believe God doesn't want them to be successful, prosperous, happy, and wealthy should carefully study these parables. He commended the guys for using their talents and condemned the one who hid his talent, calling him "wicked." God also gets angry at those who do nothing with their talents.

You can only be you and for that matter you can do something in a way that only you can do, so stop comparing yourself with other people.

Let's Make God Proud

My dear friend, God is not against you saving and investing yourself and becoming wealthy; He delights in your success. Several ancient prophets captured God's attitude toward success perfectly. He is proud when His children are prosperous. We read this passage before, but the occasion warrants reading it again.

> Let them shout for joy, and be glad, that favor my righteous cause: yea, let them say continually, let the LORD be magnified, which hath pleasure in the prosperity of his servant. (Psalm 35:27 KJV)

And under the inspiration of the Holy Spirit, the apostle John also penned these affirming words.

> Beloved, I wish above all things that thou mayest prosper and be in health, even as thy soul prospereth. (3 John 1:2 KJV)

I pray you really absorbed those verses. God wants you to be wealthy, so you should desire that yourself. God isn't opposed to your enjoying the fruits of your labors; that's why God gave you the talents in the first place. It will be satisfying to hear God say, "Well done" for making a noble contribution to the world with the talents He gave you.

God's affirmation is the bedrock of my belief and confidence that acquiring wealth is possible. Note I didn't say it was easy! That's why we should make good use of the opportunity that has been given to us, and I'll die trying to do just that. You can put this on my tombstone: "R.I.P. At least he tried!"

Key Phrase

Poor management of your talents will disqualify you from your next dimension of wealth, equally proper management of them will promote you to your next dimension of wealth.

Final Word

We all have different abilities; some of us are musical, while others are good at math. Some are great tailors, and others are great salespeople. Some are great speakers, and others have wonderful planning abilities. Some love working with children, and some thrive when they work with the elderly. There are as many abilities as there are people, and God has distributed them all.

> We all have different gifts, each of which came because of the grace God gave us. (Romans 12:6 NCV)

> God gives gifts, not miserly, but abundantly. And not randomly, but carefully: to each according to each one's unique ability. (Matthew 25:15 NKJV)

Most people are using only 20 percent of their talents. Can you imagine what you'd be capable of if you used that other 80 percent? You'd have treasures instead of trinkets, prosperity instead of pennies, and wealth instead of worries. Just imagine!

Tap into that multimillion-dollar investment God has made in you and become wealthy. Remember, God doesn't directly give anyone personal wealth, but He does give everyone the ability to acquire wealth.

My Personal Wealthy Notes

My Wealthy Place

Psalm 66:12

Chapter 6

Use What God Has Given You to Create Wealth

"What shall I do for you?" he asked. "Tell me, what do you have at home?" "Nothing at all, except a small jar of olive oil," she answered.
—2 Kings 4:2 GNB

I f you still harbor lingering doubts about your God-given abilities to become wealthy, allow me to share another biblical story, one of many human stories in this great book that has a supernatural power to change lives. It's not just words in print, a catalogue of human ideas, a pamphlet of pop psychology. It is the Word of God; it is *theopneustos*, God-breathed. That's why you can have what it says you can have.

The biblical story I share here is a biblical classic and one of my favorites. This story coupled with the two parables we dealt with in the previous chapter and in fact all the lessons on stewardship in the Bible overwhelmingly reinforce the fact that you're never down on anything, not even your luck. Even if you're facing overwhelming personal, physical, spiritual, or financial challenges, the Almighty has never left you void, empty, or without a seed.

The word *seed* here simply implies potential, possibilities, or opportunities. God very seldom gives us a harvest. Instead, He gives us talents and gifts only in seed form with which we can start. However, God will multiply only the seed you sow, not the seed you store. When the seed reaches the right soil—opportunity—it will produce abundantly.

Key Phrase

God will multiply only the seed you sow, not the seed you store. When the seed reaches the right soil—opportunity—it will produce abundantly.

> And God, who supplies seed for the sower and bread to eat, will also supply you with all the seed you need and will make it grow and produce a rich harvest from your generosity. (2 Corinthians 9:10 GNB)

What Do You Have?

My friend, do not despise little things or small beginnings; start with what you have. Remember that Moses used a simple staff to divide the sea, David used a common sling to defeat a towering giant, Samson used a jawbone to defeat thousands of his enemies, Rahab used just a piece of string to save herself, and Dorcas used an everyday needle to build wealth. And the person we're ready to deal with had just a little jar of oil.

The Widow: From Broke to Blessed

Don't miss the drama of this simple but touching story. Keep in mind that we've been debating the most common excuses people give for not making their lives purposeful and powerful: "I just don't have anything to offer."

> Now the wife of one of the sons of the prophets cried to Elisha, "Your servant my husband is dead, and you know that your servant feared the LORD, but the creditor has come to take my two children to be his slaves." And Elisha said to her, "What shall I do for you? Tell

me; what have you in the house?" And she said, "Your servant has nothing in the house except a jar of oil."

Then he said, "Go outside, borrow vessels from all your neighbors, empty vessels and not too few. Then go in and shut the door behind yourself and your sons and pour into all these vessels. And when one is full, set it aside." So she went from him and shut the door behind herself and her sons. And as she poured they brought the vessels to her.

When the vessels were full, she said to her son, "Bring me another vessel." And he said to her, "There is not another." Then the oil stopped flowing. She came and told the man of God, and he said, "Go, sell the oil and pay your debts, and you and your sons can live on the rest." (2 Kings 4:1–7 ESV)

This poor widow had just lost her husband, who had left her in debt up to her neck through imprudence, improvidence, sickness—we can only speculate. One way or the other, he left a bill rather than a will. Sounds familiar, doesn't it? The widow told the prophet, "He feared the Lord" as if to make an important point: you can be a godly person, a prophet, a teacher of truths, or a dispenser of divine ideas. You can love the Lord with all your heart and serve Him all your life, but if you aren't careful, you can die broke and leave your family in debt.

A good man leaveth an inheritance to his children's children. (Proverbs 13:22 KJV)

The Good News Bible puts it this way.

Good people will have wealth to leave to their grandchildren. (Proverbs 13:22 GNB)

I consider myself an amateur when it comes to Scripture, but this is my interpretation of that story. The widow ran to the prophet in distress crying for

Key Phrase

You can love the Lord with all your heart and serve Him all your life, but if you aren't careful, you can die broke and leave your family in debt.

financial assistance probably with tears running down her face: "Your servant my husband is dead, and you know that he revered and served the Lord faithfully," She lamented, "and the creditors are coming to take my children into servitude as a means for debt payment." Observe the prophet's fascinating counsel: "What shall I do for you? What have you in the house?" "Nothing" she said. "Except a little jar of oil."

Her response to the questions revealed a very typical mind-set: she automatically devalued the little oil she had. Never underestimate the value of a gift or talent the Lord has given you. No matter how grim it looks, you always have something. I remember years ago when I was down on my luck for years— No money in the bank, none at hand, and none expected. I'd say to folks, "The only money I have is my testimony," a testimony the Lord would provide as He always provided. I lived off my testimony for years.

The widow assumed the prophet would bail her out. Notice her emotional blackmail: "Thy servant my husband is dead; and thou knowest that 'thy servant did fear the Lord' and the creditor is come to take unto him my two children to be bondmen." This is a very typical behavior of so many of us when we're in debt. We tend to overlook or undermine our wealth-creating abilities and run to other people for quick fixes or ways out. But this "I have nothing" mentality must always be challenged, and that's what the prophet did; he didn't offer her a loan or collect an offering for her for a number of reasons. It would have reinforced her "I have nothing" mentality; he didn't fall for her emotional blackmail; rather, he showed her she could become a multimillionaire. He showed her that the little pot of oil that she called nothing was

Key Phrase

Our talents were poured into us by the divine hand. We waste time praying for what we already possess; all we need to do is activate our gifts.

---

the key to the abundance she needed. God is saying the same to you: do not despise the little things; you—no one else—has the key to your wealth.

Second, the prophet wanted to break her cycle of debt; instead of enabling her, he empowered her to pay the price for her financial future. He challenged her to start a home business with the little she had. She probably named it, "The Widow and Sons Oil Enterprise."

The Business Plan

Here's the business strategy: the prophet instructed her to borrow empty vessels because buying them would have plunged her deeper into debt. Empty containers implied she would tap into her own ability to transform her life of poverty into prosperity, to go from being broke to being blessed.

"Borrow not a few empty vessels" implied that she should think big, dream big, plan big, and expect great things from the Lord. It also implied she had to lift the ceiling on her earnings potential, the mature way to conduct business.

Treasure in Human Vessels

I love the word *vessel*; it can describe our human capacity. An ancient script described the human capacity—the body—as a vessel of clay in which treasures are stored.

But we have this treasure in earthen vessels, so that the excellence of the power may be of God and not of us. (2 Corinthians 4:7 MJKV)

This is heavyweight stuff that will bless you. Think of yourself as a human vessel containing heavenly treasures—gifts, talents, capabilities, possibilities, and potentials. Let's talk about the second word, *treasure*. In ancient times, it was the custom of eastern kings to store their treasures in earthenware vessels and hide them. Paul used this metaphor as the human vessel in which talents and capability were poured.

Power Packed for a Purpose

The widow's vessels had been filled by a divine hand; in the same manner, our talents were poured into us by the divine hand. We waste time praying for what we already possess; all we need to do is activate our gifts. The apostle Peter provided a noteworthy perspective on the power of the gifts in us.

According as his divine power hath given unto us all things that pertain unto life and godliness, through the knowledge of him that hath called us to glory and virtue. (2 Peter 1:3 KJV)

God has given us all the power we need for a successful life; all we need to do is flip the switch.

Stir up the gift of God, which is in thee by the putting on of my hands. (2 Timothy 1:6 KJV)

The apostle didn't say we should pray for the gift: "Timothy, you have the power of God in you; just flip the switch." That's the understanding of your self-worth.

Understanding Self-Worth

My favorite blogger has this to say about self-worth: "You're worth everything this world has to offer,

Key Phrase

God has given us all the power we need for a successful life; all we need to do is flip the switch.

and you have more to offer than this world."[2] If you're serious about possessing your wealthy place, recognize your worth, value, treasures, abilities, and talents already poured in you not by an ancient king but by the King of the universe. The same way earthly treasures must be unearthed by the spade of an archeologist, the treasures in you must be unearthed by the spade of self-worth.

The poor widow did this with her oil. She borrowed empty vessels and poured her oil into them until all the empty vessels were filled. She at first said, "I have nothing except a little oil." Let's consider that more deeply because it's loaded with truths.

The Value of Oil—Your Gift

Every time the Bible uses the word oil, it is referring to olive oil.

> She went back to Elisha, the prophet, who said to her, "Sell the olive oil and pay all your debts, and there will be enough money left over for you and your sons to live on." (2 Kings 4:7 GNB)

The widow's potential customers included cooks, religious institutions, apothecaries, warriors, shepherds, perfumers, embalmers, traders, and so many more willing to pay for it. This is the same when it comes to your talents. Make a list of the potential customers you have for your gifts. You'll be paid not for the hours you work but for their value—top dollar.

First, her oil was a dietary staple. It was spread on bread and used for cooking and baking.

> When you bring a grain offering baked in the oven as an offering, it shall be unleavened loaves of fine flour mixed with oil or unleavened wafers smeared with oil. (Leviticus 2:4 ESV)

Second, her oil was employed in religious ceremonies as an offering to identify, consecrate, or anoint people, places, and items, setting them apart exclusive for God's use.

> With it you shall anoint the tent of meeting and the ark of the testimony, and the table and all its utensils, and the lampstand and its utensils, and the altar of incense, You shall anoint Aaron and his sons, and consecrate them, that they may serve me as priests. And you shall say to the people of Israel, "This shall be my holy anointing oil throughout your generations. It shall not be poured on the body of an ordinary person, and you shall make no other like it in composition. It is holy, and it shall be holy to you." (Exodus 30:26–32 ESV)

Third, as a medical agent, her oil was used for healing, as a remedy for stomach distress, and as a balm for wounds.

> And went to him, and bound up his wounds, pouring in oil and wine, and set him on his own beast, and brought him to an inn, and took care of him. (Luke 10:34 KJV)

Fourth, her oil was used to fuel lamps.

> But the wise took oil in their vessels with their lamps. (Matthew 25:4 KJV)

Fifth, her oil was used by warriors to preserve their weaponry; it was massaged into leather shields to keep them from becoming brittle.

> Ye mountains of Gilboa, let there be no dew, neither let there be rain, upon you, nor fields of offerings: for there the shield of the mighty is vilely cast away, the shield of Saul, as though he had not been anointed with oil. (2 Samuel 1:21 KJV)

Sixth, her oil was used by shepherds on their sheep to protect them from bugs. I don't have scriptural support for this point, but it is well documented that in biblical times, flies, bugs, and other insects would plague sheep, especially their ears, eyes, and noses. That could lead to disease and even death.

Seventh, her oil was used in the making of expensive perfumes and fragrant ointments. A perfumer would boil root and bark powders, tree resins, and spices in the oil to make costly perfumes. One jar of oil-based myrrh, frankincense, cinnamon, and aloe ointment could fetch as much as a laborer's yearly income.

According to the gospel, the oil from the jar the woman used to anoint our Lord and Savior was argued to be of great value or worth.

> A woman came up to him with an alabaster flask of very expensive ointment, and she poured it on his head as he reclined at table. And when the disciples saw it, they were indignant, saying, "Why this waste? For this could have been sold for a large sum and given to the poor." (Matthew 26:7–9 ESV)

Finally, her oil was used by elders as an accompaniment of miraculous power in connection with exorcism and the prayers of faith for the healing of the sick.

Are any among you sick? They should send for the church elders, who will pray for them and rub olive oil on them in the name of the Lord. This prayer made in faith will heal the sick; the Lord will restore

Key Phrase

The greatest opportunity to become wealthy can be right in front of your eyes but you don't recognize its true value because it's too familiar.

them to health, and the sins they have committed will be forgiven. (James 5:14–15 GNB)

They drove out many demons, and rubbed olive oil on many sick people and healed them. (Mark 6:13 GNB)

This is how important and valuable oil was to the economy in biblical times. Oil was a multibillion-dollar industry; everyone depended on it one way or another. If you were poor, you'd be happy to have some olive oil to sell. Can you imagine this poor woman possessed one of the most lucrative products and wasn't aware of it?

In Plain Sight

This is a typical problem with most people. I learned from bitter experience that sometimes, the greatest opportunity to become wealthy can be right in front of your eyes but you don't recognize its true value because it's too familiar. You reckon you already know what it's about, and you have a standard way of dealing with it. Open your eyes to wealth opportunities that are in plain sight.

The prophet showed her what she called "nothing" and "just a little" was the key to unlocking the door to wealth. Your overlooked talents could be the key to your success. This is why understanding your self-worth is so important, my friend.

It's Good to Believe in Yourself, But It Helps to Have Someone Else Believe in You

Key Phrase

Humans don't lack capabilities or talents, but they can lack a belief in them.

It's important to believe in yourself, but sometimes, it's good if other people believe in you also. The prophet saw the potential in that little pot of olive oil that the widow couldn't see. Sometimes, it takes others to point out our overlooked potentials and abilities hidden in the "house" of our lives. It's important not to disregard this important counsel.

The Missing Number

Humans don't lack capabilities or talents, but they can lack a *belief* in them. That missing number could be a trusted and tested teacher, a praiseworthy prophet, a passionate pastor, a caring coach, a model motivator, a convincing counselor, a faithful father, or a mindful mother. And for that matter, even an aggressive opponent, because at times, it takes an adversary to get the best out of us.

The people in the widow's life, in this case her sons, limited her earning potential when she asked for another empty vessel and they said, "There is not another." Then the oil stopped flowing. Our acquisition of wealth might be limited by our incapacity to receive and the willingness of others to go the extra mile to help us. The oil stopped flowing only when they stopped receiving. God is always willing to pour into us if we have the vessels to contain it; the limiting factor is the recipient, not the giver.

I'm disappointed that she stopped when the blessing started flowing. She should have gone to the next level of wealth instead of settling for less. I'd still be gathering empty vessels to this day if I'd been her.

God doesn't limit you; there's no limit to His power to bless you financially. You're limited only by your mind and the people in your life. Sometimes, your friends,

Key Phrase

Just because something has little value to you doesn't mean it's of no value to others. Be proud of your God-given talents; let them be a source of pride.

associates, and business partners won't help you achieve the next level of wealth, so you'll have to go it alone.

The Idiot Check

Have you ever checked out of a hotel sure you've packed everything but find yourself going back for a second look anyway? That's an idiot check. Review the "house" of your life to make sure you haven't overlook a talent, skill, or ability.

Just because something has little value to you doesn't mean it's of no value to others. Be proud of your God-given talents; let them be a source of pride. If you put your talents to work, they'll work for you. Let's travel back in time and check out what God said about you.

> The LORD God formed the man of dust from the ground and breathed into his nostrils the breath of life, and the man became a living creature. (Genesis 2:7 ESV)

God has breathed into you far more than you can imagine. The capability in you far exceeds what people are applauding. It was not just breath God breathed into you; it was potential, passion, privilege, purpose, power, skills, talents, and abilities. We were all created with the potential to become wealthy. If not, what's the alternative, my friend?

The So-Called Gifted Child

I don't subscribe to the gifted-child concept. God enriches us all with talents; some of us get ten, others get five, some get two, and others get one. The same thing God said about the prophet Jeremiah He said about you.

> Before I made you in your mother's womb, I knew you. Before you were born, I chose you for a special work. (Jeremiah 1:5 ERV)

The apostle Paul made this amazing statement.

> God has made us what we are. In Christ Jesus, God made us new people so that we would spend our lives doing the good things he had already planned for us to do. (Ephesians 2:10 ERV)

Key Phrase

Your assignment is simply to breathe out what God has breathed in you; you exhale what God has given you to inhale.

Waiting to Exhale

Let me sum up the purpose of the God breath or the God "gene" in you: your assignment is simply to breathe out what God has breathed in you; you exhale what God has given you to inhale.

In 1989, I toured Israel and visited the Dead Sea, which is in stark contrast to the Sea of Galilee, which is lush with trees, flowers, and other vegetation. It receives waters from the mountains of Lebanon that passes through the Jordon River and enters the Dead Sea. That sea takes in but never gives out. That's why it's stagnant—dead.

The potential value of the potash, bromine, and other chemicals in the Dead Sea is estimated to be four times the wealth of the United States. What about that? The sea is dead because it doesn't give out what it has received. Many people have had so much poured into them by God— so much freshness, so many talents and abilities—but they refuse to give it out. The application is that there must

be a balance in your life to remain fresh and stay useful for God; there must be an outflow as well as an inflow in your life.

All Balloons Can Fly

All kinds of balloons can fly. It's not the color of the balloon that makes it fly but rather what's inside it. What God breathes into you makes the difference. That's why I'm fascinated with the human *potential*, an inspiring word! I'm intrigued with my uniqueness and my story, my possibilities and my potential, how I started with nothing as a barefooted farm boy and got to where I am today. People can start from nowhere and end up somewhere. Some start in debt and end up with big deposits. Some start at the bottom and end up at the top; some start way behind and come in first. Some start with enormous struggles but rise above them and do something noble, magical, and powerful with their lives. I call these godlike results.

God Started with Nothing

God also started out with nothing and ended up with something—this beautiful world. Out of the womb of nothingness, God said, "Let there be …" and there was. Okay, I know we humans can't do that, but we can come close in producing godlike results with the talents He has given us.

Doing the Remarkable

Yes, we can do remarkable things with our talents. We're born hungry for air and nourishment, and we stay that way throughout life. We also hunger for knowledge, wealth, affection, respect, power, prestige and influence—you name it—but our most important hunger is for God. Some of us have bigger appetites than others, but we need not lack an appetite for doing remarkable things with our lives, and here's why.

Other forms of life are driven by instincts and genetics, but we humans were custom designed by His hands and in His image. We're full of possibilities, and we can do the remarkable by recognizing there's something unique about us.

Do you know these facts?

- You give birth to 100 billion red blood cells every day.
- When you touch something, it sends a message to your brain at 124 mph.
- By this time tomorrow, your heart will have beaten around 100,000 times.
- You have over 600 muscles.
- Your eyes can distinguish up to one million colors.
- You make about a quart of saliva every day.
- Your lungs are large enough to cover half a tennis court.
- When you smile, you exercise thirty muscles.
- Your eyes can see more than the largest telescope can.
- You have copper, zinc, and nickel in your body and gold in your toenails.
- Your body can withstand impacts that would dent steel plate.
- Your body can repair itself without leaving a mark.
- You can take to the air more gracefully than a rocket.

You're amazing! God made you that way. The psalmist wrote,

> You formed the way I think and feel. You put me together in my mother's womb. (Psalm 139:13 ERV)

> I praise you because I am fearfully and wonderfully
> made; your works are wonderful, I know that full well.
> (Psalm 139:14 NIV)

So what can you do with your amazing self in spite of the challenges you face? What can you accomplish if you learn the lessons, adopt the disciplines, and feed on ideas? No telling!

With your divine gifts and abilities, you can produce godlike results. You can tear up your old life script that isn't working and write a new one. You can turn and head in the opposite direction. You can turn nothing into something. You can turn pennies into fortunes. You can turn rocks and weeds into gardens. And you can do so much more. You can transform forests into cities. You can turn small ideas into mega businesses. You can turn words into sentences, paragraphs, pages, chapters, and books. You can make money work for you instead of working for your money. Other people have done it, and so can you. If you can dream it, you can do it. If you can conceive it, you can birth it. If you can imagine it, you can invent it!

Final Word

The pursuit of your unique wealth requires you to seek God's help. Be creative! Don't despise small beginnings. Start with what you have. Let the story of the widow who went from being broke to being blessed inspire you to use what you have. You're a depository of divine gifts and talents, and not to be intrigued and excited about them is a tragedy.

A simple but powerful statement followed every creative act of God in Genesis 1 and 2; it was a statement of satisfaction and accomplishment. Each time God created something, He said, "Behold it was very good." God must've had a blast! He took a day off.

If you deploy your creativity as your Creator did, one of these days, you'll also sit back and look at all you've created, invented, or accomplished and say, "That's good."

My Personal Wealthy Place Notes

My Wealthy Place

Psalm 66:12

Chapter 7

Identifying Your Wealth-Creating Abilities

*Make a careful exploration of who you are and the work you
have been given, and then sink yourself into that.*
—Galatians 6:4 MSG

Okay, in the previous chapter, we determined that the acquisition of wealth is a worthy biblical ambition. We've also settled the fact that we have talent, and we must unearth those talents and deploy them for God's glory and the enrichment of our lives.

However, before you can tap into your wealth-creating abilities, talents, or gifts, you have to know what they are because they aren't decided but discovered. I've assembled an extensive list of specialized abilities God has breathed into us. I call them wealth-creating abilities because that's what they are. Read them and check off your initial impression concerning yourself. Then you could confer with someone who knows you well to help bring clarity to your conviction.

Bear in mind, all of these are also God-given abilities just as are the spiritual gifts we talked about earlier. Remember now, God didn't create you to be a jack of all trades; He created you special. Before you were born, God set you apart for a special assignment (Jeremiah 1:5). Hence, to be special, you have to specialize.

Specialized Wealth-Creating Abilities

1. **Welcoming Ability:** the God-given ability to convey warmth, build friendship, and make people feel happy and comfortable.
   - ☐ I definitely possess this wealth-creating ability.
   - ☐ I may possess this wealth-creating ability.
   - ☐ I definitely do not possess this wealth-creating ability.

2. **Entertaining Ability:** the God-given ability to perform, act, dance, speak, DJ.
   - ☐ I definitely possess this wealth-creating ability.
   - ☐ I may possess this wealth-creating ability.
   - ☐ I definitely do not possess this ability.

3. **Recruiting Ability:** the God-given ability to recruit, inspire, and motivate people to get involved and live out their life purposes.
   - ☐ I definitely possess this wealth-creating ability.
   - ☐ I may possess this wealth-creating ability.
   - ☐ I definitely do not possess this wealth ability.

4. **Interviewing Ability:** the God-given ability to evaluate and elicit information from others to discover their purpose, potential, and passion.
   - ☐ I definitely possess this wealth-creating ability.
   - ☐ I may possess this wealth-creating ability.
   - ☐ I definitely do not possess this wealth-creating ability.

5. **Researching Ability:** the God-given ability to read, gather material, and assemble data.
   - ☐ I definitely possess this wealth-creating ability.

☐ I may possess this wealth-creating ability.

☐ I definitely do not possess this wealth-creating ability.

6. **Creative or Artistic Ability:** the God-given ability to intellectualize, draw, paint, photograph, or make representations.

☐ I definitely possess this wealth-creating ability.

☐ I may possess this wealth-creating ability.

☐ I definitely do not possess this wealth-creating ability.

7. **Graphics or Visual Ability:** the God-given ability to lay out, design, and create visual displays or banners.

☐ I definitely possess this wealth-creating ability.

☐ I may possess this wealth-creating ability.

☐ I definitely do not possess this wealth-creating ability.

8. **Evaluating Ability:** the God-given ability to analyze, examine carefully, appraise data, and come to a conclusion.

☐ I definitely possess this wealth-creating ability.

☐ I may possess this wealth-creating ability.

☐ I definitely do not possess this wealth-creating ability.

Key Phrase

Before you were born, God set you apart for a special assignment (Jeremiah 1:5). Hence, to be special, you have to specialize.

---

9. **Planning Ability:** the God-given ability to strategize, design, and organize programs and events.

☐ I definitely possess this wealth-creating ability.

☐ I may possess this wealth-creating ability.

☐ I definitely do not possess this wealth-creating ability.

10. **Managing Ability:** the God-given ability to direct people to accomplish a task or event.

   ☐ I definitely possess this wealth-creating ability.

   ☐ I may possess this wealth-creating ability.

   ☐ I definitely do not possess this wealth-creating ability.

11. **Counseling Ability:** the God-given ability to provide advice and support to people to help them deal with problems and make important decisions.

   ☐ I definitely possess this wealth-creating ability.

   ☐ I may possess this wealth-creating ability.

   ☐ I definitely do not possess this wealth-creating ability.

12. **Teaching Ability:** the God-given ability to explain, train, coach, instruct demonstrate to, or tutor others.

   ☐ I definitely possess this wealth-creating ability.

   ☐ I may possess this wealth-creating ability.

   ☐ I definitely do not possess this wealth-creating ability.

13. **Writing Ability:** the God-given ability to use written words to express your ideas or opinions in any form.

   ☐ I definitely possess this wealth-creating ability.

   ☐ I may possess this wealth-creating ability.

   ☐ I definitely do not possess this wealth-creating ability.

14. **Editing Ability:** the God-given ability to proofread, rewrite, alter, adapt, or refine the written word and video and audio productions.

   ☐ I definitely possess this wealth-creating ability.

☐ I may possess this wealth-creating ability.

☐ I definitely do not possess this wealth-creating ability.

15. **Promoting Ability:** the God-given ability to successfully advertise events, people, and activities.

☐ I definitely possess this wealth-creating ability.

☐ I may possess this wealth-creating ability.

☐ I definitely do not possess this wealth-creating ability.

16. **Repairing Ability:** the God-given ability to fix and restore damaged or broken things.

☐ I definitely possess this wealth-creating ability.

☐ I may possess this wealth-creating ability.

☐ I definitely do not possess this wealth-creating ability.

17. **Feeding/Cooking Ability:** the God-given ability to cook for large or small groups.

☐ I definitely possess this wealth-creating ability.

☐ I may possess this wealth-creating ability.

☐ I definitely do not possess this wealth-creating ability.

18. **Recall Ability:** the God-given ability to remember what has been learned or experienced in the past.

☐ I definitely possess this wealth-creating ability.

☐ I may possess this wealth-creating ability.

☐ I definitely do not possess this wealth-creating ability.

19. **Mechanical Operating Ability:** the God-given ability to operate small or large equipment, tools, and machinery.

☐ I definitely possess this wealth-creating ability.

☐ I may possess this wealth-creating ability.

☐ I definitely do not possess this wealth-creating ability.

20. **Resourceful Ability:** the God-given ability to deal competently with new or difficult situations and find solutions to problems.

    ☐ I definitely possess this wealth-creating ability.

    ☐ I may possess this wealth-creating ability.

    ☐ I definitely do not possess this wealth-creating ability.

21. **Counting Ability:** the God-given ability to work with figures, data, or money.

    ☐ I definitely possess this wealth-creating ability.

    ☐ I may possess this wealth-creating ability.

    ☐ I definitely do not possess this wealth-creating ability.

22. **Classifying Ability:** the God-given ability to arrange books, data, records, and materials in classes or according to subject matter.

    ☐ I definitely possess this wealth-creating ability.

    ☐ I may possess this wealth-creating ability.

    ☐ I definitely do not possess this wealth-creating ability.

23. **Public Relations Ability:** the God-given ability to deal with complaints and provide information about people, organizations, or companies to others so they will regard that person or organization in a favorable manner.

    ☐ I definitely possess this wealth-creating ability.

    ☐ I may possess this wealth-creating ability.

    ☐ I definitely do not possess this wealth-creating ability.

24. **Composing Ability:** the God-given ability to create and write music or lyrics.

    ☐ I definitely possess this wealth-creating ability.

    ☐ I may possess this wealth-creating ability.

☐ I definitely do not possess this wealth-creating ability.

25. **Landscaping Ability:** the God-given ability to work with plants and improve the appearance of a tract of land.

☐ I definitely possess this wealth-creating ability.

☐ I may possess this wealth-creating ability.

☐ I definitely do not possess this wealth-creating ability.

26. **Decorating Ability:** the God-given ability to make a setting beautiful and attractive especially for a special event.

☐ I definitely possess this wealth-creating ability.

☐ I may possess this wealth-creating ability.

☐ I definitely do not possess this wealth-creating ability.

The purpose of this next exercise is to help you determine what you like doing and what you don't like doing. Support your choice by giving an example from your achievements or accomplishments in life. I did the first one as an example.

1. **Designing and Developing Ability:** the God-given ability to create something out of nothing or from scratch.

☐ Indeed, I love to create something out of nothing.

☐ I hate getting project started. I'm just not a starter.

❖ **My Example:** I designed and developed a website and data system from scratch for my church. The parishioners frequently tell me how user friendly the site is. Since then, I've had many offers to build websites for other churches.

2. **Pioneering Ability:** the God-given ability to take risks and try out new concepts.

☐ I love to take risks and venture into the unknown.

☐ I need assurances before I step out. I hate taking risk. I need security.

❖ **Give an Example:**

3. **Organizing Ability:** the God-given ability to bring order out of chaos or to make an evolving organization better.

☐ Indeed, I love to make an existing structure more effective and profitable.

☐ I hate getting involved in what other people have started. I hate cleaning up other people's mistakes.

❖ **Give an Example:**

4. **Maintaining and Operational Ability:** the God-given ability to effectively and efficiently sustain that which is already organized.

☐ I love working with effective and efficient structures and systems.

☐ I cannot stand routine. I love adventure. I strive on chaos.

❖ **Give an Example:**

5. **Serving or Helping:** the God-given ability to assist others and make it easier for them to do their jobs.

☐ I love and enjoy seeing or helping others succeed.

☐ I'm not a people's person. I hate working with people. I work better by myself.

❖ **Give an Example:**

6. **Acquiring and Possessing Ability:** the God-given ability to collect or obtain things (dilapidated buildings, furniture) by sustained effort or natural selection and repurpose them for profit.

☐ This is definitely me. I love to shop and come in possession of things. I always get quality at the best price. I'm a real collector.

☐ I hate shopping and collecting stuff. This is not me.

❖ **Give an Example:**

7. **Excelling and Developing Ability:** the God-given ability to surpass in accomplishment or achievement.

☐ I love to be the best, never settling for less than the best.

☐ I tend to get discouraged very easily. I normally start a project and do not finish. I'm not self-motivated.

❖ **Give an Example:**

8. **Influencing Ability:** the God-given ability to persuade people to my way of thinking, to join a cause, or to shape the attitudes and behavior of others.

☐ I love to convert people and shape their attitudes.

☐ No, this is not me. I tend to just leave people alone. Let them do what they wish.

❖ **Give an Example:**

9. **Performing Ability:** the God-given ability to entertain others by singing, acting, dancing, speaking, etc.

☐ I love to be on stage and get the attention of others. I love the limelight. This is me.

☐ I hate being up-front. I'm a background person. I'm shy.

❖ **Give an Example:**

10. **Leadership Ability:** the God-given ability to be in front, to give oversight and supervision to people.

☐ I love to lead the way.

☐ People are too difficult to lead. This is not me for sure.

❖ **Give an Example:**

11. **Perseverance Ability:** the God-given ability to see things through to completion, to not give up until a task is finished.

☐ I love to see things through to completion.

☐ This is not me. If things are too difficult, I just leave them alone.

❖ **Give an Example:**

Key Phrase

The things that are easy for me to do are also easy not to do, so I'm always experiencing tension between these two "easies." My advice is, if you want to be successful and wealthy, don't neglect the easy things.

---

12. **Following the Rules:** the God-given ability to follow structure, policies, and procedures.

☐ I love and enjoy meeting or fulfilling the expectations of my company or boss.

☐ I hate to work with policies and procedures; that's too restricting.

❖ **Give an Example:**

13. **Prevailing/Fighting Ability:** the God-given ability to fight for what is right and for others and to oppose injustice in any form.

☐ I feel God has called me to fight for the right of others.

☐ This is not me. You won't see me the street protesting injustice.

❖ **Give an Example:**

The Purpose of These Gifts

God endows you with abilities that will serve as an internal GPS for your life. They determine why you pursue a particular career.

Key Phrase

You must discover and live out the Creator's master plan for your life if you want to prosper.

They determine what your interests are and what will bring you the most success in the marketplace and life in general.

God-given abilities also help you determine what you instinctively feel deeply about and what you care less about. Your God-given life work will be something you will love and enjoy doing.

Talents Are Easy

It's easy to tell if you're naturally talented at something; if you're a talented singer, singing will be easy for you. Some people will ask, "If it's that easy, why I can't bring myself to do it?" I've discovered that sometimes, the things that are easy for me to do are also easy not to do, so I'm always experiencing tension between these two "easies." My advice is that if you want to be successful and wealthy, don't neglect the easy things.

The following exercise will help you to clarify our discussion. On the line below, please print your name.

> But remember the LORD your God, for it is He who gives _____ the ability to produce wealth, and so confirms his covenant, which he swore to your ancestors, as it is today. (Deuteronomy 8:18 NIV)

Again, print your name on the line below, but this time with your opposite hand. _____. I can hear you asking, "What's the catch?"

If you're right handed, writing your name was tough with your left hand, right? And vice versa. It took more time, and you still ended up doing a poor job. The same principle applies when you try to succeed or create wealth in a field where you're not naturally gifted. One law governing wealth and prosperity is that you must function in the area of your giftedness if you want to be paid well. You must discover and live out the Creator's master plan for your life if you want to prosper. God suited you for a unique life's work; He didn't intend for you to become a jack-of-all-trades.

If you wish to be special, you have to specialize. You alone can do your life's work better than anyone else. If this isn't clear, spend some time with God and get it clarified. You cannot develop your talents until you first identify your talents. Remember that you don't choose your talents; God already did that. What you have to do is discover what they are. Think what could happen if you determined what your talents were and invested them in the marketplace (however small you may think it is). The possibilities would be mind-blowing. Yes, you could be extremely happy and successful if you did.

But you'll make money only if what you're offering will also make money for others. The key to success is to find out what the marketplace is looking for and ask yourself, *What is the one thing I do better than anyone else in my field?* Look out for emerging trends and find a solution to the problems you hear about.

Final Word

Let me challenge you to treat your life as a time of sacred opportunity. Make good use of the talents or skills you've been given. The parables of the talents and the pounds remind us that even the smallest talent can be put to good use.

From the story of the widow, we learn we are never left without a choice, a seed, an option. We also learn God doesn't use what is gone. Rather, He uses what you're left with. He gives to each of us talents and says, "Engage in business till I come."

My Personal Wealthy Place Notes

Section III

My Wealthy Place
Psalm 66:12

Chapter 8

Wiping Out the Number-One Enemy of Wealth Creation

Sir, my husband has died! As you know, he was a God-fearing
man, but now a man he owed money to has come to take away
my two sons as slaves in payment for my husband's debt.
— 2 Kings 4:1b GNB

The Three Worst Human Illnesses

Here they are: stupid, broke, and sick! What a combination! Stupid, broke, and sick. It doesn't get any worse than that. Well, not so fast. There's probably one more—ugly.

You can tell by my opening joke that this chapter discusses a very serious subject, the D word, *debt*, which is no joke. It's your number-one enemy to wealth and prosperity. Therefore, no cat-and-mouse game here. You didn't make this investment for me to kid you. I congratulate you if you're not in debt. Well done! As a special gift to you, please skip this chapter if you wish.

In America and the world over, many people are deeply in debt. Years and years ago, debt was regarded as a very serious matter. Back then, the rule was that if someone didn't pay his or her debts, that person was regarded a thief; it was that simple.

People Would Rather Die

In ancient times, the matter of debt was taken so seriously that if people were unable to pay their debts, they would commit suicide rather than be dishonorable. I'm certainly not suggesting you do that. But today, credit cards have led people to get so deeply into debt that being indebted is the norm, and it doesn't bother us. Not only that—we put off paying our debts as long as possible or even avoid paying them altogether. Folks will borrow money without the slightest thought of repaying it. That's wrong. If you're indebted to someone, make it your goal to pay that debt off.

Debt is devastating, and by delaying paying your debt, you're simply delaying the pain. It will be a small fire that grows and grows and threatens you.

The Effect of Debt

> The rich rule over the poor, and the borrower is slave to the lender. (Proverbs 22:7 NIV)

- Debt puts you in bondage.
- Debt makes you a slave.
- Debt is like a millstone around your neck.
- Debt can affect your relationship with your spouse.
- Debt causes emotional, physical, and mental pain.
- Debt can bog you down and hold you back.
- Debt can cause anxiety and frustration.
- Debt can keep you from the flexibility you require to execute your God-given passion and purpose.
- Debt can affect your testimony as a believer.
- Debt can cause all kinds of pain.
- Debt can cause you to be gloomy, discouraged, depressed, frustrated, and angry.
- Debt can make you sick.

Ben Franklin said, "Think what you do when you run in debt: you give to another power over your own liberty."

Bad Debt vs. Good Debt

Though the word *debt* can invoke feelings of panic, dread, and fear, it doesn't always have to. One type of debt can move you forward; good debt and bad debt are both debt just as good cholesterol and bad cholesterol are both cholesterol. The difference is that good cholesterol and good debt can improve your physical and financial health.

A debt is generally considered good if it will ultimately put you in a better financial situation. Think about mortgages, investments in businesses, or college loans.

Bad debt is the opposite. An example is using credit cards for day-to-day purchases and paying high interest rates. On the other hand, when used smartly, a credit card can allow you to buy things that increase in value; that would be good debt, but not everyone uses their cards for this purpose.

Borrowing for a new car is generally considered bad debt because the car depreciates in value quickly. But if that new car is cheaper to operate or maintain than your old car, that could be considered good debt. It's a fine line at times; you'll have to calculate the difference over the long haul.

Debt can be good if you make smart spending decisions. Like bad cholesterol, often called the silent killer, bad debt can kill you. The downside with this good debt vs. bad debt philosophy is that when we label something good, it diminishes the urgency or the need to deal with it. So if you will, the only good debt is no debt.

Key Phrase

The downside with this good debt vs. bad debt philosophy is that when we label something good, it diminishes the urgency or the need to deal with it. So if you will, the only good debt is no debt.

Weight Watchers

Pounds are easy to put on but hard to take off; it's the same with debt—it's very easy to get into but very hard to get out of. If you're serious about going from

Key Phrase

Many people are poor not because of circumstances such as their backgrounds, the color of their skin, or a lack of opportunities but because they made poor spending decisions.

being broke to your wealthy place, you have to deal with debt, however painful that can be. Before we look at some specific ways to lose the weight of debt, let's explore the reasons why folks gain that debt weight in the first place.

First, folks gain debt when they don't watch their spending habits. How do we pack on the extra pounds? By not watching our eating habits and not exercising. The same applies to debt obesity. That's the simplest way I can say it! Many people spend far more than they earn. Their yearnings exceed their earnings. That's madness, but so many people ignore this simple fact. Someone said, "When your output exceeds your income, your upkeep will be your downfall."

The second reason for gaining debt weight is closely connected with the first: "I see it and I want it. Now!" I believe we have more money and stuff today than at any time. So what's the problem? Our expensive lifestyles and our desires for more stuff. The Scripture is correct.

> Human desires are like the world of the dead—there is always room for more. (Proverbs 27:20 GN)

Most of the debt we get into is not motivated by our needs but by our wants. The more we have, the more we want, and the more we're willing to get into debt for it. We're not willing to resist the urge to splurge. Even the wealthy can get into debt if their yearnings exceed their earnings. If you want out of debt, you have to control your wants!

The "buy now pay later" philosophy and the adverting industry are constantly telling us we need this and that to make our lives better, and that's gotten many of us into serious trouble. Are you still paying for things you bought on credit years ago that you're no longer using?

Many of us could easily finance our present lifestyle and save for the future if we weren't still paying off credit card debt. Folks, most of the stuff we spend money on we don't really need, but because of this "want it now" mentality, we got into debt by making unwise purchases. Many people are poor not because of circumstances such as their backgrounds, the color of their skin, or a lack of opportunities but because they made poor spending decisions. King Solomon, the richest man ever, said,

> Careful planning leads to profit. Acting too quickly (impulse spending) leads to poverty. (Proverbs 21:5 ERV)

The third reason folks gain debt weight is what I call situational factors. This may be due to sickness, the loss of a job, divorce, or the death of a loved one. It's tough to control debt in such situations. This was the case of the poor widow we talked about in the previous chapter.

> Now the wife of one of the sons of the prophets cried to Elisha, "Your servant my husband is dead, and you know that your servant feared the LORD, but the creditor has come to take my two children to be his slaves." (2 Kings 4:1 ESV)

Her predicament was aggravated by the fact that her creditors planned to sell her children as slaves to settle the debt; that was the law in those days. I pray you'll never have to go into debt due to loss of income or health. That's why it's important to save for rainy days and not get into debt in the first place if you can avoid it.

The fourth reason why folks gain debt weight is because they cosign for other people's loans. If you cosign a loan for anyone and that person can't repay it, you're legally required to repay

Key Phrase

True security is not determined by earthly riches such as stocks, shares, and savings but by trusting Jesus Christ exclusively as our Savior.

it. Consider carefully what you're doing. Cosigning is a promise to pay, and you could be putting what you have at risk. I'm amazed at how many people flout this fact. I beseech you not to cosign for anyone unless you're prepared to be legally responsible for that person's debt. And that's debt-free advice. Even God is opposed to cosigning for loans.

> Do not be one who shakes hands in pledge or puts up security for debts; if you lack the means to pay, your very bed will be snatched from under you. (Proverbs 22:26–27 NIV)

If God's opposed to this, so should you be. And this same rules applies to lending money to anyone. Always objectively assess a person's ability to repay a loan before you lend any money. If the borrower will not use your money wisely, you will have left the borrower in further debt and you without the money. Don't lend money unless you're prepared to write it off. And that's certainly debt-free advice.

The fifth reason people gain debt weight is by making shaky investments. I go into detail on this in chapter 13, so all I'll say here is that shaky investments can put you in a lot of doo-doo. Losing a little money is no big deal, but if you lose plenty, it can leave you in debt for the rest of your life. You probably know many people who made big-ticket investments without professional help and wound up in big debt.

There are no investments without risk, but the Bible warns us specifically about shaky investments.

> Here is a terrible thing that I have seen in this world: people save up their money for a time when they may need it, and then lose it all in some bad deal and end up with nothing left to pass on to their children. (Ecclesiastes 5:13–14 GNB)

The sixth reason people gain debt weight is due to self-delusion, the psychological and emotional reason for our indebtedness. This is based on three common misconceptions. The first misconception is what I call the satisfaction factor—the desire to possess more and more thinking that will bring satisfaction, but it never does.

If you purchase a nice painting, it will remain the same, and pretty soon, you'll get bored with it. You'll buy another, but your satisfaction with it will also go away in time. Wealth doesn't bring happiness, nor do those things that wealth can buy.

King Solomon made this observation.

> Those who love money will never be satisfied with the money they have. Those who love wealth will not be satisfied when they get more and more. This is also senseless. (Ecclesiastes 5:10 ERV)

Solomon wasn't saying it was wrong to acquire wealth; his point was that worldly wealth will never bring long-lasting satisfaction. Only Jesus can do that.

The second misconception I call the significance factor. We live in a society that focuses on status, and people unfortunately get into debt in vain attempts to raise their status. "It's so cool, and it'll make me look cool and make people look up to me!" All too often, people who say this don't even like those they're trying to impress; they're looking to prop up their own sense of identity. Thank God that many of us despise the idea that things make us

Key Phrase

All too often, people who say this don't even like those they're trying to impress; they're looking to prop up their own sense of identity.

important. We know they bring only a temporary thrill. Are you still excited about the computer you bought last year?

It's human nature to want bigger, better, newer, faster, but we have to keep in mind that our self-worth isn't based on our net worth but on our relationship with Jesus Christ. He thought we were worth dying for; that's how valuable we are. How many people would die for us? Jesus reminded us,

> Watch out and guard yourselves from every kind of greed; because your true life is not made up of the things you own, no matter how rich you may be. (Luke 12:15 GNB)

We find our self-worth not in things or designer labels. I'm not preaching we should remain old fashioned; I'm just saying our self-worth comes from knowing God.

The third misconception is what I call the security factor. People get into debt because they think that will bring them added security. Real security comes from trusting your life exclusively to God. The richest and wisest man ever said,

> Those who depend on their wealth will fall like the leaves of autumn, but the righteous will prosper like the leaves of summer. (Proverbs 11:28 GNB)

Consider the story of the rich fool, a great example in Scripture of someone seeking to find security through riches.

> There was a rich man who had some land. His land grew a very good crop of food. He thought to himself, "What will I do? I have no place to keep all my crops." Then he said, "I know what I will do. I will tear down my barns and build bigger barns! I will put all my wheat and good things together in my new barns. Then I can say to myself, 'I have many good things stored. I have saved enough for many years. Rest, eat, drink, and enjoy life!'" But God said to that man, "Foolish man! Tonight you will die. So what about the things you prepared for yourself? Who will get those things now?" (Luke 12:16–20 ERV)

True security is not determined by earthly riches such as stocks, shares, and savings but by trusting Jesus Christ exclusively as our Savior. It's not worth getting into debt based on these psychological and emotional factors. That's what Paul thought.

> I pray that the eyes of your heart may be enlightened in order that you may know the hope to which he has called you, the riches of his glorious inheritance in his holy people. (Ephesians 1:18 NIV)

Perhaps there's one more reason get into debt. It's one simple word we don't like to acknowledge: *envy*. I mean, you see other people sporting cool stuff and you say, "I have to get one too." Your neighbor redecorates, and you say, "Got to redecorate too." Someone buys a new car, and you say, "Got to change my car too." Know what I mean?

Let's turn our attention how to lose the debt weight and keep it off.Losing the Debt Weight

It's so easy to gain weight, but it's so difficult to lose it. If you've been on a diet high in fat, sugar, and sodium, you'll find it hard to change that at first. Ask me. I know. According to nutritionists, if we want to lose weight, we have to change our lifestyles as well as our diets. For that matter, any life changes can be very hard.

The same principle applies to debt—easy to gain, hard to lose. If you want off the debt cycle, you have to change your spending habits. According to the Bible, success in life require that we

> Lay aside every weight, and sin which clings so closely, and let us run with endurance the race that is set before us. (Hebrews 12:1)

Take note that the text says to lay aside every "weight" and "sin." Not every weight is sinful. The word *weight* denotes anything that is hindering a runner's progress. We have to shed whatever it is in life that's slowing us down and keeping us from our goal, and that includes debt.

With this diet metaphor in mind, I'll suggest four easy, or should I say difficult, exercise routines to help you lose your debt weight. I'll use the acronym DEBT for this workout.

Exercise 1: D—Determine Your Income and Outgo

Have you ever said in regard to money, "I just don't know where it all goes?" Can you imagine being the chief financial officer of a corporation and telling your superiors that? You'd be out of a job. You have to know where all your dollars are going. The prophet Elisha asked the widow who was in debt when she came begging for help, "What shall I do for you?" and "Tell me, what you have at home?" (2 Kings 4:2

Key Phrase

Though God hates debt, it's not a sin to get into debt, but it is a sin to walk away from it.

GNB). He was assessing her financial situation. This applies to you also. Getting out of debt starts with being aware of your financial reality. Hence, determining your weekly or monthly income and expenditures is the first step in shedding the debt weight. Say these aloud.

- I will determine all my assets.
- I will determine all my debts.
- I will determine my income.
- I will determine where all my money is going.

There's only one way to do this—by keeping accurate financial records. Otherwise, you won't know where your money went. Proverbs reminds us of that truth.

> Riches can disappear fast ... so watch your business interests closely. Know the state of your flocks and herds. (Proverbs 27:23–24 LB)

> Your money can be gone in a flash, as if it had grown wings and flown away like an eagle. (Proverbs 23:5 GNB)

I know that to be a fact. As you just read, keeping good financial records is a biblical principle as well as a sound accounting principle.

Determine How Much You Owe People

Let's talk about the above point, probably the most painful to confront. You might have to get a financial counselor to help you here. Fortunately, you're blessed with the greatest financial counselor, God, and He has some sound advice in regard to this. His plan for your life is not to owe money or get into debt in the first place. He issued this command.

> You should owe nothing to anyone, except that you will always owe love to each other. The person who loves others has done all that the law commands. (Romans 13:8 ERV)

> The wicked borrow and never pay back, but good people are generous with their gifts. (Psalm 37:21 GNB)

Paying Your Debts Is a Spiritual Obligation

We have a spiritual obligation to pay our debts. We might be tempted to walk away from this obligation, but if we did, we'd be dishonoring God. Though God hates debt, it's not a sin to get into debt, but it is a sin to walk away from it; it makes you "wicked."

God says we must repay what we owe. This is His financial counsel for our peace of mind. God wants to bless us and see us prosper by using our talents and repaying our debts; that's how we'll get to our wealthy place.

First Things First

As soon as the widow of 2 Kings 4 received her first paycheck, the prophet told her to take care of her debt.

> She went back to Elisha, the prophet, who said to her, "Sell the olive oil and pay all your debts, and there will be enough money left over for you and your sons to live on." (2 Kings 4:6–7 GNB)

Many financial experts say we should set aside emergency funds. I understand the rationale behind having some emergency money set aside, and if that makes you feel more

Key Phrase

With planned spending, you tell your money where to go rather than hearing it tell you where it went on its own.

comfortable, do so. But I believe paying off loans and debts (not mortgages) should be our priority. What's the point of putting money into a saving account that's paying 2 percent while carrying credit card debt that's costing you 25 or 30 percent?

Next, determine your income and expenditures. You can find budget templates and money diaries online. Print one and be diligent about keeping it up to date. List monthly income to the left and expenses to the right. You'll also find it helpful to complete an asset and liability sheet. Deduct the second from the first to determine your net worth.

Exercise 2: E—Eliminate Nonessential Expenses

Frugality was a very difficult one for me. Especially giving up cappuccino. Hey, relax. I'm not asking you to give up your "cappuccino," whatever it is. That won't get you out of debt; it'll just make you depressed. Rewarding yourself with something reasonable every time you pay down on your debt is a great idea; it will foster a sense of discipline and contentment with what you have.

> It is better to be satis-fied with what you have than to be always wanting something else. (Ecclesiastes 6:9 GN)

Be careful about spending money on things you don't really need, including eating out, buying new clothes, and going to the movies except on special occasions. Consider vacationing at home or buying a less-expensive television.

I know that this is extreme, but getting out of debt requires taking extreme measures. Use up what you have, make do with what you have, or do without. Except for your cappuccino of course!

Exercise 3: B—Budgeting

Some people call them budgets while others call them spending plans because the word *budget* makes them nervous. We'll call them spending plans here for their sake. With planned spending, you tell your money where to go rather than hearing it tell you where it went on its own. It's a step-by-step plan for meeting expenses and gives you control over you finances, helps you reduce stress, and builds assets.

For years, I thought being financially secure meant having lots of money. I didn't know I could be financially free regardless of how much I made. So I got a second job, but I was still getting into debt even with more money coming in.

Financial freedom doesn't come from earning more but from spending less regardless of how much you're earning. It's so important to understand this concept. Budgeting teaches you how to live on less now so you'll have more in the future.

Listen, I've discovered it's a myth that if you reach a certain level of income, you'll be financially free. I know many millionaires who aren't enjoying financial freedom. Sometimes, more income means more expenses, and if you cannot manage your money at level one, you aren't going to manage it at levels two or three either. But you can enjoy financial freedom at any level of income.

Because our culture is designed to trigger impulse buying, life dictates that you must develop a domestic budget, break the habit of impulsive spending, take the ceiling off your earning potential, and live a debt-free lifestyle as much as possible.

Plan carefully and you will have plenty; if you act too quickly, you will never have enough. (Proverbs 21:5 GNB)

Planning carefully is budgeting and acting too quickly is impulse purchasing.

Exercise 4: T—Time

Please also understand that there are no shortcuts to getting out of debt; that takes time. It can take ten years to pay off a $3000 credit card purchase if you make only the minimum payments. Credit card companies are strict with late-payment or underpayment fees. Such debt is your chief obstacle to getting to your wealthy place.

Your ascent to your wealthy place will take you through three financial levels, none of which you can skip over, and they all will take time.

The Three Financial Levels: Stability, Security, and Sovereignty

I listen to many people setting goals to become millionaires while they're drowning in debt; they're living in a fantasy world. It's okay to talk about earning millions, but you have to focus on one level at a time. If you're in debt, your first step is to get out of it and achieve financial stability.

1. Financial Stability

I do not have a specific definition of 'financial stability.' The word stable means not easily moved or the strength to stand or endure changes or threats. With regards to your finances, it means the strength to endure economic threats or disasters. At the very least, financial stability is your ability to pay your bills, save and invest some of your money and have at a minimum three months of emergency savings.

2. Financial Security

Invester Dictionary.com defines financial Security as follows: "Having an appropriate financial plan and enough financial resources to adequately fulfill any needs or most wants of an individual or business.

To me, financial security means to build a financial wall around myself and my family that nothing can touch me regardless of the economic wind.

3. Financial Sovereignty

Most people would refer to this as financial independence: But I love the word Sovereignty because the word is *'godlike'* and it speaks of someone in authority. Sovereignty is used to describe someone who is in total control of their money and not the other way around. It also means to possess an abundance of personal wealth or assets generated income to live, without the need to work actively for daily needs.

In addition to the principles that I have shared in this book, here are some tips for achieving financial sovereignty.

- Make a plan to pay off your credit card debt and stick to it.
- Talk with your creditors if you're having difficulties paying your debt and come to some agreement. You'll be surprised how willing they'll be to work with you.
- Avoid high-interest debt consolidation pranks or loans and any get-rich-quick schemes.
- Pay off debt rather than moving it around to other accounts.
- Set up repayment agreements for any unpaid amounts.
- Keep investing.
- Purchase income generating assets.
- Don't borrow money unless you really have to. Borrowing money from friends and family can damage relationships, and it's never simple.
- Above all, spend much less than you earn.

What to Do When Your Expenses Exceed Your Income

What payments should you take care of first? Glad you asked.

- Think about the well-being of your family first when you're prioritizing bills.
- Take care of your necessary_household expenses first—rent or mortgage and food.
- Seek assistance to help cover expenses.
- Seek credit counseling (2 Kings 6; Proverbs 15:22).
- Last resort: declare bankruptcy
- Ask for God's help. You can never tell. He might just give you a miracle. My favorite book says, "This poor man called, and the LORD heard him; he saved him out of all his troubles." (Psalm 34:6

I believe the poor man's trouble was financial; he was probably in a lot of debt, but God helped him when he called out to Him.

Final Word

If you're in debt, I can relate to you. I was in debt up to my neck. I understand. Debt is devastating! We've bought into a "buy now pay later" philosophy, and that's gotten us into a lot of doo-doo. Just grit your teeth and get out of debt as soon as possible. You must start now with a strong desire. You must be internally motivated because external motivations don't last. Yes! Begin right now. Don't procrastinate.

The first thing you probably notice about those who are debt-free and financially secure is their posture and demeanor; they have an air of confidence and a sense of well-being. They feel good about themselves; it shows even in the way they relate to others. Imagine yourself as such a person walking around with an upright stance and manner coupled with self-confidence and a sense of well-being.

If you act on the principles I shared with you, before you know it, you'll be out of debt and living the dream in your wealthy place. Remember the scriptural command.

> Let no debt remain outstanding, except the continuing debt to love one another, for whoever loves others has fulfilled the law. (Romans 13:8 NIV)

I leave you with quote from Primerica, a leading financial institution.

> Of all the threats to your financial security, none is more dangerous than debt. In every family's quest to feel good financially, debt is the most common enemy. The very fact that it is so common—who doesn't have debt?—makes it one of the biggest threats to your financial well-being.[3]

Wipe out debt before it wipes you out!

My Personal Wealthy Place Notes

Section IV

My Wealthy Place

Psalm 66:12

Chapter 9

Forbes' Wealthiest People of the Ancient World

He raiseth up the poor out of the dust, He lifteth up the needy from the dunghill, to make them sit with princes, and inherit the throne of glory: For the pillars of the earth are Jehovah's, and he hath set the world upon them.
—2 Samuel 2:8 ASV

I'm holding a copy of *Forbes* magazine, volume 193 that lists the richest people in the world.

> From welfare to zillionaire, more new millionaires, more billionaires … Records weren't merely broken within our twenty-eighth annual guide to the world's wealthiest; they were shattered. The planet's 1,645 billionaires are worth some $6.4 trillion, an 18.5 percent increase from last year. Two hundred and sixty-eight of them are making their first appearances on the list, and there are now a total of 172 women billionaires—42 of them newcomers.

Consider this: the minimum to make the top twenty is $31 billion. It's official, folks; the rich are certainly getting richer, and pretty soon, it won't be special anymore to be a millionaire.

I'm motivated by some of the stories of these super rich, particularly the story of Jan Koum of Silicon Valley, the WhatsApps phenomenon. According to

Key Phrase

You don't have to read far into the Bible before you discover it's replete with men and women who commanded extraordinary wealth.

Forbes, he went from welfare to zillionaire when he sold WhatsApps for $19 billion. There are some other great financial success stories in this magazine. I encourage you to get a copy. Their story will inspire you; and you might find contact with ideas that will change your life.

So after a second helping of the *Forbes* list of the richest people in the world, I thought I'd catalog a list of the richest people in the Bible. My hope is that you would find inspiration and motivation from their lives and take advantage of what's available to us all. Most of these ancient people were not only rich, they were also righteous. The reason God included these super rich in Scripture is that He wanted us to learn from their examples.

> These things happened unto them by way of example; and they were written for our admonition, upon whom the ends of the ages are come. (1 Corinthians 10:11 ASV)

Life Lessons from the Rich and Righteous in the Bible

You don't have to read far into the Bible before you discover it's replete with men and women who commanded extraordinary wealth. There are records after records of God blessing His children with abundant wealth. Virtually all our biblical heroes commanded great wealth. In fact, you have to think very hard to find one of these Bible heroes who was very poor. Let's start with the first couple.

Adam and Eve. Many people don't think of him as wealthy, but Adam was. Fresh from the hand of God, he and Eve were placed in a favorable environment and given dominion over all earth and its wealth.

> So God created man in his own image, in the image of God he created him; male and female he created them. And God blessed them. And God said to them, "Be fruitful and multiply and fill the earth and subdue it, and have dominion over the fish of the sea and over the birds of the heavens and over every living thing that moves on the earth." And God said, "Behold, I have given you every plant yielding seed that is on the face of all the earth, and every tree with seed in its fruit. You shall have them for food." (Genesis 1:27–29 ESV)

The land God gave the first family was rich in silver and gold (see Genesis 2:10–15). God blessed them and said they were to be fruitful and multiply. These terms signify abundance, prosperity, and great wealth. You have to agree that Adam was really rich and righteous. The text also speaks of God's original intent to bless and prosper Adam and Eve's descendants.

Abraham. He was the cattle, gold, and silver businessman, a man of great wealth. God blessed him with great substance.

> Abram was a very rich man, with sheep, goats, and cattle, as well as silver and gold. (Genesis 13:2 GNB)

Another text states,

> "I am the servant of Abraham," he began. "The LORD has greatly blessed my master and made him a rich man. He has given him flocks of sheep and goats, cattle, silver, gold, male and female slaves, camels, and donkeys." (Genesis 24:34–35 GNB)

The word *rich* in the text means weighty, loaded, with an abundance. The same wealth and abundance given to Abraham is available to all who enjoy a personal relationship with Jesus Christ. But watch this—it's made available only to those who will appropriate them.

> Christ redeemed us from the curse of the law by becoming a curse for us—for it is written, "Cursed is everyone who is hanged on a tree"— so that in Christ Jesus the blessing of Abraham might come to the Gentiles, so that we might receive the promised Spirit through faith. To give a human example, brothers: even with a man-made covenant, no one annuls it or adds to it once it has been ratified. Now the promises were made to Abraham and to his offspring. It does not say, "And to offsprings," referring to many, but referring to one, "And to your offspring," who is Christ. (Galatians 3:14–16 ESV)

Lot, Abraham's nephew and business partner. Lot was a very wealthy man. The wealth and prosperity of his uncle overflowed upon him.

> And Lot also, which went with Abram, had flocks, and herds, and tents. And the land was not able to bear them, that they might dwell together: for their substance was great, so that they could not dwell together. (Genesis 13:5–6 KJV)

As a consequence of their increasing wealth, this power duo had to part ways; the land couldn't support both. There were bitter disputes between Abraham and Lot's employees. Sometimes, it will be necessary to disassociate ourselves from others for business purposes and peace of mind.

Isaac, the shy but savvy investor. He was heir to Abraham's estate. Abraham's will read,

> Abraham left everything he owned to Isaac; but while he was still alive, he gave presents to the sons his other wives had borne him. Then he sent these sons to the land of the East, away from his son Isaac. Abraham died at the ripe old age of 175. (Genesis 25:57 GNB)

Isaac built on his father's huge estate and became very wealthy in his own right.

> There was another famine in the land besides the earlier one during the time of Abraham ... Isaac sowed crops in that land, and that year he harvested a hundred times as much as he had sown, because the LORD blessed him. He continued to prosper and became a very rich man. Because he had many herds of sheep and cattle and many servants. The Philistines were jealous of him. (Genesis 26:1, 12–14 GNB)

These gentlemen were estimated to be wealthier than the king of Philistia. The most remarkable thing about Isaac was that he became wealthy during one of the worst economic recessions in the ancient world. This makes the point that you can make money even in economic downturns. His enemies envied his wealth; not many will be happy for your success.

Jacob. He was part of Isaac's dysfunctional dynasty that included Esau and Rebekah. Jacob obtained his father's (Isaac) wealth by deceit and bribery. He's known in Scripture as the cheater and fraudster. His mother, Rebekah, was the mastermind behind a plot successfully executed by her and her cheater son. They took advantage of the old man and took Esau's birthright.

Besides the wealth he inherited, which had been passed on from his grandfather, Abraham, to his father, Isaac, Jacob became very wealthy in his own

Key Phrase

The same wealth and abundance given to Abraham is available to all who enjoy a personal relationship with Jesus Christ.

right. According to the Bible, God was actually helping him.

Because of his evil schemes, he had to run out of town to escape his brother's vengeance. But after years on the run and further bribery, Jacob's wealth continued to grow.

Eventually, his fortunes turned around; he had an encounter with the God of his fathers. He reached a settlement with his brother in the sum of 550 head of livestock (Genesis 32:13). Bear in mind that in ancient times, wealth was measured in terms of livestock. Hence, a person had to be pretty wealthy to make such a generous gift. What can we learn from Jacob? We can learn it's not good to become wealthy by fraud, stealing, and cheating. Don't become wealthy through skullduggery; prosper with your integrity intact.

Esau, Jacob's twin. Although he had been cheated out of his birthright, he recovered from it and became extremely wealthy.

> And Esau took his wives, and his sons, and his daughters, and all the persons of his house, and his cattle, and all his beasts, and all his substance, which he had got in the land of Canaan; and went into the country from the face of his brother Jacob. For their riches were more than that they might dwell together; and the land wherein they were strangers could not bear them because of their cattle. (Genesis 36:6–7 KJV)

Who said you can't recover from losses, robbery, betrayal, and setbacks and become rich and powerful? Esau proves that if you don't give up, you can bounce back from financial setbacks.

Key Phrase

The most remarkable thing about Isaac was that he became wealthy during one of the worst economic recessions in the ancient world.

Joseph, the convicted sex offender. Joseph was a man of considerable means. He worked for the Egyptian government and managed the Egyptian economy; he led the country to growth and prosperity over fourteen years.

> And so Joseph was appointed governor over all Egypt. The king said to him, "I am the king—and no one in all Egypt shall so much as lift a hand or a foot without your permission." (Genesis 41:44 GNB)

This was unprecedented when you consider Joseph's background. He was hated by his brothers, sold into slavery, and imprisoned for a sex crime. But God is no respecter of persons. Joseph wrote about what he had amassed in Egypt.

> And the name of the second called he Ephraim: For God hath caused me to be fruitful in the land of my affliction. (Genesis 41:52 KJV)

Joseph married into the most wealthy and influential family in Egypt. He was second next to the great pharaoh and enjoyed all the privileges of a statesman. He also inherited most of his father's wealth.

> And Israel said to Joseph, Behold, I die. But God shall be with you, and bring you again into the land of your

> fathers. And I have given to you one portion above
> your brothers, which I took out of the hand of the
> Amorite with my sword and with my bow. (Genesis
> 48:21–22 MKJV)

We learn from this that bad spells don't last forever and that the art of overcoming obstacles personal and professional will help you make it to the top.

Nabal, the ever-divisive millionaire. This livestock businessman was quite a colorful character, a coarse and churlish man. Don't take my word for it.

> And there was a man in Maon whose business was in
> Carmel. The man was very rich; he had three thousand
> sheep and a thousand goats. He was shearing his sheep
> in Carmel. Now the name of the man was Nabal, and
> the name of his wife Abigail. (1 Samuel 25:2a ESV)

In stark contrast,

> His wife Abigail was beautiful and intelligent, but he
> was a mean, bad-tempered man. (1 Samuel 25:2b GNB)

This guy's name means "fool." He probably acquired his name by his conduct. It could have been given to him by his parents, but what parent would give a child such a name? However, what really puzzles me is why a bright and beautiful woman stay with this coarse, churlish man. How did they get together in the first place? She probably married him not for his looks and stupidity but for his wealth.

At any rate, Nabal was financially savvy enough to acquire immense wealth. We can learn from this guy that anybody can make money if he or she has half a brain.

King David, the man after God's own heart. When most people think of King David, they immediately think of his adulterous affair with Bathsheba. He wasn't known for being wealthy, but he was. Just take a look at his tax returns.

Key Phrase

Bad spells don't last forever, and the art of overcoming obstacles personal and professional will help you make it to the top.

> Moreover, in addition to all that I have provided for the holy house, I have a treasure of my own of gold and silver, and because of my devotion to the house of my God. I give it to the house of my God: 3,000 talents of gold, of the gold of Ophir, and 7,000 talents of refined silver, for overlaying the walls of the house, and for all the work to be done by craftsmen, gold for the things of gold and silver for the things of silver. Who then will offer willingly, consecrating himself today to the LORD? (1 Chronicles 29:3–5 ESV)

Experts have estimated that three thousand talents of gold was equivalent to $13.5 million today, and seven thousand talents of silver was equivalent to $2.5 million. The value of Ophir is still considered undetermined. I'm telling you, this guy was rich! He also died very wealthy. So said his epitaph.

> He (David) died at a ripe old age, wealthy and respected, and his son Solomon succeeded him as king. (1 Chronicles 29:28 GNB)

King Solomon, the first Bible billionaire. King Solomon was the Bill Gates of his time. He inherited his father's (David) immense wealth, and God blessed him with more riches. According to the Bible,

God appeared to Solomon in a vision and told him to name whatever his heart wished for.

> The Lord was pleased that Solomon had asked for this, and so he said to him, "Because you have asked for the wisdom to rule justly, instead of long life for yourself or riches or the death of your enemies, I will do what you have asked. I will give you more wisdom and understanding than anyone has ever had before or will ever have again. I will also give you what you have not asked for: all your life you will have wealth and honor, more than that of any other king." (1 Kings 3:13 GNB)

Solomon's yearly income, not including royalties, is in 1 Kings 10.

> Every year King Solomon received over twenty-five tons of gold, In addition to the taxes s paid by merchants, the profits from trade, and tribute paid by the Arabian kings and the governors of the Israelite districts. (1 Kings 10:14–15 GNB)

> And all the earth sought to Solomon, to hear his wisdom, which God had put in his heart. And they brought every man his present, vessels of silver, and vessels of gold, and garments, and armour, and spices, horses, and mules, a rate year by year. (1 Kings 10:24–25 KJV)

Read 2 Chronicles 9 for more about King Solomon's wealth and be dazzled! The queen of Sheba was when she visited him, a money magnet.

All the kings of the earth came to listen and learn from Solomon because of the wisdom God had put in his heart. His gifts and skills transcended all social, religious, and political barriers. This same principle applies to you. If you can offer the marketplace something—a skill or talent—no one else can offer, folks will pursue you and pay you for it over and over.

Boaz and Ruth, the power couple. Boaz, a man of considerable influence, power, and wealth, is the subject of one of the most heartwarming love stories in the Bible.

> Naomi had a relative named Boaz, a rich and influential man who belonged to the family of her husband Elimelech. (Ruth 2:1 GNB)

> So Boaz took Ruth, and she was his wife: and when he went in unto her, the LORD gave her conception, and she bare a son. And the women said unto Naomi, Blessed be the LORD, which hath not left thee this day without a kinsman, that his name may be famous in Israel. (Ruth 4:13–14 KJV)

Ruth, the Moabite, was David's great-grandmother. Her rags-to-riches story is fascinating. Due to severe famine in the land of Canaan, Elimelech's family, his daughter Naomi, and two sons migrated to Moab. There, Naomi's husband died, leaving her with her two sons. Later, her sons married Moabites, Ruth and Orpah. In time, tragedy hit the family— Ruth's and Orpah's husbands died, leaving three widows destitute.

Naomi decided to return to her homeland. After failing to persuade Ruth, her daughter-in-law, to return to her mother's home, both women went back to their homeland. There, Ruth met her husband Boaz, an extended family member. According to Jewish law, the next of male kin had to marry the wife of the deceased to carry on the family name. It was also a form of ancient Social Security for the women.

Naomi realized this and advised Ruth how to win Boaz's affections. The plan worked. Boaz fell in love with Ruth, and she became

Key Phrase

Once you have money, don't flaunt it. Be refined and cultured with what God has blessed you.

his wife. A very smart girl. The marriage elevated Ruth from rags to riches. If you're poor and you can help it, don't marry another poor person like yourself. Marry up if you can.

The Queen of Sheba. There were wealthy women in ancient times, one of whom was the queen of Sheba, probably the first wealthy black sista'. Sheba was in southwestern Arabia, present-day Yemen.

The Sabeans traded in precious commodities—gold, gemstones, perfumes, and spices. She probably earned her wealth from such trading or inherited her money. At any rate, she was wealthy, and she posed some difficult questions to King Solomon to satisfy her curiosity about his wisdom and of course his incredible wealth.

> And she gave the king an hundred and twenty talents of gold, and of spices very great store, and precious stones: there came no more such abundance of spices as these which the queen of Sheba gave to King Solomon. (1 Kings 10:10 KJV)

This sista' lived her life in style. She must have been truly rich to give such a gift. That is what we call living your life in style.

The Great woman of Shunem. She was another woman of substance. Wealth isn't sexist. God's principle of wealth works for everyone regardless of sex, race, color, or creed. This wealthy woman showed great hospitality to the prophet Elisha whenever he was in town.

One day Elisha went to Shunem, where a rich woman lived. She invited him to a meal, and from then on every time he went to Shunem he would have his meals at her house. She said to her husband, "I am sure that this man who comes here so often is a holy man. Let's build a small room on the roof, put a bed, a table, a chair, and a lamp in it, and he can stay there whenever he visits us." (2 Kings 4:8–10 GNB)

The fact that she was mentioned above her husband shows she was a woman of substance, perhaps the one who brought her husband the bulk of his wealth.

The Proverbs 31 woman. We don't often think of this woman as a person of wealth, but her financial statement shows she might have well had considerable wealth. She was an entrepreneur who sold the superfluous work of her hands to merchants and purchased land with the proceeds.

She looks at land and buys it, and with money she has earned she plants a vineyard. She is a hard worker, strong and industrious. She knows the value of everything she makes, and works late into the night. She spins her own thread and weaves her own cloth. She is generous to the poor and needy. She doesn't worry when it snows, because her family has warm clothing. She makes bedspreads and wears clothes of fine purple linen. Her husband is well known, one of the leading citizens. She makes clothes and belts, and sells them to merchants. She is strong and respected and not afraid of the future. (Proverbs 31:16–25 GNB)

Jehoshaphat, king of Judah. Jehoshaphat, the money master, had riches and honor in abundance thanks to his obedience and faithfulness to God. He became the first king after David to obey God's commandments, and he took delight in the Lord's ways. As a result, God established the kingdom in his hands and blessed him with unprecedented wealth.

> The LORD established the kingdom under his control;
> and all Judah brought gifts to Jehoshaphat, so that he
> had great wealth and honor. (2 Chronicles 17:5 NIV)

Hezekiah, king of Judah and wealthy bank owner. This Old Testament king was so wealthy that he built special treasury buildings to store gold, silver, precious stones, shields, spices, and other valuables. This wealthy wizard built his personal banks and cities. He also built stalls for flocks and herds and many cities for his enjoyment.

> King Hezekiah became very wealthy, and everyone held him in honor. He had storerooms built for his gold, silver, precious stones, spices, shields, and other valuable objects. In addition, he had storehouses built for his grain, wine, and olive oil; barns for his cattle; and pens for his sheep. Besides all this, God gave him sheep and cattle and so much other wealth that he built many cities. (2 Chronicles 32:27–29 GNB)

King Ahasuerus (also called Xerxes), an extravagant king. The Scripture did not say how he amassed his fortune, but he was wealthy; he hosted the most extravagant feast on record to display his wealth to the great lords of his glorious kingdom. This vain exhibition of wealth went on for 180 days. The multitudes were entertained in the palace garden, where gorgeous awnings were slung from marble pillars. The guests reclined on couches of gold and silver placed on marble pavement. They were served with delicious viands and costly wines from the cellar of the king.

Imagine being a guest there and reclining on a luxurious couch. Read the story. You can almost taste the wealth.

> From his royal throne in Persia's capital city of Susa, King Xerxes ruled 127 provinces, all the way from India to Ethiopia. In the third year of his reign he gave a banquet for all his officials and administrators. The armies of Persia and Media were present, as well as the governors and noblemen of the provinces.
>
> For six whole months he made a show of the riches of the imperial court with all its splendor and majesty. After that, the king gave a banquet for all the people in the capital city of Susa, rich and poor alike. It lasted a whole week and was held in the gardens of the royal palace. The courtyard there was decorated with blue and white cotton curtains, tied by cords of fine purple linen to silver rings on marble columns. Couches made of gold and silver had been placed in the courtyard, which was paved with white marble, red feldspar, shining mother-of-pearl, and blue turquoise.
>
> Drinks were served in gold cups, no two of them alike, and the king was generous with the royal wine. There were no limits on the drinks; the king had given orders to the palace servants that everyone could have as much as they wanted. (Esther 1:1–8 GNB)

We can learn here that the possession of wealth is not a license to display it. If you want to hold onto your wealth, use it wisely. Once you have money, don't flaunt it. Be refined and cultured with what God has blessed you.

Job, the wealthiest worshipper of the East. He prospered with integrity.

There was a man in the land of Uz, whose name was Job; and that man was perfect and upright, and one that feared God, and eschewed evil. And there were born unto him seven sons and three daughters. His substance also was seven thousand sheep, and three thousand camels, and five hundred yoke of oxen, and five hundred she asses, and a very great household; so that this man was the greatest of all the men of the east. (Job 1:1–3 KJV)

Key Phrase

If Job were with us today, he'd tell us we could lose everything—health, family, wealth—and bounce back from these losses.

Again, wealth was estimated by the amount of livestock one possessed among the nomads. The text says, "His substance," his wealth. Job went through several trials and lost all his wealth, but before he died, God had restored twice as much to him.

So the LORD blessed the latter end of Job more than his beginning: for he had fourteen thousand sheep, and six thousand camels, and a thousand yoke of oxen, and a thousand she asses. He had also seven sons and three daughters. (Job 42:12–13 KJV)

According to the *Dakes Annotated Reference Bible*, Job's initial wealth was estimated at $790,000. His total estimated wealth was $1,580,000. God gave him double for his trouble.

If Job were with us today, he'd tell us we could lose everything—health, family, wealth—and bounce back from these losses. He'd probably say, "If you fall on your back financially, don't beat yourself too much. It's not what you lost that matters; it's what you learn from that which matters. It's the next opportunity that counts. Your losses set

you up for your successes." He
believed it's a myth you cannot
be righteous and filthy rich.

*The way we handle our wealth may well
determine where we spend eternal life.*

**Wealth of the church in the
wilderness.** The church in the
wilderness wasn't poor as many people believe. Here's a copy of the
church in the wilderness's financial statement I obtained from a reliable
source.

> These are the offerings you are to receive from them:
> gold, silver and bronze; blue, purple and scarlet yarn
> and fine linen; goat hair; ram skins dyed red and
> another type of durable leather; acacia wood; olive oil
> for the light; spices for the anointing oil. and for the
> fragrant incense; and onyx stones and other gems to
> be mounted on the ephod and breastpiece. Then have
> them make a sanctuary for me, and I will dwell among
> them. (Exodus 25:3–8 NIV)

> The skilled workers said to Moses, "The people are
> bringing more than enough for doing the work the
> LORD commanded to be done." Then Moses gave an
> order and they sent this word throughout the camp:
> "No man or woman is to make anything else as an
> offering for the sanctuary." And so the people were
> restrained from bringing more, because what they
> already had was more than enough to do all the work.
> (Exodus 36:5–7 NIV)

When God instructed Moses to build the tabernacle, the first
worship center, the people gave so much that Moses had to stop them
from giving. Where did they get all that money? They were in the
wilderness and had been slaves for four hundred years. Something

remarkable had happened. God had given them favor in the eyes of the Egyptians just before the Exodus. The Egyptians paid them for their four hundred years of hard work in jewels, gold, silver, and clothing. They left Egypt extremely wealthy. Their financial statements read like this.

> And (God) I will make the Egyptians favorably disposed toward this people, so that when you leave you will not go empty-handed. Every woman is to ask her neighbor and any woman living in her house for articles of silver and gold and for clothing, which you will put on your sons and daughters. And so you will plunder the Egyptians. (Exodus 3:21–22 ESV; see 11:2)

> The Israelites had done as Moses had said, and had asked the Egyptians for gold and silver jewelry and for clothes. The LORD made the Egyptians respect the people and give them what they asked for. In this way the Israelites carried away the wealth of the Egyptians. (Exodus 12:35–36 GNB)

Take notice of the phrase "They carried away the wealth of the Egyptians"; the Egyptians, "glad at their departing," paid them to expedite their flight. The Hebrews received everything they needed—this was the first and greatest wealth transfer in history. It also confirms the wealth of the wicked is stored up for the righteous as long as they take it.

You can also count on your God to show you favor. He has a divine plan for your financial welfare. If you trust the Lord and cooperate with Him, He will cause people to show you favor.

Let's consider some of the wealthiest people of the New Testament.

Zacchaeus the tax collector. The Scripture states,

> There was a chief tax collector there named Zacchaeus, who was rich. (Luke 19:2 GNB)

Zacchaeus, the guy everybody hated, was the head of customs at the department at Jericho. Being the head, he found it easy to enrich himself at the expense of others. This may have explained his remarks to Jesus.

> Zacchaeus stood up and said to the Lord, "Listen, sir! I will give half my belongings to the poor, and if I have cheated anyone, I will pay back four times as much." (Luke 19:8 GNB)

The rich, young ruler, the youngest billionaire in the Bible. The Bible didn't say how he got his wealth, only that he had great wealth and was young. I love this story about this rich kid. He wanted to know how to have eternal life, so he went to Jesus, knelt down, and inquired,

> "Teacher, what good thing must I do to get eternal life?"

What a great question! Never leave a great question of this magnitude unanswered. He shouldn't have asked.

> "Why do you ask me about what is good?" Jesus replied. "There is only One who is good. If you want to enter life, keep the commandments." "Which ones?" he inquired. Jesus replied, "'You shall not murder, you shall not commit adultery, you shall not steal, you shall not give false testimony, honor your father and mother,' and 'love your neighbor as yourself.'" "All these I have kept," the young man said. "What do I still lack?"

> Jesus answered, "If you want to be perfect, go, sell your possessions and give to the poor, and you will have treasure in heaven. Then come, follow me." When the young man heard this, he went away sad, because he had great wealth. (Matthew 19:16–22 NIV)

This is a reminder to us that wealth can become a hindrance to gaining eternal life. It's okay to possess great wealth as long as it doesn't possess us; the way we handle our wealth may well determine where we spend eternal life.

Joseph of Arimathea. Joseph was well off and an honored member of the high council, the Sanhedrin. As were many others, he was waiting for the arrival of the kingdom of God. He was "a disciple of Jesus," one of His secret followers due perhaps to his seat on the Sanhedrin. He was also incredibly rich.

> As evening approached, there came a 'rich man' from Arimathea, named Joseph, who had himself become a disciple of Jesus. Going to Pilate, he asked for Jesus' body, and Pilate ordered that it be given to him. Joseph took the body, wrapped it in a clean linen cloth, and placed it in his own new tomb that he had cut out of the rock. He rolled a big stone in front of the entrance to the tomb and went away. (Matthew 27:57–60 NIV)

You had to be very wealthy then to have your tomb hewn out of a rock. He had to have immense power and influence to make such a request for the body of Jesus.

Joseph, Mary's husband. Again, most of us believe Joseph was poor because he was a carpenter. Carpentry wasn't considered a rich person's occupation in those days, but it all depended on the level of your skills.

At any rate, according to the Bible, he was considered a man of means.

Key Phrase

God is the God of all humanity. His purpose concerning salvation, personal health, and wealth encompasses all, not just some of us.

> And it happened in those days that a decree went out from Caesar Augustus that all the world should be taxed. (This taxing was first made when Cyrenius was governor of Syria.) And all went to be registered, each to his own city. And Joseph also went up from Galilee to be taxed (out of the city of Nazareth, into Judea, to the city of David which is called Bethlehem, because he was of the house and family line of David). (Luke 2:1–4 MKJV)

According to Luke, Joseph was a descendant of King David, an important point. The couple traveled to Jerusalem to pay taxes, and poor people don't have money to pay taxes. For that reason, I don't believe he was poor; odds are he was man of means.

The Roman centurion who believed. In Luke, we meet another wealthy believer, a centurion whose slave Jesus healed.

> Now a centurion had a servant who was sick and at the point of death, who was highly valued by him. When the centurion heard about Jesus, he sent to him elders of the Jews, asking him to come and heal his servant. And when they came to Jesus, they pleaded with him earnestly, saying, "He is worthy to have you do this for him, for he loves our nation, and he is the one who built us our synagogue." (Luke 7:2–5 ESV)

It didn't say he was wealthy, but note the obvious sign of wealth. He paid for the synagogue, owned a slave, and showed kindness to poor people; he had to be a man of some means.

Wealthy women who supported Jesus' ministry. This is my favorite story. Among the wealthiest women of the Bible, we meet a group of wealthy church sisters in Luke.

> Soon afterward he went on through cities and villages, proclaiming and bringing the good news of the kingdom of God. And the twelve were with him, and also some women who had been healed of evil spirits and infirmities: Mary, called Magdalene, from whom seven demons had gone out, and Joanna, the wife of Chuza, Herod's household manager, and Susanna, and many others, who provided for them out of their means. (Luke 8:1-3 ESV)

Some of these sisters belong to the wealthy class; some even occupied responsible and noble position in society. Joanna was the wife of Chuza, Herod's steward, a wealthy family, and she was of high rank at the court of Herod Antipas and was a person of wealth (see Luke 24:10).

These women were healed from diseases, delivered from demons, and had their dead raised back to life. They were blessed by the Master, and out of hearts of gratitude, these grateful souls underwrote Jesus' ministry and His disciples, twelve grown men some of who had families then.

We learn from the these grateful women that the best use of our money is to invest it in the kingdom of God so others can be changed, healed, delivered, set free, touched, and impacted.

Lydia, the wealthy worshipper of God. This wealthy woman had a lucrative business selling purple cloth, a very expensive material only the wealthy could afford. She responded to the message of salvation and was baptized along with her entire house. She hosted the first church in Europe in her home.

> One who heard us was a woman named Lydia, from the city of Thyatira, a seller of purple goods, who was a worshiper of God. The Lord opened her heart to pay attention to what was said. And after she was baptized, and her household as well, she urged us, saying, "If you have judged me to be faithful to the Lord, come to my house and stay. And she prevailed upon us." (Acts 16:14–15 ESV)

I like the fact she was a worshipper of God. Who said you cannot be a worshipper of God and be wealthy? That's a myth. Wealthy people are coming to the body of Christ.

Other Wealthy New Testament believers. There were other wealthy believers, maybe not millionaires, but people who possessed decent wealth. This included Philemon, who owned slaves and property. You can read his story in Philemon 1.

Next was the seemingly well-to-do dynamic duo Ananias and Sapphira, who had a real estate business. Their story (in Acts 5) is a fascinating but tragic story about how they sold some property, withheld some of the proceeds, and lied about it. The Holy Spirit took their lives. But my point here is that they were wealthy folks who had considerable assets.

> But there was a man named Ananias, who with his wife
> Sapphira sold some property that belonged to them.
> (Acts 5:1 GNB)

Next, we meet the wealthy Ethiopian queen's treasurer in Act 8. He had been to Jerusalem to worship God and was going home. As he rode along, he was reading Isaiah.

In Acts 10, we meet another well-to-do-person, Cornelius, a centurion noted for his prayer and his generosity to the poor.

> In the city of Caesarea there was a man named
> Cornelius, a Roman army officer in what was called
> the Italian Unit. He was a religious man. He and all the
> others who lived in his house were worshipers of the
> true God. He gave much of his money to help the poor
> people and always prayed to God. (Acts 10:1–2 ESV)

Note the appropriate use of money. Cornelius proved you can be prayerful and prosperous; you don't have choose one or the other.

Thoughts on the Wealth of the Early Church

The vast majority of people in the early church commanded considerable wealth and helped out any of the poor among them.

> All the believers continued together in close fellowship
> and shared their belongings with one another. They
> would sell their property and possessions, and distribute
> the money among all, according to what each one
> needed. (Acts 2:44–45 GNB)

Final Word

The Bible repeatedly shows you can be wealthy and still be a worshipper of God, who is not a respecter of person; He doesn't show favoritism. What He did for the ancients He can do for you.

God is the God of all humanity. His purpose concerning salvation, personal health, and wealth encompasses all, not just some of us. And his principles of finance work for everyone regardless of race, color, sex, or creed—so says Scripture.

> I now realize how true it is that God does not show favoritism but accepts from every nation the one who fears him and does what is right. (Acts 10:34 NIV)

Since that's true, I challenge you to reach out and appropriate all God has in store for you.

My Personal Wealth Place Notes

My Wealthy Place

Psalm 66:12

Chapter 10

Thoughts On Wealth In The Life Of Jesus

You know the grace of our Lord Jesus Christ; rich as he was, he made himself poor for your sake, in order to make you rich by means of his poverty.
— 2 Corinthians 8:9 GNB

Most of the time when we think about Jesus, we don't think of Him as a wealthy person but as a wanderer in hand-me-down clothes and dusty sandals who fed off scraps. We have inherited a religious tradition about "poor little Jesus." Preachers have delivered great sermons on the blessedness of poverty, referencing Jesus' birth in a stable as evidence that Jesus and his family were poor.

> And she brought forth her firstborn son, and wrapped him in swaddling clothes, and laid him in a manger; because there was no room for them in the inn. (Luke 2:7 KJV)

It didn't say they couldn't afford a room; it said none was available. Thousands were visiting Jerusalem at the order of Caesar Augustus, and all the hotels were filled. Their only recourse was stable.

Wise Men Gave Jesus Great Wealth

I'll make a statement that will shock you. Jesus never had a financial need in the world. The Holy Spirit compelled the wise men to give the young King valuable gifts.

Key Phrase

On the contrary, Jesus was given the customary gifts given only to kings then. These included at least seven caravans of gold, spices, ointments, and precious stones.

> Jesus was born in the town of Bethlehem in Judea, during the time when Herod was king. Soon afterward, some men who studied the stars came from the East to Jerusalem and asked, "Where is the baby born to be the king of the Jews? We saw his star when it came up in the east, and we have come to worship him." (Matthew 2:1–2 GNB)

> They went into the house, and when they saw the child with his mother Mary, they knelt down and worshiped him. They brought out their gifts of gold, frankincense, and myrrh, and presented them to him. (Matthew 2:11 GNB)

We traditionally think about three wise men based on their three gifts. Most people assume He was given three tiny gifts. On the contrary, Jesus was given the customary gifts given only to kings then. These included at least seven caravans of gold, spices, ointments, and precious stones. When the queen of Sheba visited King Solomon, they exchanged gifts of gold, silver, expensive spices, and ointments (1 Kings 10:10). So I don't believe these wise men brought the new King trinkets or knickknacks. Certainly not!

Jesus Owned Real Estate

> The foxes have holes to live in. The birds have nests.
> But the Son of Man has no place where he can rest his
> head. (Luke 9:58 ERV)

Proponents of the blessedness of poverty doctrine use this text to convince others that Christ was poor and probably homeless. This is based on an answer He gave to a "certain man" who made this offer of service to follow Him wherever He went. If we look a little below the surface of this particular text, we will find all the Master was saying here was that His ministry involved a lot of traveling and He never knew where He would be from one night to the next; He wasn't implying He was homeless. Do you believe He lived with His mother and father throughout His early ministry? Certainly not! He was a proud homeowner.

> Jesus turned, saw them following him, and asked,
> "What are you looking for?" They answered, "Where
> do you live, Rabbi?" (This word means "Teacher.")
> "Come and see," he answered. (It was then about four
> o'clock in the afternoon.) So they went with him and
> saw where he lived, and spent the rest of that day with
> him. One of them was Andrew, Simon Peter's brother.
> (John 1:38–40 GNB)

Some Bible commentators have negatively assumed the worst: "Jesus probably lived in some cave or humble shelter in the hills." The Son of God living in caves for thirty years? I believe He lived a great life. It might not have been extravagant, but it was decent. I can say with all certainty Jesus was definitely not homeless. He probably lived in a gated community.

Jesus Had a Treasurer

Jesus' financial statement suggests He was wealthy enough to own a house and hire a full-time treasurer. Poor people don't have treasurers.

In fact, He hired twelve full-time employees that took care of His business. Just think about it—traveling around with twelve grown men for three years, and most of them had families to support.

Zoom in on the details—these guys left their professions to follow Him, and according to the Gospels, they were well taken care of financially for the three years they worked for Him. Jesus' ministry was constantly receiving money, and He needed a full-time treasurer to manage it.

> Since Judas had charge of the money, some thought Jesus was telling him to buy what was needed for the festival, or to give something to the poor. (John 13:29 NIV)

Mark's gospel tells us about Jesus preaching to a huge crown in a remote place where food was scarce.

> Send the people away so that they can go to the surrounding countryside and villages and buy themselves something to eat. But he answered, "You give them something to eat." They said to him, "That would take more than half a year's wages! Are we to go and spend that much on bread and give it to them to eat?" (Mark 6:36–37 NIV)

According to Mark's gospel, they had enough money to feed a multitude in a remote place. Note that they didn't say they couldn't afford it; rather, they asked if they should spend that much. You have to think like a treasurer here; to spend half a year's wages in one day doesn't make much financial sense.

Jesus Wore Designer Clothes and Drove a New Car

Oh yes, Jesus wore designer clothes. At birth, the child Jesus was wrapped in swaddling clothes, garments made for a king. At His death, soldiers gambled for His robe.

> When the soldiers crucified Jesus, they took his clothes, dividing them into four shares, one for each of them, with the undergarment remaining. This garment was seamless, woven in one piece from top to bottom. "Let's not tear it," they said to one another. "Let's decide by lot who will get it." This happened that the scripture might be fulfilled that said, "They divided my clothes among them and cast lots for my garment." So this is what the soldiers did. (John 19:23–24 NIV)

It was customary practice at executions for the soldiers to take the victims' garments and divide them among themselves. These included the headdress, the large outer robe with its girdle, and sandals. But take note of the soldiers' attitude toward Jesus' seamless garment: they said, "Let's not tear it ... Let's decide by lot who will get it." Why? The inner garment was seamless, woven in one piece from top to bottom. This garment was certainly not a beggar's rag; it was probably a design of a top fashion designer at the time comparable to Vera Wang. There had to be something of great monetary value about the material to explain why they didn't want to destroy it. This seamless, expensive garment was a royal coat made for a king. Tradition tells us it normally took up five years to make.

When Jesus traveled to Jerusalem for His triumphal entry, what did He ride? A new (car) donkey! In those days, donkeys were the ride of the day, and only the very

Key Phrase

In those days, donkeys were the ride of the day, and only the very wealthy could afford one. Poor people walked in those days while the wealthy rode.

wealthy could afford one. Poor people walked in those days while the wealthy rode.

Jesus, Chief Enemy of Poverty

According to the Scriptures, Jesus was the biggest enemy of poverty; He preached against it. Many of His messages were about money. He empowered and showed people how to prosper and get ahead financially in life.

He taught the principles of investment and financial success in most of His parables. No one would have listened to His teaching on finances if He had been poor, especially the wealthy. Jesus was a friend of the poor but was never poor himself. His messages empowered people to get out of poverty. Check out His antipoverty message here.

> Then Jesus went to Nazareth, where he had been brought up, and on the Sabbath he went as usual to the synagogue. He stood up to read the Scriptures and was handed the book of the prophet Isaiah. He unrolled the scroll and found the place where it is written, "The Spirit of the Lord is upon me, because he has chosen me to bring good news to the poor. He has sent me to proclaim liberty to the captives and recovery of sight to the blind, to set free the oppressed and announce that the time has come when the Lord will save his people."

Jesus rolled up the scroll, gave it back to the attendant, and sat down. All the people in the synagogue had their eyes fixed on him, as he said to

them, "This passage of scripture has come true today, as you heard it being read." They were all well impressed with him and marveled at the eloquent words that he spoke. They said, "Isn't he the son of Joseph?" (Luke 4:16–22 GNB)

Anatomy of the Poor and the Gospel

Jesus' sermon previewed the purpose of His public ministry. The Holy Spirit anointed Him to preach the gospel to four groups of people. Let us examine these groups separately.

The Poor

After He was handed the scroll, He said, "The Spirit of the Lord is upon me, because he has chosen me to bring good news to the poor." This is the most significant and foremost of the Messiah's work. Here's the $60 million question—what was the gospel to the poor? Before we answer that crucial question, let's talk about the other groups of people to whom Jesus preached the gospel.

The Captives

What was His messages to the captives—suppression, bondage, and servitude? Certainly not! His message to them was about freedom, liberty, deliverance, emancipation! Jesus announced total deliverance to the captives.

The Brokenhearted

What was Jesus' message to the brokenhearted— more broken heartedness, suffering, sickness, and sadness? I hardly think so!

Jesus preached healing, comfort, and wellness to the heartbroken.

The Blind

Jesus preached to those who were spiritually, morally, and physically blind not about staying that way but about how they could recover their sight.

I think we're ready to answer our first question for the first group of people: What was Jesus' gospel to the poor? That they would be poverty-stricken, sickly, and live meager existences for the rest of their lives? Certainly not! The text says He preached good news to the poor—the gospel of salvation, abundance, and prosperity. He was never in the business of destroying people; He was in the people-building business.

> The thief comes only in order to steal, kill, and destroy. I have come in order that you might have life—life in all its fullness. (John 10:10 GNB)

Jesus' War on Poverty

When Jesus announced that the Lord had anointed Him to preach the gospel, it was a declaration of war against the kingdom of Satan. It was also a declaration of war not just against sin, sickness, sufferings, lack, captivity—you name it; it was also a declaration of war on poverty. His arrival on earth was an invasion by the forces of heaven.

If Jesus was poor, He certainly wouldn't have empowered poor people to prosper. His message would have been at odds with His lifestyle. Many people who were attracted by Jesus' teaching were not the peasants, the poor, or the laborers; He attracted some wealthy people, and I don't think many wealthy folks would have followed a poor man around. Most of the religious groups ridiculed Him for hanging out with poor people.

Jesus' Wealthy Business Partners

Have you ever wondered who financed Jesus' ministry? He never performed a money miracle to support His ministry because He was constantly receiving money from grateful, wealthy donors. His ministry was never hindered by a lack of financial resources.

According to Scripture, each receiving town was expected to feed and support Him and His disciples. This was clear from Jesus' instructions to His disciples as they went from city to city to share the message of the kingdom.

> Jesus sent out these twelve, commanding them, saying, Do not go into the way of the nations, and do not enter into any city of the Samaritans. But rather go to the lost sheep of the house of Israel. And as you go, proclaim, saying, The kingdom of Heaven is at hand. Heal the sick, cleanse the lepers, raise the dead, cast out demons. You have received freely, freely give. Do not provide gold nor silver, nor copper in your purses, nor a bag for the journey, nor two coats, nor sandals, nor staves. For the workman is worthy of his food. (Matthew 10:5–10 ESV)

In addition, Jesus had wealthy partners such as Joseph of Arimathea, a member of the Jewish court who commanded great wealth and underwrote Jesus' ministry.

Wealthy Women Partners

Jesus also had wealthy women partners; the vast amount He received came from them. Here is one of the clearest references as to how Jesus' ministry was financed.

> Soon afterward he went on through cities and villages, proclaiming and bringing the good news of the kingdom of God. And the twelve were with him, and also some women who had been healed of evil spirits and infirmities: Mary, called Magdalene, from whom seven demons had gone out, and Joanna, the wife of Chuza, Herod's household manager, and Susanna, and many others, who provided for them out of their means. (Luke 8:1–3 ESV)

The majority of these grateful people evidently belonged to the wealthy class. Some of them even occupied high positions in society. Most of them experienced miracles that delivered them from addiction and infirmity. They were touched and blessed by Him, and they invested in His ministry so others would be delivered, healed, blessed, and changed as well.

The Understatement of the Century

From the evidence we've just considered, I believe we can say Jesus wasn't poor. On the other hand, to call Him very wealthy is an incredible understatement; He had created and owned all the wealth in the world.

> For every beast of the forest is mine, and the cattle upon a thousand hills. I know all the fowls of the mountains: and the wild beasts of the field are mine. If I were hungry, I would not tell thee: for the world is mine, and the fullness thereof. (Psalm 50:10–12 KJV)

More Good News

Every blessing has been purchased by Christ; His blood has made them all available to us. The believer is blessed beyond belief.

Most importantly, if Jesus is poor we are all in trouble because we are all relying on Him to meet our needs.

> Let us praise God for his glorious grace, for the free gift he gave us in his dear Son! For by the blood of Christ we are set free, that is, our sins are forgiven. How great is the grace of God, which he gave to us in such large measure! In all his wisdom and insight. (Ephesians 1:6–8 GNB)

Every blessing for the believer resides in Christ.

> Blessed be the God and Father of our Lord Jesus Christ, who has blessed us in Christ with every spiritual blessing in the heavenly places. (Ephesians 1:3 ESV)

Every blessing flows out to you, the believer, through Christ. In His sacrificial death on the cross, Jesus sacrificed His riches that we might become rich.

> For ye know the grace of our Lord Jesus Christ, that, though he was rich, yet for your sakes he became poor, so that you through his poverty might be rich. (2 Corinthians 8:9 NIV)

If It Was Good for Jesus, It's Good for Me

Poverty is a reality, but it's not so by divine appointment. God wants you to prosper. Don't you think that if it was okay for virtually all the Bible heroes and Jesus to be wealthy, it's also okay for you? Claim all God has made available to you. Be encouraged by God's intent concerning wealth for His chosen people when they enter their wealthy place.

> The LORD your God will bless you in the land that he is giving you. Not one of your people will be poor if you obey him and carefully observe everything that I command you today. The LORD will bless you, as he has promised. You will lend money to many nations, but you will not have to borrow from any; you will have control over many nations, but no nation will have control over you. (Deuteronomy 15:4–6 GNB)

Final Word

Friends, what an awesome promise! "Not one of your people will be poor." That's why it was called the wealthy place. God is such an enemy of poverty that He passed an antipoverty laws. It's by divine appointment that everyone should have at the very least enough food, a good place to sleep, and good clothes. God promises financial peace and prosperity to individuals and nations alike if they obey and live in harmony with God's plan governing wealth and abundance.

His plan to take you into your wealthy place won't work without your working and cooperating with Him. The streets of heaven are garnished with jewels and gold, the gates are solid pearls, and the houses are mansions (John 14:1–3; Revelation 21). Why would God be opposed to your having something He created and is enjoying Himself?

Most importantly, if Jesus is poor we are all in trouble because we are relying on Him to meet our needs.

My Personal Wealthy Place Notes

Section V

My Wealthy Place

Psalm 66:12

Chapter 11

Thoughts on Work and Wealth

Lazy people always want things but never get them. Those who work hard get plenty.
—Proverbs 13:4 ERV

Work, Work, Work and You'll Be Wealthy

Well, not necessarily. I know many hard-working people who are just barely making ends meet. There may be many reasons for this, and we'll explore some ways you can increase your chances of becoming wealthy by working for others or yourself.

There are basically two ways to become wealthy—inheriting it or working hard for it. Many folks are opposed to the latter; they want God's wealth but not God's work. These days, many people don't associate hard work with wealth. They believe if they pray hard enough and believe God hard enough, untold wealth will come to them. They want more money for less work. But if you want to increase your chances of becoming wealthy, you must be prepared to work hard.

You simply have to put yourself through the paces—staying up late, getting up early, and doing the uncomfortable until it becomes comfortable. Becoming wealthy is not about sprouting propositional truths and prophetic pronouncements. You can *decree* this and that as much as you like, but unless you *do*, nothing will change.

Friends, there's no new life or miracle without labor pains. All mothers know that the only way to produce new life involves pain. The only way to create a new financial future for yourself and the people depending on

Key Phrase

Lazy people don't get rich and become powerful and influential in the marketplace. Work on your plan or your dream until it becomes a reality.

you is through labor. Without labor, your desires, dreams, and visions will be stillborn. We may also apply the same term to inspiration without perspiration leads to frustration. The ancient prophet said, "Faith without works is dead."

Let me quote you a couple of key phrases from ancient wisdom.

> Hard work means prosperity; only fools idle away their time. (Proverbs 12:11 NLT)

> How long will you lie there, you sluggard? When will you get up from your sleep? A little sleep, a little slumber, a little folding of the hands to rest—and poverty will come on you like a thief and scarcity like an armed man. (Proverbs 6:6–11 NIV)

Underline the word *poverty.* The consequence of laziness is poverty, while the consequence of hard work coupled with strong financial intelligence is wealth. Lazy people don't get rich and become powerful and influential in the marketplace. Work on your plan or your dream until it becomes a reality.

Wealth Is Reward for Hard Work

No amount of praying and pondering will make you wealthy. You have to get up off your "blessed assurance" and work. The marketplace is not interested in your dreaming, decreeing, and declaring, only your doing. The marketplace won't pay you for what you know, only for what you do. For a huge part of the population, there's a big gulf between what they know and what they do.

Key Phrase

I wonder if it's the people they work with that are the major reason people don't like their work.

I challenge you in this chapter to shift the weight off your blessed assurance onto your feet. Acquiring wealth is simply a reward for hard work. It's a direct result of thinking and working smart.

In this section, we'll be talking about your attitude toward work, increasing your value in the marketplace, building multiple income streams, and working for yourself vs. working for someone else. Think about your job. Some people lament, "I just work to pay the bills," others say, "I work to retire," and some say, "I work to get rich." That's sad considering we'll spend approximately 40 percent of our waking lives working.

According to a recent survey, about a third of those in the workforce claim they're in the wrong jobs because their jobs don't line up with their gifts and abilities. The same survey also reveals that a vast majority of people complain how much they hate their work. I find that incredible, because God wants us to enjoy our work. The same survey also shows that we can make lots of money and not be in the job that we're best suited for or were created to do. However, I wonder if it's the people they work with that are the major reason people don't like their work.

Since the average person will spend most of his or her life at work, it's important that we explore our attitude toward work in line with God's Word. Probably out of sheer frustration, one ancient writer asked,

> What do we gain from all our work? (Ecclesiastes 3:9 GNB)

Let's explore six reasons why we work. The first reason is because God created us to work and commands us to work. We might want to call

Work is a blessing from God; He created us to work, and it's His will that we find fulfillment in work.

this the high calling of work. Most people would say work is a curse, but it's a blessing; God created us to work, and we give Him glory through our work. Long before the fall and the so-called curses pronounced on the human race, God commanded us to work.

> So God created humans in his own image. He created them to be like himself. He created them male and female. God blessed them and said to them, "Have many children. Fill the earth and take control of it. Rule over the fish in the sea and the birds in the air. Rule over every living thing that moves on the earth." (Genesis 1:27–28 ERV)

> And in the next chapter before the curse, "The LORD God put the man in the Garden of Eden to work the soil and take care of the garden." (Genesis 2:15 ERV)

God Himself is a worker, and He created us in His image. God took six days to create the universe and has continued to work to this day. Jesus said this of Himself and His Father.

> My Father never stops working, and so I work too. (John 5:17 ERV)

If we want to be like God and Jesus, we must work. The Bible speaks of six working days of twelve hours each. So quit complaining about the forty hours you work because they are less than the seventy-two mentioned in the Word. Being a Christian means being a good worker.

I pray you take on a new perspective about work.

Work itself is not a curse, but the daily grind, pain, disappointment, and the difficult people we work with can make it seem a curse. This all happened after sin entered the world. Work is a blessing from God; He created us to work, and it's His will that we find fulfillment in work.

The second reason we work is for financial compensation so we can pay our bills and get ahead financially. I never want to be a freeloader. What wakes me up each day is not my alarm clock but the opportunity to earn money and put it to good use.

> Work brings profit: talk brings poverty. (Proverbs 14:23 LB)

Work supplies our financial needs and prevents us from becoming burdens to our friends, families, and society. You don't stand a chance of becoming wealthy if you don't work. God wants to bless you and make you wealthy through your work.

Third, we should work because it builds our character and develops our competence. Studies have concluded that the more free time we have, the less significant and unfulfilled our lives become. The good Lord means for the workplace to be a proving and pruning ground or a university for developing character and competence. Our work is the place where we translate theory into practice.

You will develop many of your characteristics and competences only at your place of work, not in any classroom: accountability, adaptability, honesty, dependability, loyalty, sensitivity, patience, purpose, self-control, faithfulness, confidence, integrity, self-respect, and many others. You can also learn to work with those difficult people. So at work, ask yourself, *What am I becoming here?* rather than *How much am I getting paid?*

Work develops competence and character, and you can become wealthy if you develop these two personal attributes.

Key Phrase

Your secular job is your full-time ministry, your calling. God has strategically placed you there to represent Him, to infiltrate your organization, your company, your institution, or system and get paid at the same time. Life doesn't get better than that!

Wealth is not something you pursue; rather, it's something you attract by your competence and character.

> Do you see someone skilled in their work? They will serve before kings; they will not serve before officials of low rank. (Proverbs 22:29 NIV)

Fourth, we should work as a witness of God to our community. We communicate the love of God through our work. Most people think they aren't working for God unless they're working at a church. Traditionally, full-time ministry meant proclaiming the gospel, leading people to Jesus Christ, healing the sick, and driving out demons. But this shortsighted view limits God's purpose for our lives and confines us to church pulpits. I talk with Christians all the time who say, "I can't wait to give up my secular job and go into the ministry full-time. I want to get away from those wicked, mean, bad, foul-mouthed, nasty, unsaved people. I can't put up with their bad language."

Listen up! Your secular job is your full-time ministry, your calling. God has strategically placed you there to represent Him, to infiltrate your organization, your company, your institution, or system and get paid at the same time. Life doesn't get better than that!

Most of our Bible heroes, including Joseph, Daniel, Esther, Mordecai, Nehemiah, Nicodemus, and Joseph of Arimathea, were righteous people working in secular settings. Joseph worked for the Egyptian government. Daniel served as a political figure in Babylon. As you will recall from the previous chapter, all these people were amazingly wealthy. Friends, this is the epitome of what the wealthy place is all about—showing the love of God in the secular world and amassing wealth at the same time.

> Do all you can to live a peaceful life? Mind your own business, and earn your own living, as we told you before. If you do these things, then those who are not believers will respect the way you live. And you will not have to depend on others for what you need. (1 Thessalonians 4:11–12 ERV)

Underline the phrase, "Then those who are not believers will respect you." God wants you out there not just to become wealthy but to be light and salt, an influence (Matthew 5:13–16) in the secular world. He doesn't want you to be working with just other Christians; He wants you to work in secular settings or with people who don't know Him so you can be a witness of His love while you're amassing wealth.

The fifth reason we need to work is to be charitable.

> [We] must work, doing something useful with our own hands, so that we may have something to share with those in need. (Ephesians 4:18 GN)

We shouldn't work just to meet our needs; we should work so we can be generous. I don't have a problem with helping those who have fallen on hard times and legitimately need support, but the Bible is strongly against us dishing out money to freeloaders.

For you yourselves know how you ought to follow our example. We were not idle when we were with you, nor did we eat anyone's food without paying for it. On the contrary, we worked night and day, laboring and toiling so that we would not be a burden to any of you. We did this, not because we do not have the right to such help, but in order to offer ourselves as a model for you to imitate.

For even when we were with you, we gave you this rule: "The one who is unwilling to work shall not eat." We hear that some among you are idle and disruptive. They are not busy; they are busybodies. Such people we command and urge in the Lord Jesus Christ to settle down and earn the food they eat. (2 Thessalonians 3:7–11 NIV)

Those are pretty strong words. The Bible is saying here there's no free lunch. Note that it didn't say, "If a person can't work." It was addressing those who were lazy.

The lazy man is full of excuses. "I can't go to work," he says. "If I go outside, I might meet a lion in the street and be killed!" (Proverbs 22:13 LB)

Work for More than You Need

Many of us would like to be a blessing to other people, but big problem! Many of us struggle to meet our needs and can't be generous as we want to be. But we can become more-than-enough workers. According to Ephesians 3:20, there are three levels of living or wealth. Let's read the passage.

Now to him who is able to do far more abundantly than all that we ask or think, according to the power at work within us. (Ephesians 3:20 ESV)

The first level of wealth is the not-enough level at which your needs are greater than your income. That's why you need to aspire to the next level of wealth, the enough level,

Key Phrase

It's God's will for you to produce more than you need for yourself so you can bless your colleagues, community, church, and country.

where you have at least enough for your needs if not for others. Many stop at this level because they feel comfortable there. Most people even opt for early retirement at this level. If that's you, I challenge you to keep on working so you have enough to give away.

The third level is the more-than-enough level. God wants you to work and be wealthy so you can be generous, propagate the gospel, and build churches, schools, and health facilities. He told Adam and Eve to be fruitful and multiply. It's God's will for you to produce more than you need for yourself so you can bless your colleagues, community, church, and country. Work allows you to do this. Move up higher, my friend.

Limitless Possibilities in Life

Take a second look at the above Scripture, which is addressing the imaginaries. When it comes to wealth, God doesn't put a limit on what we can acquire; we do that! The poverty of thought keeps many at the enough level of living. If we're limited in our thinking, we'll be limited in our asking and receiving. If we take the limit off ourselves and our wealth prospects, there's no limit with God, who created us with unlimited possibilities.

Something unique happens when we give. Ours and our beneficiaries' lives are transformed, and isn't transformation what we're looking for? Maybe we just drop by at the right time in a person's life.

Perhaps the person has three of the numbers to a combination lock; if we give that person the fourth, we can transform his or her life.

Giving also creates room for philanthropists to receive more. If you're a giver, when your bounty is poured out on the economy, you'll get more in return and thus have even more to give.

Final Word

Believers are to work as though they're working for Christ.

> In all the work you are given, do the best you can. Work as though you are working for the Lord, not any earthly master. Remember that you will receive your reward from the Lord, who will give you what he promised his people. Yes, you are serving Christ. He is your real Master. (Colossians 3:23–24 ESV)

That's the attitude we need to embrace. We should work as if we're working for Christ rather than earthly bosses. God requires us to work and create more wealth than we need for ourselves so we'll have more to give away. Remember that wealth is connected with your work, not your wishes.

My Personal Wealthy Place Notes

My Wealthy Place

Psalm 66:12

Chapter 12

Working for Yourself vs. Working for Others

Lord our God, may your blessings be with us. Give us success in all we do!
—Psalm 90:17 NIV

If you've considered working for yourself, that's noble. However, working for yourself won't necessarily make you wealthy. On the other hand, working for someone else might not make you wealthy either. There's no guarantee either way. If you work for someone cutting lawns, that won't make you wealthy, but starting your own lawn service just might.

Some people are far better off working for themselves, but I know some who are doing extremely well financially by working for other people. The key here is to pursue what works best for you. If you have the entrepreneurial spirit, put it to work, but keep in mind that most new business fail in the first three years, so do your research carefully.

Working for yourself requires hard work, the right product for the demand, the right people, and the right timing. It's also fun. Here are seven fundamentals to consider.

Fundamental One: Protect Your Business Idea from Premature Death

You might be excited about your new business venture, and at some point, you'll have to share it with somebody, but for the moment, keep it under your hat.

> There is a time to be silent and a time to speak. (Ecclesiastes 3:7 ERV)

Wait for the right time, the right place, and the right people before you share your business idea. Here's what Nehemiah did when he worked on the broken-down wall in Jerusalem.

> I went to Jerusalem and stayed there three days. Then at night I started out with a few men. I had not said anything to anyone about what my God had put on my heart to do for Jerusalem. There were no horses with me except the horse I was riding. While it was dark I went out through the Valley Gate. I rode toward the Dragon Well and the Gate of the Ash Piles.
>
> I was inspecting the walls of Jerusalem that had been broken down and the gates in the wall that had been burned with fire. Then I rode on toward the Fountain Gate and the King's Pool. As I got close, I could see there was not enough room for my horse to get through. So I went up the valley in the dark, inspecting the wall. Finally, I turned back and went back in through the Valley Gate.
>
> The officials and important Israelites didn't know where I had gone. They didn't know what I was doing. I had not yet said anything to the Jews, the priests, the king's family, the officials, or any of the other people who would be doing the work. (Nehemiah 2:11–16 ERV)

This wise businessman prayed, previewed the work, and planned. He did his homework; he didn't take the words of other people as

Key Phrase
Successful businesspeople protect their plans from premature death and the wrong partnership.

final. And he did all this in the dark. Successful businesspeople protect their plans from premature death and the wrong partnership.

Fundamental Two: Understand that You Can Be Your Own Worst Boss

Many people set up businesses to be free from the demands of a boss and end up being their own worst boss. Their business becomes their new boss that doesn't let them go home early or even draw a paycheck. Create your own business with the goal of gaining the wealth that will free you, not to avoid work.

Fundamental Three: Don't Let Your Business Depend Solely On Your Skills

Any business that depends solely on you alone will work you harder than your worst employer. It takes more than one person to run a business. If your business cannot function without your being there, something's wrong with your system of operation.

> Two are better off than one, because together they can work more effectively. If one of them falls down, the other can help him up. (Ecclesiastes 4:9–10 GN)

Fundamental Four: Understand that the Skills Required to Start a Business Are Different from Those Needed to Sustain It

Great cooks don't nece-ssarily know how to run a whole restaurant. Many people are overwhelmed after they set up business; they suddenly realize they have to deal with accountants, lawsuits, suppliers, payrolls, taxes, policies and procedures, complaints, stocks, security issues, and many more things they're not prepared to handle.

Fundamental Five: Before You Set Up Your Business, Get a Vision of Opening Many Branches

Doing this will get you thinking like an entrepreneur, a strategist. You'll transition from the backroom to the ballroom, and you'll start making your business work for you instead of you working for the business. A smart business plan will help you think ahead.

Fundamental Six: Realize that Some of Your Colleagues Will Resent Your Climb

When you transition from the backroom to the ballroom, many of those you started your business with will resent your climb. People who start at the first phase of a business are rarely there for the business's subsequent stages. You must be prepared for this; don't let it discourage you when it happens.

Fundamental Seven: Realize You Just Might Fail

But please hear me out before you get discouraged. Most people who start businesses fail at least three times before they succeed. But the fourth time, they succeed, and it's often with their original business idea. Isn't that incredible?

If you fail, get back on track. Failures are part of life. Even successful people fail; it's just that they learn from their failures.

Wisdom from the Parable of the Sower

Consider the parable of the sower, one of Jesus' better-known parables. This one is about life, hard work, averages, and success and failure. This parable can be applied to all aspects of life.

Key Phrase

When things don't go as you planned, be disappointed, but don't let it stop you, let it educate you. Let it teach you. Let it coach you. Let it guide you.

> Listen! Behold, a sower went out to sow. And as he sowed, some seed fell along the path, and the birds came and devoured it. Other seed fell on rocky ground, where it did not have much soil, and immediately it sprang up, since it had no depth of soil. And when the sun rose, it was scorched, and since it had no root, it withered away.
>
> Other seed fell among thorns, and the thorns grew up and choked it, and it yielded no grain. And other seeds fell into good soil and produced grain, growing up and increasing and yielding thirtyfold and sixtyfold and a hundredfold. (Mark 4:2–8 ESV)

The first thing that catches our attention is the birds that were eating the seed. I think they represent negative people who try to talk us out of great opportunities for whatever reason. These birds were eating away at a business, company, enterprise, or idea. And on the day the sower launched his business, he lost almost everything. Sometimes, you'll lose some of your seeds to such birds, but if you're prepared for that, you won't end up discouraged.

Next, some of his seed fell on rocky ground, but something went wrong. The seeds sprouted, but on the first hot day, because the roots hadn't grown deep enough, they died. Consider the birds and the sun as representing the trials and tests of life.

But hold on. That isn't the end of the story. He had more seeds than the birds and the sun could devour, and you have more seeds in you than any forces working against you can destroy.

Some of his seed was chocked out by the thorns, the little cares of the world, the deceitfulness of riches, and the desire for other things. He was probably just involved in too many projects—too many irons in the fire. You have to admit this guy was ambitious! He continued to sow, invest, refine his skills, and learn from his mistakes. He must have been excited at the prospect of success, building a great company, an enterprise, and great wealth.

When things don't go as you planned, be disappointed, but don't let it stop you; let it educate, teach, coach, and guide you. Discipline your disappointment and move on.

We're told, "and other seeds fell into good soil and produced grain, growing up and increasing and yielding thirtyfold and sixtyfold and a hundredfold." What a relief for the sower!

Final Word

If you have a good business idea, dream—whatever—and you work hard, it too will eventually fall on good ground (circle those two words) and make you wealthy. But first, you must go through the birds, the weather, and the thorns, and they may cause you to experience failure, but be diligent like the sower and never give up.

My Personal Wealth Place Notes

My Wealthy Place

Psalm 66:12

Chapter 13

Creating Multiple Income Streams

Blessed shall you be in the city, and blessed shall you be in the field. Blessed shall be the fruit of your womb and the fruit of your ground and the fruit of your cattle, the increase of your herds and the young of your flock.
—Deuteronomy 28:3–4 ESV

I want to share my thoughts on creating multiple income streams. The best-kept secret to becoming wealthy is having multiple income streams. The successful have done this. If you want to become wealthy, brainstorm ways you can start money flowing to you apart from your main job. Here are some ideas about that.

- Teach classes or offer technical support online in your area of expertise.
- Start a computer class for seniors or for English as a second language.
- Park some of your emergency cash into investments that produce dividends.
- Turn a hobby (photography?) into an income stream.
- Type and research for a fee.
- Offer to check emails for busy people who don't have the time.
- Invest in assets that will earn you money without your having to be present.

- Become a proofreader or a ghostwriter. (Do you know how much it cost me to have this proofread? That could be you!)

In short, explore ways you can put your skills, talents, and expertise to work in different settings. Reread chapter 5, "Tapping into Your Wealth-Creating Abilities" to identify your talents or gifts. Sharpen them and sell them.

By the way, thanks for buying this book. It's a secondary source of income for me. Have you considered writing?

Creating multiple in-come streams can be fun and rewarding, and that can help you out in economic downturns whether personal or national. Here are some rules about multiple income streams.

Rule One: Don't Burn the Candle at Both Ends

There are only so many income streams you can create and sustain without doing serious damage to your physical, emotional, social, mental, relational, and spiritual life. I used to work a full-time job and some part-time jobs that took a toll on me. I fell asleep at the wheel one morning and hit the mirrors of two parked cars. Only by the grace of God am I alive today. What's the use striving for a pot of gold you get to hold in your hands only as you're taking your last breath? This violates the kingdom principle of rest and restoration.

> Here is someone who lives alone. He has no son, no brother, yet he is always working, never satisfied with the wealth he has. For whom is he working so hard and denying himself any pleasure? This is useless, too—and a miserable way to live. (Ecclesiastes 4:8 GNB)

> For what shall it profit a man, if he shall gain the whole world, and lose his own soul? Or what shall a man give in exchange for his soul? (Mark 8:36–37 KJV)

Rule Two: Passive Income Streams Are More Valuable than Active Incomes Streams

Key Phrase

The best-kept secret to becoming wealthy is having multiple income streams. The successful have done this.

Passive income streams keep flowing even when you're not working or are no longer able to work. It will still be coming even after you're dead.

Rule Three: A Second Income Stream Needs to Be without a Ceiling

With some jobs, it doesn't matter how hard you work, you'll still get the same money. Focus on creating multiple revenues that reflect your work.

Rule Four: Don't Give Up Your Day Job

A second job must not control your time. You can choose when you want to work. I write and speak as secondary sources of income, and I write and speak whenever I want to.

Rule Five: Understand the Power of the Internet

Start an ecommerce business. There are many twenty-one-year-olds who are making millions on the Internet. And you won't have to deal with most of the barriers you'd otherwise face because of biases against gender, race, or color. Today, a person can become a multimillionaire working in a basement due to the power and reach of the Internet.

Rule Six: Retain the Rights to Your Intellectual Property

This includes songs, poetry, poems, music, lyrics, sermons, concepts, ideas, and so on because they could become sources of income. If you don't own it, you can't sell it or charge for it.

Rule Seven: Don't Give Away Your God-Given Gifts

God gave you ways of generating wealth, but some think that because those ways come from the Lord, they shouldn't profit by them. Many times, that attitude can be false humility. I challenge you to maximize your God-given talents to increase your income. By all means give back, but ensure that your skills are earning money for you as well. Remember that King Solomon was compensated for his gift of wisdom.

> And all the earth sought Solomon, to hear his wisdom which God had put in his heart. And every man brought his presents, vessels of silver and vessels of gold, and clothing and armor, and spices, horses and mules, so much year by year. (1 Kings 10:24 MKJV)

Rule Eight: Investigate before Investing

If you're careful, investing can be a great way of producing an income stream. The common reason I've heard why people don't invest in stocks is, "I don't understand investing." So here's a quick Q&A crash course on investing.

Q. What's a stock?

A. A stock is a partial ownership in a company. This means if the company whose stocks you own does well, you make money, but if it does poorly, you can lose it.

Q. What are dividends?

A. That's money some companies pay quarterly or annually to those who own its stock based on the profit it makes. But keep in mind that companies can also lose money and not pay any dividends.

Q. What's a bond?

A. An amount of money you lend a company on which it pays you interest. You might buy a bond for $5,000 and receive 3 percent interest on it yearly. When the bond "matures," say in three or five years, you get your original $5,000 back. Bonds aren't as risky as stocks, but if the company whose bond you bought goes out of business, you could lose your money.

Q. What are income investments?

A. Bonds are considered income investments because they yield a certain amount yearly, though it's not that much. Then again, the risk is lower than with stocks.

Q. What are certificates of deposit (CDs) and money market accounts?

A. These are also known as cash equivalents and are considered the safest forms of investments, but then, they offer low rates of return.

Q. What's a mutual fund?

A. Consider it an arranged marriage between a group of stocks and bonds selected by investments professionals and combined. Mutual funds comprise hundreds of stocks and bonds. In theory, these shares rise and fall based on their collective performance.

This means you'll get more diversification than you'd be able to on your own if you purchase individual stocks. The downside to this is that when you buy and sell shares of a mutual fund, you might have to pay fees.

Q. Should I have a retirement account?

A. If you have a 401(k), a 403(b), or an IRA, you already have one. Study your statements carefully and ensure your portfolio has the best assets allocation. If you don't have an IRA, start one without delay and set a goal of investing 10 percent of your income. Up the percentage as your income grows. You'd be amazed how as little as $50 a month could make a big difference over the long haul. Once you max out your 401(k) and your IRA, you can open an investment account.

Investing money for retirement thirty years away requires a different strategy from investing for retirement five years away. Long-term goals will allow for the stock market to fall and recover, which means you can afford to have a portfolio of more growth-oriented investments. Again, the conventional wisdom is not to invest money in stocks for short-term goals you are seeking to achieve in less than five years.

Q. How much risk can I afford to take?

A. That depends on a number of factors. When will you need the money? How much do you have stashed away for emergencies? How sure are you about your future income? The golden rule here is to do your due diligence before you invest.

> Only a simpleton believes what he is told. A prudent man checks to see where he is going. (Proverbs 14:15 LB)

Find a good financial adviser or broker to help you set financial goals. They can help with a wide range of issues such as diversification, how to minimize risks, and how you can multiply your income streams. You can also attend financial seminars to increase your financial literacy. Through these avenues, you'll come up with information or ideas that will change your life. Always pay for financial advice, and ask your financial advisor what's in it for him or her. God said you should.

> Get the facts at any price, and hold on tightly to all the good sense you can get. (Proverbs 23:23 LB)

Invest only money that you are prepared to lose. According to financial experts, one of the smartest ways to invest is to use dollar-cost averaging. That means investing the same amount each month in a mutual fund or an investment account. This will ensure that you purchase more shares when the price is low and fewer shares when the price is high. Ask your financial adviser about The Bankers Rule of 72.

Rule Nine: Understand the Three Ps for Marketing Success
Positioning

The *Business Dictionary* defines positioning as "a marketing strategy that aims to make a brand occupy a distinct position, relative to competing brands, in the mind of the consumer." It's about finding a unique place or niche for what you're selling. This shouldn't be too difficult since God created us uniquely different.

Packaging

This is the manner in which you present yourself, your product, or company to the public. Design your package to build up a favorable image or response.

Performance

The *Business Dictionary* defines performance as "the accomplishment of a given task measured against preset known standards of accuracy, completeness, cost, and speed." A distinctive characteristic of good performance is customer satisfaction.

Rule Ten: Understand the Difference between Value and Volume

This is an important but often overlooked factor in increasing income. Your value is what you get paid for in the marketplace, not the number of hours you put in. I'm talking about the monetary worth of your skills. Your value is the extent to which customers consider their need met by your products or services.

Key Phrase

You become wealthy by adding value to others' lives, the company you work for, the church you serve, the organization you work for, and the general marketplace.

Why would a company pay one employee the minimum wage but pay another twice that? It's because the company considers one to be more valuable. You might be a valuable brother, sister, friend, husband, and wife, and you are definitely a valuable person in the sight of God, but if you or your business isn't adding value to the marketplace, you won't be paid much. Since we don't get paid for our volume of hours but for our value, is it possible to increase our value in the marketplace? Of course! When we increase our value, we also increase our income.

Is it possible to increase our value twice as much and earn twice as much? Of course! We can increase our value four, five, six, ten times as much and earn that much more.

Is it possible to increase our value to be worth a million? Yes! To earn more, we simply have to become more. We become wealthy by adding value to others' lives, the companies we work for, the churches we serve, the organizations we work for, and the general marketplace.

The Blessing of Multiple Streams of Income Passage

Having more than one income stream is supported by Scripture as long as you obey the above rules. Check out Deuteronomy 28, a powerful passage on the blessings of multiple income streams.

> If you obey the lord your god and faithfully keep all his commands that I am giving you today, he will make you greater than any other nation on earth. Obey the lord

your god and all these blessings will be yours: The lord will bless your towns and your fields. The lord will bless you with many children, with abundant crops, and with many cattle and sheep.

The lord will bless your grain crops and the food you prepare from them. The lord will bless everything you do. The lord will defeat your enemies when they attack you. They will attack from one direction, but they will run from you in all directions. The lord your god will bless your work and fill your barns with grain. He will bless you in the land that he is giving you.

If you obey the lord your god and do everything he commands, he will make you his own people, as he has promised. Then all the peoples on earth will see that the lord has chosen you to be his own people, and they will be afraid of you. The lord will give you many children, many cattle, and abundant crops in the land that he promised your ancestors to give you.

He will send rain in season from his rich storehouse in the sky and bless all your work, so that you will lend to many nations, but you will not have to borrow from any. (Deuteronomy 28:1–12 GND)

Sometimes, years of poverty can condition you to think in a certain way contrary to God's will. A poverty mentality tends to develop a poverty vocabulary. Don't let your words sabotage your chance of getting you to your wealthy place. Announce these intentions and make them personal.

- I proclaim that God has set me on high above poverty and lack.
- I proclaim that I am blessed in the city and the field.

- I proclaim that my basket and storehouses will be filled with good things.
- I proclaim that I shall produce perfect offspring and leave and inheritance for them.
- I proclaim that my crops will increase.
- I proclaim that my flocks will increase.
- I proclaim that I am prosperous in investments, goods, children, and real estate.
- I proclaim that the heavens will give me rain (wealth) in due season.
- I proclaim that I have victory over all my enemies.
- I proclaim that the Lord will open to me His treasures and bless my work.
- I proclaim that I will be prosperous enough to lend and not need to borrow.
- I proclaim that the Lord shall make me the head, not the tail.
- I proclaim that I will be a witness and example to all people of the blessings of God.
  Sign here: _____

Final Word

Reader, God wants to bless you and make you wealthy through your work, and whatever you decide to do, whether to work for yourself or other people, ensure that you focus on what will pay you well.

My Personal Wealthy Place Notes

My Wealthy Place

Psalm 66:12

Chapter 14

Climbing the Wealth Ladder

Then this Daniel was made overseer of the presidents and
satraps, because an excellent spirit was in him. And the
king was planning to set him over all the kingdom.
—Daniel 6:3 MKJV

As you work through this chapter, keep in mind that most developing countries' economic systems are ladders we climb, not beds we sleep on. Here in America, we call it climbing the "corporate ladder." At the top of the ladder are the super-rich, the 1 percent, and at the bottom are those on minimum wage. Some people are so poor they aren't even on the first rung of this ladder.

This ladder is exasperating because it's very crowded at the bottom, and many are content to remain there. But there's plenty of room at the top, and you don't have to stay anywhere below that! Let that inspire you to take your next step to the top.

Option One

Many people campaign for a higher minimum wage, but you have options beyond that. If you intend to stay at the bottom of this corporate ladder, you need to take to the streets with banners and a loud voice. While it might be tempting to petition the government to raise the minimum wage, it will always be too little and too late. Your life is too important to put on hold as you wait for the government to act.

You'll make a living by working hard on your job, but you'll make a fortune if you work harder on yourself.

It's much better to bet on a sure principle that has worked for the wealthy. I'll share with you twelve specific, practical steps you can take right away, eleven in this chapter and the twelfth in the next. These steps will get you moving up the ladder quicker than the government could. But before we address these specific steps, let me give you the broad answer in option two.

Option Two

The key to reaching the top of this ladder is to work harder on yourself than you do on your job. When I learned this truth years ago, it transformed my life. Thousands of people are working harder on their jobs than their friends are but aren't having the success their colleagues are enjoying. If they work forty or fifty hours, they get the same money. They've worked hard on the job, but they haven't worked on improving themselves. You'll make a living by working hard on your job, but you'll make a fortune if you work harder on yourself. Skills, my friends, are the keys to the top. Those who have made it to the top have done so by continually improving their skills and themselves.

> Do you see someone skilled in their work? They will serve before kings. (Proverbs 22:29 NIV)

> If the ax is dull and its edge unsharpened, more strength is needed, but skill will bring success. (Ecclesiastes 10:10 NIV)

With that firmly embedded in your mind, here are the first of twelve steps. You cannot skip any; to obtain great wealth you must achieve A+ at all levels.

Step 1: Ambition

Ambition is a strong desire to become something extraordinary, do something remarkable and noble with your life, or possess or achieve something extraordinary. Notice the progression: become something, do something, and possess something. What you become in life is far more important than what you do or possess. The Bible says, "Life does not consist of the abundance of things you possess." Your goal in life is to work on your person, not on your performance or possessions. Nothing noble is ever achieved without ambition. Ambition, not money, will buy you a future, not money.

> Nothing that they have a mind to do will be impossible for them! (Genesis 11:6b ISV)

Make sure you have ambition before you become wealthy. I've seen many people who won the lottery end up broke within a few years. They had the money, but they didn't have the ambition to complement it.

We need to be ambitious, but at times, our ambition needs to be tempered. A good example of this is Joseph. You can almost feel his passion and see the fire in his eyes as he talked about his ambition to his family.

> One time Joseph had a dream, and when he told his brothers about it, they hated him even more. He said, "Listen to the dream I had. We were all in the field tying up sheaves of wheat, when my sheaf got up and stood up straight. Yours formed a circle around mine and bowed down to it."

"Do you think you are going to be a king and rule over us?" his brothers asked. So they hated him even more because of his dreams and because of what he said about them. Then Joseph had another dream and told his brothers, "I had another dream, in which I saw the sun, the moon, and eleven stars bowing down to me." He also told the dream to his father, and his father scolded him: "What kind of a dream is that?

Do you think that your mother, your brothers, and I are going to come and bow down to you?" Joseph's brothers were jealous of him, but his father kept thinking about the whole matter. (Genesis 37:5–11 GNB)

You can almost hear Joseph saying, "I was born for this." Guys, you don't see me until you see me in my element. Some people say it was unwise for Joseph to talk about his ambition because it almost got him killed. I think you should as long as the timing is right. But life with no challenges or dreams or ambitions is boring!

Step 2: Attitude

Our attitude determines our altitude; it's our frame of mind. Have you ever worked with someone who grumbles and gripes all day? "It's not fair. I don't deserve this. No one ever appreciates me. Nothing will ever change. If that's all they pay me, I won't come early or stay late." No one wants to live and work with someone with that attitude. People like this don't get promoted or rise to the top. On the other hand, have you ever been around someone who said, "It doesn't matter how much they pay me. I'll always be on time and work late if required."

People who reach the top of the ladder maintain positive attitudes even under pressure, during times of change, and in spite of unrealistic expectation from their bosses. Here's how a supervisor described one employee: "John is always cordial and happy, looks for ways to assist others, and comes to work early every day, always upbeat and optimistic. John exceeds company expectations; he's always pleasant to be around."

Key Phrase

Attitude is first input then output, personality that becomes performance.

Here's how the same supervisor described another employee: "Joseph is always negative and quarrelsome. He very seldom assists others, is pessimistic, always late and leaves early, and frequently criticizes others."

Same job, different attitude.

One of the best displays of a great attitude under pressure in the Bible is Daniel, who worked his way out of prison and to the top.

> Then this Daniel was preferred above the presidents and princes, because an excellent spirit was in him; and the king thought to set him over the whole realm. (Daniel 6:3 KJV)

What promoted Daniel to the top of the corporate ladder? His excellent attitude. The king was thinking about promoting him because of what he saw in him. Attitude is first input then output, personality that becomes performance.

Ask yourself, *What does my boss see in me and my future? A promotion or a demotion based on my attitude?* Develop and maintain a positive, passionate, and persistent attitude about yourself and your work and watch yourself rocket to the top. Someone said, "A bad attitude is like a flat tire; you won't get anywhere with it unless you change it." Don't let your attitude conflict with your ambition; they need to work together to produce wealth.

Step 3: Activities

Activities are about what you do with your professional, personal, and people time. To be successful, your activities

We should be constantly working on self-improvement.

must be consistent with your ambition and attitude. You cannot be like the man who dreams about becoming wealthy while he's engaging in impulsive spending.

> An intelligent person aims at wise action, but a fool starts off in many directions. (Proverbs 17:24 GNB)

Do you know people who are great talkers who never take action? They have great plans but never act on them. They're always dreaming, never doing. When someone tells me, "I'm waiting for my ship to come in," I want to ask, "Why don't you swim out to it?"

People who excel don't waste time on projects that aren't consistent with their destination. All successful people devote their time to activities that pay them well.

> It is stupid to waste time on useless projects. (Proverbs 12:11 GNB)

> People who waste time will always be poor. (Proverbs 28:19 GNB)

> Much dreaming and many words are meaningless. (Ecclesiastes 5:7 NIV)

Success begins with action that gets you closer to your wealthy place, so get in the habit of asking yourself, *Is what I'm doing with my time taking me toward or away from my dreams?*

Thoughts on Activities and Results

Life is a numbers game. This is so because the numbers tell the whole story. It's so easy to confuse movement for

Develop and maintain a positive, passionate, and persistent attitude about yourself and your work and watch yourself rocket to the top.

achievement. You might be busy, but if you're not progressing, something's wrong not with you as a person but with your activities, ambition, or attitude.

Where Are The Figs?

This question was posed by the owner of a certain fig tree to his landscaper.

> A man had a fig tree growing in his vineyard, and he went to look for fruit on it but did not find any. So he said to the man who took care of the vineyard, "For three years now I've been coming to look for fruit on this fig tree and haven't found any. Cut it down! Why should it use up the soil?" "Sir," the man replied, "leave it alone for one more year, and I'll dig around it and fertilize it." (Luke 13:6–8 NIV)

Wow! A fig tree and no figs! Unacceptable! I believe Jesus told this story to show the relationship between activities and results and most important, to see who gets to stay. The parable can be interpreted to be about individual lives, people, companies, businesses, or organizations. It's about production, fruitfulness, profits—you name it. The purpose of the individual is to produce results. The purpose of companies, businesses, and churches is to be productive and fruitful.

The owner of the fig tree came three years looking for fruit but had found none. He lost his cool and ordered the tree cut down. "Why should

Key Phrase

A bad attitude is like a flat tire; you won't get anywhere with it unless you change it.

it use up the soil?" he asked in response to the lack of result. Life requires us to make reasonable progress in a reasonable time.

The caretaker beseeched the owner not to cut down the tree. He said he'd work with it for another year and if it didn't produce, he could have it removed. I love it; when you're not getting the results you want, you look into what's wrong and make changes.

When to Stick or When to Quit

Winners never quit and quitters never win, it's said. I don't believe that to be true in every case. I believe that sometimes you need to quit in order to win. Every successful person you meet understands time thinking. It's foolish to keep laboring at something that isn't working. But how long should a person devote time and energy to a project that isn't working out? I wish I had the answer to that. You do so for a reasonable amount of time depending on circumstances; that could be an hour, a day, a month, or a year. Remember, life is a numbers game.

Regardless of what your job is, work with a goal in mind. Plan your work daily and refine your skills as necessary to ensure you're profitable and productive for yourself and those you're accountable to. Always ask yourself, *Where are the figs?* before someone asks you that.

Step 4: Your Alliances

Never underestimate the power of the alliances you have with people, influential and otherwise. People shape us, and we shape people. Influences can be strong or subtle. Most of the time, it's the subtle influences we're not prepared for. We'll resist being pushed off course, but we might not notice something that slowly, subtly nudges us off course.

You cannot succeed by yourself; you'll need someone to hold the ladder you climb. The key is to hang out with the right people. Have you ever noticed that successful people tend to hang out with other successful people? When you associate with people with a wealth mentality and a larger-than-life mind-set that will rub off on you.

There may be some people in your life who aren't growing or adding credibility to your life. So because your alliances are critical, ask yourself,

- Who am I around?
- What do they have me thinking?
- What do they have me reading?
- What do they have me listening to?
- What do they have me saying?
- What do they have me doing?
- What do they have me becoming?
- Is that all right with me?

You simply cannot afford to give a minute of your time to some folks or they'll empty your soul, heart, mind, and pocketbook, so disassociate from them if you must, and think about making alliances with those whose attitude is more like yours.

> Whoever walks with the wise becomes wise, but the companion of fools will suffer harm. (Proverbs 13:20 ESV)

> Don't let the world around you squeeze you into its own mold. (Romans 12:2 Phillips)

> Do not associate with a man given to anger; or go with a-hot-tempered man, lest you learn his ways, and find a snare for yourself. (Proverbs 22:24, 25 NASB)

> Iron sharpeneth iron; so a man sharpeneth the countenance of his friend. (Proverbs 27:17 KJV)

Enlarge your network of friends. Connect with the world around you to find wise, influential, successful, and substantial people. Connect with every culture, context, and color. Just ensure they complement your ambition, attitude, and activities and add credibility to you.

The "Ain't It Awful" Club

I believe getting wealthy is pretty easy to figure out; just study what unsuccessful people do and don't do that. Don't read what they read. Don't watch what they watch. Don't go where they go. Don't spend how they spend. Don't talk how they talk, and don't dress how they dress. It's that simple.

Take another look at the people you're around; you might conclude you have to disassociate with some of them. Jack Canfield puts it in his book *The Success Principles*, "Drop out of the 'Ain't It Awful' Club … and Surround Yourself with Successful People." An *(Imprint of HarperCollinsPublishers, 2007), 191-2.*

Step 5: Approach

Are you easy to talk to or deal with? How do you meet and greet people? Are you hot or cold? Do you make eye contact? Do you smile? Your approach is crucial to your success. What we're talking about here is not your substance but the style and strategy with which you pursue a goal. It's not about what you do but how you do it. The difference between a good pitch and a bad pitch is the pitcher's approach. A successful landing depends on a pilot's approach. A pitcher's approach can influence the dynamics of a game, and a pilot can have either a successful or disastrous landing based on approach. A bad approach can ruin a business deal and get you demoted and even fired.

Key Phrase

Work very hard on your approach so when your opportunity comes, you'll have the style as well as the substance and sharpness to deal with it.

People say, "I just speak what's on my mind and let the chips fall where they may." That's not smart. This and all the others steps are essential skills to master. They might not be easy to master, but if you make the investment in this intellectual process, it will make a difference in how your life turns out socially, economically, and financially.

Work very hard on your approach so when your opportunity comes, you'll have the style as well as the substance and sharpness to deal with it. If you have something worthwhile saying, say it well. Learn how to express, not impress. Be bold, but don't be a bully. Be assertive without being aggressive. Be gentle but not weak. Even Jesus took great care in how He spoke to people.

> The Father who sent me commanded me what to say and how to say it. John 12:49 (NIV)

> Your speech should always be pleasant and interesting, and you should know how to give the right answer to everyone. (Colossians 4:6 GNB)

Your approach matters; it must be in sync with your ambition, activities, attitude, and alliances.

Step 6: Appearance

There's been lots of talk about the connection between appearance and achievement in spite of the success of Steve Jobs and Mark Zuckerberg,

Key Phrase

If you look shabby, people will treat you accordingly. Dress looking wealthy and people will assume you are and treat you accordingly.

who amassed unprecedented wealth while dressed casually.

Does dressing wealthy really make you wealthy? Yes and no. Many people feel they don't need to look wealthy to become wealthy. Do people treat you the way you look? Yes, they do. Some people say, "People shouldn't judge you by the way you look." Maybe they shouldn't, but they do! After people get to know you, they'll treat you differently, but when they first make contact with you, your appearance is the only thing they have to go by. Outward appearance matters especially if your work requires you to have face time with strangers.

> For man looketh on the outward appearances, but the Lord looketh on the heart. (1 Samuel 16:7 KJV)

> Be ready for whatever comes, dress for action and with your lamps lit. (Luke 12:35 GNB)

Dress appropriately for your job and in a way that's consistent with your goal. Since people look at the outside and God looks at the inside, work hard on the outside for people and on the inside for God. Dress simply and smartly and look clean and elegant. Neat haircut, please— step out and radiate attractiveness, and please, no bling.

When the king sent for Joseph for his first job interview as a dream interpreter, Joseph dressed for the occasion.

> Then Pharaoh sent and called Joseph, and they quickly brought him out of the pit. And when he had shaved

himself and changed his clothes, he came in before Pharaoh. (Genesis 41:14 ESV)

Have you ever wondered why people get poor service? Could it be because they dress poorly? If you look shabby, people will treat you accordingly. Dress looking wealthy and people will assume you are and treat you accordingly. And it's not the clothes you wear but the way you wear them that allows people to promote or demote you in their minds.

Don't be lazy with your appearance as it may make a great difference in how your economic life turns out. And remember to smile; there's nothing more pitiful than a well-dressed person who doesn't smile. Another thing—wear clean underwear; that will make you feel powerful and confident. My grandmother used to say that if I got run over by a bus, at least my underpants would be clean.

Do all in your power to improve your dress so it complement your ambition, activities, attitude, alliances, and approach.

Step 7: Adaptability

Adaptability is the ability to change to fit or work better in a situation or for a purpose; it connotes strength without rigidity. It's the recognition that you cannot control things beyond your control and the discipline to behave accordingly.

Consider the skyscrapers that are able to survive earthquakes; they were designed to sway without compromising their strength. You have to live the same way if you want to withstand economic, social, and political earthquakes. Jesus compared the wise man who built his house on the rock to the foolish man who built his on the sand.

> "So then, anyone who hears these words of mine and obeys them is like a wise man who built his house on rock. The rain poured down, the rivers flooded over, and the wind blew hard against that house. But it did not fall,

because it was built on rock. But anyone who hears these words of mine and does not obey them is like a foolish man who built his house on sand. The rain poured down, the rivers flooded over, the wind blew hard against that house, and it fell. And what a terrible fall that was!" When Jesus finished saying these things, the crowd was amazed at the way he taught. (Matthew 7:24–28 GNB)

The same wind blows on us all, but that doesn't determine our success; our ability to sway in that wind does. The Bible talks about a group of men who really knows what it means to be adaptable.

From the family of Issachar there were 200 wise leaders. These men understood the right thing for Israel to do at the right time. (1 Chronicles 12:32 ERV)

The world is changing; that calls on us to adapt and change as well, and we all can if we want to. If we don't, who knows what will happen to us? Perhaps the same thing that happened to the dinosaurs.

I bet you're working with some dinosaurs. They're brain dead because they never opened a book since they graduated. They stopped learning, growing, and developing and became inflexible, rigid.

The way to stay flexible is to never stop learning and developing new skills. The more you learn, the more you earn. High earners are learners, and when you become rigid and inflexible, that stops your earning power. A rapidly changing world requires growing and changing people—that's a real no-brainer.

You've heard people say, "What you don't know can't hurt you." That's not necessarily true. The information you miss won't help you, and it could hurt your health, marriage, and bank account. It doesn't matter how much you know; there's room to learn more. Don't be lazy in learning. Don't miss any opportunity to grow and change. Don't miss seminars and lectures, books, and conferences! Stay teachable and adaptable, and never stop developing new skills and perspectives.

A rapidly changing world requires growing and changing people—that's a real no-brainer.

Intelligent people are always eager and ready to learn. (Proverbs 18:15 GNB)

Do yourself a favor and learn all you can; then remember what you learn and you will prosper. (Proverbs 19:8 GNB)

Intelligent people want to learn, but stupid people are satisfied with ignorance. (Proverbs 15:14 GNB)

Step 8: Achievements

People who get to the top and have bounty poured into their lives have learned one of life's greatest secrets for becoming wealthy: they've learned to enjoy what they have and not waste time complaining about what they don't have.

You might say, "I don't achieve much in life. I don't have any money in the bank, and I'm in debt." I understand. I lived in that camp for a long time. But even in times of so-called lack, you're never really down to nothing; there's always something to be thankful for. In those times, it's easy to become a cynic by overlooking, cursing, undermining, and even ignoring your past achievements. That cynicism blocks the flow of all the treasures that are available to us all.

You have to stop complaining and be grateful for what you have. Legitimate complaining is okay, but constant complaining isn't. Through a series of miracles, God delivered the Israelites from Egypt and promised to take them to a place of wealth. On their way, they complained about the leader: "He doesn't know what he's doing." They complained about the food and water: "It doesn't taste good." They complained about the weather: "It's too hot" or "Too cold!" The Lord heard their complaining and said, "Enough! Trip canceled!" One Old Testament writer captured this dramatic occasion.

Act One

The Israelites complained against Moses and Aaron. All the people came together and said to Moses and Aaron, "We should have died in Egypt or in the desert. Did the LORD bring us to this new land to be killed in war? The enemy will kill us and take our wives and children! It would be better for us to go back to Egypt." Then the people said to each other, "Let's choose another leader and go back to Egypt." (Numbers 14:2–4 ESV)

Act Two

And the LORD said to Moses, "How long will this people despise me? And how long will they not believe in me, in spite of all the signs that I have done among them?" (Numbers 14:11 ESV)

Act Three

None of the people I led out of Egypt will ever see the land of Canaan. They saw my glory and the great signs that I did in Egypt and in the desert. But they disobeyed me and tested me ten times. (Numbers 14:11–22 ESV)

Act Four

I promised their ancestors that I would give them that land. But none of those people who turned against me will ever enter that land! But my servant Caleb was different. He follows me completely. So I will bring him into the land that he has already seen, and his people will get that land. (Numbers 14:23–24 ESV)

Key Phrase

Giving thanks opens the door for more. It's the reservoir from which not just bounty flows but also information and ideas.

God was making the point that if we're not grateful for where He has brought us and for the things we have achieved and continue with senseless complaining, we'll have our future canceled—no promotion, no increase, no successful business.

Thank You Power

If you're to get to your wealthy place, you must recognize what you've already achieved or possess and be thankful for that. Giving thanks opens the door for more. It's the reservoir from which not just bounty but also information and ideas flow.

You might not be where you want to be financially, but God hasn't left you with nothing. Take an inventory of your life; you'll be amazed at how many beautiful things you have that you're not enjoying. You have your life and are probably are in reasonably good health, right? You have ambition, a positive attitude, faith, family, friends, unique abilities, and twenty-four hours to change anything you wish to change. And you live in a great country; America is a remarkable and exceptional country, a land of incredible wealth. Here in America, if you make $10,000 to $15,000 a year, you're considered poor, but most of the world would consider you rich.

I've lived in three countries including America, and I've found them to be truly exceptional. As well, the Internet has erased the distances between us. So let's be thankful and not curse what we have. Let's all find something to embrace and be thankful for.

> When you have all you want to eat and have built good houses to live in and when your cattle and sheep, your silver and gold, and all your other possessions have increased, be sure that you do not become proud and forget the LORD your God who rescued you from Egypt, where you were slaves. (Deuteronomy 8:12–14 GNB)

> So then, you must never think that you have made yourselves wealthy by your own power and strength. Remember that it is the LORD your God who gives you the power to become rich. He does this because he is still faithful today to the covenant that he made with your ancestors. (Deuteronomy 8:17–18 GN)

> Give thanks to the LORD, for he is good; his love endures forever. (Psalm 118:1 NIV)

Step 9: Your Adversaries

Adversaries! Oh boy, we all have them. In your desire to climb the corporate ladder, not many people will appreciate your climb to success and will do everything they can to pull you down. One of the tragedies of life is that those who seek to improve their lives will be marginalized by those who choose not to. People who set lofty goals for themselves will always be criticized by those who set no goals.

One key to success is the ability to recognize enemies. Sometimes, a friend can be an adversary to your success, and sometimes, an adversary can be a friend to your success. You have to be smart enough to recognize the difference.

Category One: Adversaries from Without

I wish it weren't so, but you'll face major opposition in your line of work. I don't know why this is because I wasn't in on it when it was worked out in God's council.

Key Phrase

One of the tragedies of life is that those who seek to improve their lives will be marginalized by those who choose not to. People who set lofty goals for themselves will always be criticized by those who set no goals.

You and I didn't set up the setup. When we get our own planets, we can do what we wish. But here's what I know: all treasure and value will be attacked, and they must be defended.

> And Isaac dug again the wells of water that had been dug in the days of Abraham his father, which the Philistines had stopped after the death of Abraham. And he gave them the names that his father had given them. But when Isaac's servants dug in the valley and found there a well of spring water, the herdsmen of Gerar quarreled with Isaac's herdsmen, saying, "The water is ours." So he called the name of the well Esek, because they contended with him.
>
> Then they dug another well, and they quarreled over that also, so he called its name Sitnah. And he moved from there and dug another well, and they did not quarrel over it. So he called its name Rehoboth, saying, "For now the LORD has made room for us, and we shall be fruitful in the land." (Genesis 26:18–22 ESV)

Isaac named the first well Esek, Hebrew for "to strive with, to contend for." The name of the second well, Sitnah, is Hebrew for "to experience violent opposition." We get the word *Satan* from that word.

The name of the final well was Rehoboth, Hebrew for "to flourish, to be in a wealthy place." Prior to Isaac getting to his wealthy place (Rehoboth), he had to overcome conflict (Esek)

and violence (Sitnah). To ascend to the top, you must deal with opposition in your life with maturity. Never retaliate; God will take care of your enemies.

> The LORD will defeat your enemies when they attack you. They will attack from one direction, but they will run from you in all directions. (Deuteronomy 28:7 GNB)

> When a man's ways please the LORD, he maketh even his enemies to be at peace with him. (Proverbs 16:7 KJV)

Consider one more Old Testament scenario, that of Nehemiah and the rebuilding of the broken wall around Jerusalem.

> Even those who carried building materials worked with one hand and kept a weapon in the other. (Nehemiah 4:16–17 GNB)

What do you suppose the tool the workers carried with one hand was for? What do you think the weapon they had in other hand was for? The tool was to build their future, and the weapon to defend their future. What can we learn from this? If we're to win the high life, we must build our future as we battle our adversaries.

Category Two: Adversaries Within

Key Phrase

If we're to win the high life, we must build our future as we battle our adversaries.

Sometimes, we focus on the adversaries outside and ignore those within our minds. We're so afraid of the guy waiting to steal our identity, the guy waiting in the alley to snatch our purse, or the guy trying to break into our home that we ignore our major internal enemies. The adversaries within are far more deadly than those from without. Let me list at least nine adversaries you need to be aware of and protect yourself from.

- Adversary 1: Fear of failure
- Adversary 2: Timidity
- Adversary 3: Indecision
- Adversary 4: Over-caution
- Adversary 5: Procrastination
- Adversary 6: Limited worldview
- Adversary 7: Low self-esteem
- Adversary 8: Doubt
- Adversary 9: Worry

Another adversary we don't often think about is ill health. The reason many don't do well is because they've neglected their health and end up with a willing mind but an unwilling body. Terrible combination. Poor health is an enemy to success and wealth, so do battle with it.

Many times, you don't have control over what's going on out there, but you have control over what's going on in your mind. The same way you can protect yourself from external adversaries is how you can protect yourself from the enemies within. Build up your courage and destroy your fear of failure before it destroys you. Do the same with your timidity and all your other internal foes because they're all adversaries of your opportunities.

As silly as this might sound, you should be grateful for your adversities because even in the midst of them, you can grow and change.

Go after your limited worldview and low self-esteem. Broaden your horizon. Refuse to settle for the bottom of the ladder. Do battle with doubt, and don't allow your worries to worry you. Finally, do battle with ill health; you'll need good health if you want good wealth. Get your cholesterol under control, and start a health and fitness plan today. Start with an apple a day or a glass of water instead of that 79¢ soda.

Take the sword to all your adversaries, inside and out, if you wish to win the high life. You ignore them at your peril.

Step 10: Your Adversities

This step is akin with the last step but with a twist. The biblical words for adversity are trials, tribulations, troubles, sufferings, and others. Life can be viewed as a series of adversities; to expect to live without adversity is naïve. You'll face adversity on your journey to the wealthy place. Jesus reminded His followers of this.

> I have spoken these things to you so that you might have peace in Me. In the world you shall have tribulation, but be of good cheer. I have overcome the world. (John 16:33 MKJV)

For the simple reason that you'll face adversities, it makes sense to prepare yourself for them and learn from them as they come. As silly as this might sound, you should be grateful for your adversities because even in the midst of them, you can grow and change. When you're flat broke, there's only one way to go—up.

Adversities can get you to build your faith, enhance your talents, polish your gifts, commend your capabilities, and transcend yourself beyond familiar boundaries and into new territories. Don't be intimated by adversity; rather, treat it as a stepping stone to your wealthy place. Let's take another look at the psalm that is the inspiration for this project.

> Thou hast caused men to ride over our heads; we went
> through fire and through water: but thou broughtest us
> out into a wealthy place. (Psalm 66:12 KJV)

This makes it clear there's no shortcut to your wealthy place. You have to go through something. The writer used the words *fire* and *water* to describe the bitter experiences God's people endured in Egypt. Yet God delivered them out of it and deposited them in their wealthy place, the Promised Land.

One biblical character triumphed over much adversity and ended up super rich. I bet you know whom I mean. You're right—Job. He started out at the top of the wealth ladder but through a series of unfortunate blows lost it all. He faced a series of adversities on the day of one of his son's birthday celebrations.

Blow 1: His Wealth

> The LORD told Satan, "Everything he has is in your
> power, but you must not lay a hand on him!" Then
> Satan left the LORD'S presence. One day when Job's
> sons and daughters were eating and drinking wine in
> their oldest brother's home, a messenger came to Job.
> He said, "While the oxen were plowing and the donkeys

were grazing nearby, men from Sheba attacked. They took the livestock and massacred the servants. I'm the only one who has escaped to tell you."

While he was still speaking, another messenger came and said, "A fire from God fell from heaven and completely burned your flocks and servants. I'm the only one who has escaped to tell you." While he was still speaking, another messenger came and said, "The Chaldeans formed three companies and made a raid on the camels. They took the camels and massacred the servants. I'm the only one who has escaped to tell you."

Blow 2: His Family

While he was still speaking, another messenger came and said, "Your sons and your daughters were eating and drinking wine at their oldest brother's home when suddenly a great storm swept across the desert and struck the four corners of the house. It fell on the young people, and they died. I'm the only one who has escaped to tell you."

Job stood up, tore his robe in grief, and shaved his head. Then he fell to the ground and worshiped. He said, "Naked I came from my mother, and naked I will return. The LORD has given, and the LORD has taken away! May the name of the LORD be praised." Through all this Job did not sin or blame God for doing anything wrong. (Job 1:12–22 GW)

Blow 3: His Health

Then Satan answered the LORD and said, "Skin for skin! All that a man has he will give for his life. But stretch out your hand and touch his bone

and his flesh, and he will curse you to your face."
And the LORD said to Satan, "Behold, he is in
your hand; only spare his life." So Satan went out
from the presence of the LORD and struck Job with
loathsome sores from the sole of his foot to the
crown of his head.

And he took a piece of broken pottery with which to
scrape himself while he sat in the ashes. Then his wife
said to him, "Do you still hold fast your integrity? Curse
God and die." But he said to her, "You speak as one of
the foolish women would speak. Shall we receive good
from God, and shall we not receive evil?" In all this Job
did not sin with his lips. (Job 2:4–10 ESV)

It all happened in two days. Before he could recover from the first
adversity, along came another and another. He lost his wealth, family,
and health in one day—a triple blow. Job's response to it all speaks of
his character—he was willing to accept adversity as well as prosperity
from the hand of the Almighty. He goes on record as one of if not the
most patient man of all times who bounced back from adversity to
prosperity. According to the text, the Lord gave him twice the amount
of wealth he had before.

Then all his brothers, all his sisters, and all those who
had been his acquaintances before, came to him and
ate food with him in his house; and they consoled him
and comforted him for all the adversity that the LORD
had brought upon him. Each one gave him a piece of
silver and each a ring of gold. And Jehovah blessed the
latter days of Job more than the beginning. For he had
fourteen thousand sheep, and six thousand camels, and
a thousand yoke of oxen, and a thousand she asses. He
also had seven sons and three daughters. (Job 42:11–13
MJKV)

The lesson here is to never quit on your dream during times of adversity because there's always a hidden purpose behind every pain.

Step 11: Asking

> Ask, and you will receive, Seek, and you will find; Knock, and the door will be opened to you. (Matthew 7:7 GNB)

This is a major step on the corporate ladder. Everything you need to become powerful, wealthy, and sophisticated is within asking reach, but you have to learn how to ask for what you want. You might be a good, hard-working person, but if you don't know how to ask for help, you can end up broke. Let me pass on a few tips about how to ask for what you need.

Ask Intelligently

Making intelligent requests and address questions such as what? where? when? how? who? why? and what then? Don't beg or moan. Learn to articulate your need intelligently. Explore questions about government, society, country, taxes, investments, risks, capitalism, the marketplace, people, races, cultures, religions—everything. You can't let these major questions go by causally as they probably will leave you broke.

Ask Specifically

Don't mumble. Be specific. Asking is an art. State what you need politely, concisely, and clearly especially about how to make and invest money.

> You ask and do not receive, because you ask wrongly, to
> spend it on your passions. (James 4:2–3 ESV)

Ask Persistently

If at first you don't succeed, try, try again. Perhaps the first time
you asked someone for something, that person was in the middle of a
bad day. Go back the next day.

> In a certain town there was a judge who neither feared
> God nor respected people. And there was a widow in
> that same town who kept coming to him and pleading for
> her rights, saying, "Help me against my opponent!" For
> a long time the judge refused to act, but at last he said to
> himself, "Even though I don't fear God or respect people,
> yet because of all the trouble this widow is giving me, I
> will see to it that she gets her rights." (Luke 18:1–5 GNB)

We can learn a great deal from kids about persistent asking. They
don't take no for an answer; they keep asking. "But Dad!" "But Mom!"
They master the value of persistence; they have nothing to lose and
everything to gain by asking.

Ask Expectantly

"If you could ask the Lord for anything in this whole world, what
would you ask for?"

> If you don't ask with faith, don't expect the Lord to give
> you any solid answer. (James 1:7–8 LB)

Asking expectantly also means asking someone who is able to give
you what you need. Remember, you can never ask for too much, but if
you don't ask, you won't get anything.

Let us wrap up this point with the all-time classical biblical example of the man who became the richest man who ever lived. He became wealthy by mastering the art of asking. According to the text God appeared to Solomon in a dream:

> At Gibeon the LORD appeared to Solomon in a dream
> by night, and God said, "Ask what I shall give you."

And Solomon said, "You have shown great and steadfast love to your servant David my father, because he walked before you in faithfulness, in righteousness, and in uprightness of heart toward you. And you have kept for him this great and steadfast love and have given him a son to sit on his throne this day.

> And now, O LORD my God, you have made your servant king in place of David my father, although I am but a little child. I do not know how to go out or come in.
>
> And your servant is in the midst of your people whom you have chosen, a great people, too many to be numbered or counted for multitude.
>
> Give your servant therefore an understanding mind to govern your people, that I may discern between good and evil, for who is able to govern this your great people?"
>
> It pleased the Lord that Solomon had asked this.
>
> And God said to him, "Because you have asked this, and have not asked for yourself long life or riches or the life of your enemies, but have asked for yourself understanding to discern what is right,

behold, I now do according to your word. Behold, I give you a wise and discerning mind, so that none like you has been before you and none like you shall arise after you.

I give you also what you have not asked, both riches and honor, so that no other king shall compare with you, all your days. (Kings 3:5-13 ESV)

Because this king knew how to *ask*, God exceeded his expectation by granting him not only wisdom but untold wealth. Why? Because he knew how to ask.

Final Word

I challenge you to develop these skills that lead to success. Successful people don't wish for things to be easy; rather, they strive to be better. If you want the extra dollar, you have to do the extra learning. Stay up late, rise early, and apply the seat of the trousers to the seat of the chair until you have mastered a subject.

My friend, you become wealthy, powerful, unique, and sophisticated by refining your skills and enlarging your knowledge. That's how you gain upward mobility. When you get to the top, you'll look back and exclaim (with a humble heart of course), "My God, there's nothing quite like the view from the top!"

My Personal Wealth Place Notes

My Wealthy Place

Psalm 66:12

Chapter 15

Promotion to Your Wealthy Place
by the Anointing

*The LORD will make you be like the head, not the tail. You will be on top,
not on the bottom. This will happen if you listen to the commands of the LORD
your God that I tell you today. You must carefully obey these commands.*
—Deuteronomy 28:13 ERV

As I promised, this chapter will deal with step 12, your anointing.
There are many functions of your anointing, and my friend,
promotion to your wealthy place is one. The anointing has unlimited
capabilities but fulfils nine functions: identification, educational,
magnetic, protective, destructive, optical, positional, and promotional.

I can't elaborate on all these functions in this book, so I'll focus
on the promotional function of the anointing as it relates to climbing
the ladder to your wealthy place. Let's first deal with two other kinds
of promotion.

Self-Promotion

In its simplest form, this is promoting one's own interests or profile.
This can take an aggressive form in organizations whose members are
trying to get to the top at all costs. And by *organizations*, I mean businesses,
churches, associations, political parties, and so many other places.

Organizational politics comes into play everywhere organizations exist, including your church. Organizational politics dictate that you might have to pull someone down in order to move up.

Key Phrase

The "anointing" is a sophisticated piece of software installed by God into the operating system of your life. It has unlimited capabilities but fulfils nine unique functions.
—Bishop Wayne Malcolm

People Promotion

What happens here is an individual seeks out key figures in an organization and becomes a "pal-pal" with them to help their cause. Most promotions by people usually come with strings attached: as long as you can serve their purpose, they'll keep supporting your climb up the ladder. When you can no longer serve their purposes, they'll pull it out from under you. Many times, you get all tied up with a rope of gratitude and have to beg, creep around, and serve them with a slave's mentality for the rest of your days. If someone offers to open a door for you, ask or figure out what's in it for him or her.

Promotion by God or by the Anointing

To anoint simply means to be officially chosen and endued by the Holy Spirt to do or be something. In his book *Live the Dream*, my dear friend Bishop Wayne Malcolm made this great statement about the anointing.

> The "anointing" is a sophisticated piece of software installed by God into the operating system of your life. It has unlimited capabilities but fulfils nine unique functions.[4]

The Magnetic Function of Your Anointing

Did you know you have a magnetic function of the anointing on your life that will make people seek you out and bless you? I remember speaking at a church. A businessman came to me after the service and told me how blessed he was by the Word. A few weeks later, he invited my wife and me out and blessed us. He said, "There was something in you that just made me want to bless you." I cannot tell you how many times this has happened to me. The anointing on your life will force people to bless you. What do you think caused the Egyptians to dispose of their wealth on the redeemed people?

Key Phrase

Most promotions by men usually come with strings attached: as long as you can serve their purpose, they'll keep supporting your climb up the ladder. When you can no longer serve their purposes, they'll pull it out from under you.

> Then the Israelites did what Moses asked them to do. They went to their Egyptian neighbors and asked for clothing and things made from silver and gold. The LORD caused the Egyptians to be kind to the Israelites, so the Egyptians gave their riches to the Israelites. (Exodus 12:35–36 ERV)

The simple answer is the magnetic function of the anointing. We also witness this function of the anointing in the ministry of Jesus. The wise men traveled hundreds of miles just to dispose of their wealth on Him.

> And going into the house they saw the child with Mary his mother, and they fell down and worshiped him. Then, opening their treasures, they offered him gifts, gold and frankincense and myrrh. (Matthew 2:11 ESV)

I declare that wise men are seeking you out to bless you because of the anointing on your life. Check it out; the Egyptians had no peace until they blessed the people of God. There is an anointing on you to get wealth, and God will bring key people into your life who will have no peace until they dispose of their wealth on you.

Though all the eleven points we dealt with in the previous chapter are essential steps up the ladder, your move to the top is also a key function of the anointing on your life.

> For promotion cometh neither from the east, nor from the west, nor from the south. But God is the judge: he putteth down one, and setteth up another. (Psalm 75:6–7 KJV)

Most people of faith understand what I'm saying here. This doesn't contradict what I have previously said; you should never stop learning and developing skills and competence. I'm simply saying your anointing will promote you but won't keep you there unless you keep on working on yourself. This process never stops.

How do you know when your promotion to your wealthy place is a function of your anointing? Answer—your experience will be autographed with seven divine trademarks.

Trademark One: You achieve your desired wealthy place against all odds

Take for example Joseph, a Hebrew boy sold as slave to the Egyptians by his jealous brothers. Consider the odds against his incredible promotion to a place of wealth and honor. All the odds were against him.

Odds One: He was hated by his brothers.

And when his brethren saw that their father loved him
more than all his brethren, they hated him, and could
not speak peaceably unto him. (Genesis 37:4 KJV)

Odds Two: He was sold by his brothers.

"Let's sell him to these Ishmaelites. Then we won't
have to hurt him; after all, he is our brother, our own
flesh and blood." His brothers agreed, and when some
Midianite traders came by, the brothers pulled Joseph
out of the well and sold him for twenty pieces of silver
to the Ishmaelites, who took him to Egypt. (Genesis
37:27–28 GNB)

Odds Three: He was seduced at work by Egypt's first lady and
wrongly accused of rape.

From then on, because of Joseph the LORD blessed
the household of the Egyptian and everything that
he had in his house and in his fields. Potiphar turned
over everything he had to the care of Joseph and did
not concern himself with anything except the food he
ate. Joseph was well-built and good-looking, and after
a while his master's wife began to desire Joseph and
asked him to go to bed with her. He refused and said
to her, "Look, my master does not have to concern
himself with anything in the house, because I am here.
He has put me in charge of everything he has.

I have as much authority in this house as he has, and he
has not kept back anything from me except you. How
then could I do such an immoral thing and sin against
God?" Although she asked Joseph day after day, he
would not go to bed with her. But one day when Joseph
went into the house to do his work, none of the house
servants were there.

She caught him by his robe and said, "Come to bed with me." But he escaped and ran outside, leaving his robe in her hand. When she saw that he had left his robe and had run out of the house, she called to her house servants and said, "Look at this! This Hebrew that my husband brought to the house is insulting us. He came into my room and tried to rape me, but I screamed as loud as I could." (Genesis 39:5–14 GNB)

Odds Four: He was framed and put on death row as a convicted rapist.

And Joseph's master took him and put him into the prison, the place where the king's prisoners were confined, and he was there in prison. (Genesis 39:20 ESV)

Odds Five: He was forgotten in prison by someone whom he had helped.

Within three days Pharaoh will lift up your head and restore you to your position, and you will put Pharaoh's cup in his hand, just as you used to do when you were his cupbearer. But when all goes well with you, remember me and show me kindness; mention me to Pharaoh and get me out of this prison. (Genesis 40:13–14 NIV)

He restored the chief cupbearer to his position, so that he once again put the cup into Pharaoh's hand—but he impaled the chief baker, just as Joseph had said to them in his interpretation. The chief cupbearer, however, did not remember Joseph; he forgot him. (Genesis 40:21–23 NIV)

What was the likelihood of a convicted rapist getting out of jail and promoted to the vice presidency of a foreign country? Zilch. But when you study the life of Joseph, you'll come across this neat little phrase: "But the Lord was with Joseph." That phrase holds the key to your breakthrough: it doesn't matter who is against you as long as God is with you. If God is with you, you don't need to worry about the odds against you no matter what they are

☑ Academically
☑ Biographically
☑ Biologically
☑ Economically
☑ Educationally
☑ Emotionally
☑ Ethnically
☑ Financially
☑ Genetically
☑ Geographically
☑ Legally
☑ Linguistically
☑ Medically
☑ Mentality
☑ Morally
☑ Physically
☑ Physiologically
☑ Politically
☑ Psychologically
☑ Racially
☑ Relationally
☑ Socially
☑ Statistically
☑ Stigmatically
☑ Systematically

☑ Technically

☑ Technologically

Now, pay attention to this! Sovereignly, if the odds aren't against you, you are in good shape. That's right, as long as God's odds aren't against you, you don't have to worry. When God targets you for promotion, my dear friend, you're on your way up, and there's nothing the devil can do about it. You better believe you're on your way to the top and can't be stopped.

Key Phrase

As long as God's odds aren't against you, you don't have to worry. When God targeted you for promotion, my dear friend, you're on your way up, and there's nothing the devil can do about it.

After Joseph served two years on death row, God showed him favor; his promotion was occasioned by a midnight crisis. The king had a bad dream his chief people couldn't interpret. The king's chief cupbearer remembered Joseph.

> Then the chief cupbearer said to Pharaoh, "I remember my offenses today. When Pharaoh was angry with his servants and put me and the chief baker in custody in the house of the captain of the guard, we dreamed on the same night, he and I, each having a dream with its own interpretation. A young Hebrew was there with us, a servant of the captain of the guard. When we told him, he interpreted our dreams to us, giving an interpretation to each man according to his dream. And as he interpreted to us, so it came about. I was restored to my office, and the baker was hanged."
>
> Then Pharaoh sent and called Joseph, and they quickly brought him out of the pit. And when he had shaved himself and changed his clothes, he came in before Pharaoh. (Genesis 41:9–14 ESV)

And he said to them, "We will never find a better man than Joseph, a man who has God's spirit in him." The king said to Joseph, "God has shown you all this, so it is obvious that you have greater wisdom and insight than anyone else. I will put you in charge of my country, and all my people will obey your orders. Your authority will be second only to mine. I now appoint you governor over all Egypt."

The king removed from his finger the ring engraved with the royal seal and put it on Joseph's finger. He put a fine linen robe on him, and placed a gold chain around his neck. He gave him the second royal chariot to ride in, and his guard of honor went ahead of him and cried out, "Make way! Make way!" And so Joseph was appointed governor over all Egypt. The king said to him, "I am the king—and no one in all Egypt shall so much as lift a hand or a foot without your permission." (Genesis 41:38–44 GNB)

Joseph's authority was second only to the great man's. If you see yourself in Joseph, please be encouraged that your promotion will come. I love this part: "Then Pharaoh sent and called Joseph, and they quickly brought him out of the pit."

Trademark Two: You're promoted to your wealthy place in the face of your enemies

Study the plight of David as a young shepherd. He was left out of the anointed lineup by his father when Samuel came to anoint the new king of Israel perhaps because he was illegitimate. David seemingly made reference to it in one of his psalms: "In sin my mother conceived me" (Psalm 51:5). He wrote in another, "When my mother and father forsake me the Lord took me up!" (Psalm 27:10). He was referring to the guilt of been born out of wedlock and expressing his childhood abandonment and his burden.

I believe David's father had conveniently kept him out of sight to cover up the affair he'd had with David's nameless mother. Out of sight, out of mind? No! When God sent Samuel to anoint the next king of Israel, He targeted Jesse's household; the Almighty was after one person, the rejected and abandoned David. Just imagine the occasion and the lineup for the next king of Israel.

> The LORD said to Samuel, "How long will you mourn for Saul, since I have rejected him as king over Israel? Fill your horn with oil and be on your way; I am sending you to Jesse of Bethlehem. I have chosen one of his sons to be king." Jesse had seven of his sons pass before Samuel, but Samuel said to him, "The LORD has not chosen these."
>
> So he asked Jesse, "Are these all the sons you have?" "There is still the youngest," Jesse answered. "He is tending the sheep." Samuel said, "Send for him; we will not sit down until he arrives." So he sent for him and had him brought in. He was glowing with health and had a fine appearance and handsome features. Then the LORD said, "Rise and anoint him; this is the one." So Samuel took the horn of oil and anointed him in the presence of his brothers, and from that day on the Spirit of the LORD came powerfully upon David. (1 Samuel 16:1, 10–12 NIV)

Don't you just love the part that says all the sons of Jesse passed by one by one? The first son passed by, and the Holy Spirit said, "I have not chosen this one." The second, and the Holy Spirit said, "I have not chosen this one." The third, fourth, fifth, and sixth stepped up, and the Holy Spirit said, "I have not chosen these either."

The prophet asked Jesse, "Are these all the sons you have?" Jesse probably scratched his head and sighed, thinking his sin had caught up with him, and said, "It's funny you asked. I do have another son, but he's tending the animals."

Key Phrase

When God is your friend, it doesn't matter who's your enemy. When God is speaking well of you, it doesn't matter who's speaking ill of you. You're on your way up, and there's nothing the devil can do about it.

Don't you just love God's sense of humor? He targeted David for promotion, and there was nothing his father or anyone else could do to prevent it. The prophet said, "We will not sit down until he comes." The prophet anointed David in the presence of his brothers. Take note of the following psalm David composed acclaiming his promotion by the anointing.

> You prepare a table before me in the presence of my enemies. You anoint my head with oil; my cup overflows. (Psalm 23:5 NIV)

You don't have to worry about the odds being against you. When God targets you for a promotion, it doesn't matter who targets you for demotion. When God accepts you, it doesn't matter who rejects you. When God is your friend, it doesn't matter who's your enemy. When God is speaking well of you, it doesn't matter who's speaking ill of you. You're on your way up, and there's nothing the devil can do about it.

Trademark Three: Promotion to your wealthy place by humility

Promotion by humility is the opposite of self-promotion. It's allowing God to exalt you when the time, people, and place are right.

Humility is hard to explain, but you know when you see it. There's something wondrous and godly about the word. Humility is a sense

Key Phrase

Whenever you are promoted by humility, you will be overwhelmed with a sense of awe and inadequacy.

of your being close to God while at the same time realizing the distance between you and Him.

Jesus gave us the most accurate description of what promotion by humility looks like in one of His teachings. He was the special guest at a certain Pharisee's home. He observed guests file in to the banquet and secure for themselves the loftiest seats. These guys considered themselves really important. It's my bet they had no idea how much sweat, tears, and sacrifices were poured into those seats. Let's read the Master's teachings on humility.

> When he (Jesus) noticed how the guests picked the places of honor at the table, he told them this parable: "When someone invites you to a wedding feast, do not take the place of honor, for a person more distinguished than you may have been invited. If so, the host who invited both of you will come and say to you, 'Give this person your seat.' Then, humiliated, you will have to take the least important place. But when you are invited, take the lowest place, so that when your host comes, he will say to you, 'Friend, move up to a better place.' Then you will be honored in the presence of all the other guests. For all those who exalt themselves will be humbled, and those who humble themselves will be exalted." (Luke 14:7–11 NIV)

How do you know when you're promoted by humility? When someone tells you, "Friend, come move up to a better place." Whenever you are promoted by humility, you will be overwhelmed with a sense of awe and inadequacy. Humility says, *I don't really deserve what I have; it's all because of the favor of God.*

The Towel vs. the Title

Jesus demonstrated humility when He shared the last supper with His disciples.

> So while they were eating, Jesus stood up and took off his robe. He got a towel and wrapped it around his waist. Then he poured water into a bowl and began to wash the followers' feet. He dried their feet with the towel that was wrapped around his waist. (John 13:4–5 ERV)

Note the other disciples were fighting for a title. They were all about the ego (edging God out) and the logo. But Jesus asked for a towel, not a title. Jesus himself was the perfect embodiment of humility; He was promoted to the highest place of honor because of it.

The apostle Paul has the rest of this story.

> Who, being in the very nature God, did not consider equality with God something to be grasped, But made himself nothing, taking the very nature of a servant being made in human likeness. And being found in appearance as a man, he humbled himself by becoming obedient to death—even death on a cross! Therefore God exalted him to the highest place and gave him the name that is above every name. (Philippians 2:6–9 NIV)

Be like Jesus. Don't do your own press. Let God speak on your behalf. Always bear in mind the key to self-abasement is self-promotion. Ancient wisdom says, "Humble yourself in the mighty hands of God and he will promote you in due season."

The relationship between David and Saul is a great story of humility lived out. A prophet had told David he would be king of Israel. When Samuel anointed him king, effectively giving him the throne, David did not walk over to Saul and say, "Excuse me, you're sitting on my throne." Even when David had the chance to kill King Saul and take the throne, he refused to do so. David had multiple opportunities to destroy his rival Saul and take the throne, but he chose to honor the call on Saul's life by not hurting him.

> Don't harm my chosen servants; do not touch my prophets. (1 Chronicles 16:22; Psalm 105:15 GNB)

David was anointed king but not enthroned until Saul died. He worked as a servant and became one of the Saul's armor bearers. That is real humility.

Trademark Four: Promotion to your wealthy place by special favor

When you're promoted by favor, you won't be able to explain it; neither will it make any sense in the eyes of the beholder and the begetter. You probably were the least qualified, but God gave you favor with key people in your company. They often remarked, "I don't even know why I'm doing this. You're not qualified for the position, but I'm going to offer it to you anyhow." The phrase *"Favor ain't fair"* is old, but it still sounds fresh to me.

Let us again consider Joseph as another example of promotion by favor. God showed Joseph favor in Potiphar's house when he was appointed manager of his household.

> Joseph found favor in his eyes and became his attendant. Potiphar put him in charge of his household, and he entrusted to his care everything he owned. From the time he put him in charge of his household and of all

that he owned, the LORD blessed the household of the Egyptian because of Joseph. The blessing of the LORD was on everything Potiphar had, both in the house and in the field. So Potiphar left everything he had in Joseph's care; with Joseph in charge, he did not concern himself with anything except the food he ate. (Genesis 39:4–6 NIV)

God also showed Joseph favor in prison when he was appointed warden.

The LORD was with him; he showed him kindness and granted him favor in the eyes of the prison warden. So the warden put Joseph in charge of all those held in the prison, and he was made responsible for all that was done there. (Genesis 39:21–22 NIV)

God gave this former convicted felon favor in all Egypt when the great pharaoh made him president of the kingdom.

Then Pharaoh said to Joseph, "Since God has made all this known to you, there is no one so discerning and wise as you. You shall be in charge of my palace, and all my people are to submit to your orders. Only with respect to the throne will I be greater than you." So Pharaoh said to Joseph, "I hereby put you in charge of the whole land of Egypt."

Then Pharaoh took his signet ring from his finger and put it on Joseph's finger. He dressed him in robes of fine linen and put a gold chain around his neck. He had him ride in a chariot as his second-in-command, and people shouted before him, "Make way!" Thus he put him in charge of the whole land of Egypt. Then Pharaoh said to Joseph, "I am Pharaoh, but without your word no one will lift hand or foot in all Egypt." (Genesis 41:39–44 NIV)

Notice at each stage of Joseph's promotion, the Almighty worked through someone. You never can rule out human involvement in your promotion. Your promotion to your wealthy

Key Phrase

Your promotion to your wealthy place will always involve people, but it doesn't depend on human personnel. God uses them to hold the ladder, but He provides the ladder.

place will always involve people, but it doesn't depend on human personnel. God uses them to hold the ladder, but He provides the ladder.

Trademark Five: Promotion to your wealthy place by crisis

As painful and uncomfortable as crises can be, they're not as bad as you can imagine. Sometimes, God will promote you to be the head of a company, church, or organization because of a crisis within it. I have been called upon to manage organizations that were in crisis. On these occasions, I discovered that in most cases, it was a good idea to take over a bad situation.

Joseph was promoted to avert an economic crisis in Egypt and save Israel. He didn't understand that until years later at a family reunion.

> Joseph said to his brothers, "Come near to me, please." And they came near. And he said, "I am your brother, Joseph, whom you sold into Egypt. And now do not be distressed or angry with yourselves because you sold me here, for God sent me before you to preserve life. For the famine has been in the land these two years, and there are yet five years in which there will be neither plowing nor harvest. And God sent me before you to preserve for you a remnant on earth, and to keep alive for you many survivors. So it was not you who sent me

here, but God. He has made me a father to Pharaoh, and lord of all his house and ruler over all the land of Egypt." (Genesis 45:4–8 ESV)

David became king of Israel because of a crisis. According to 1 Samuel 16, David's predecessor, Saul, had backslidden and was rejected by God.

And Esther was promoted after the king had a midnight crisis and ordered Queen Vashti, his wife, to parade her beauty before a host of drinking men. Vashti snubbed the king. You never snub the king. The king consulted with his nobles as to what he should do about it.

> For the queen's conduct will become known to all the women, and so they will despise their husbands and say, "King Xerxes commanded Queen Vashti to be brought before him, but she would not come." This very day the Persian and Median women of the nobility who have heard about the queen's conduct will respond to all the king's nobles in the same way. There will be no end of disrespect and discord.
>
> Therefore, if it pleases the king, let him issue a royal decree and let it be written in the laws of Persia and Media, which cannot be repealed, that Vashti is never again to enter the presence of King Xerxes. Also let the king give her royal position to someone else who is better than she. Then when the king's edict is proclaimed throughout all his vast realm, all the women will respect their husbands, from the least to the greatest. (Esther 1:17–20 NIV)

This was breaking news! A law was enacted that women had to honor their husbands, and Vashti would never again appear before the king. Esther became the king's new queen after she won the beauty contest.

> The king loved Esther more than all the women, and she won grace and favor in his sight more than all the virgins, so that he set the royal crown on her head and made her queen instead of Vashti. (Esther 2:17 ESV)

There wouldn't have been a beauty contest if the king hadn't had that midnight crisis. Sometimes, God will bring you into prominence because of a crisis or even to avert one; you must be prepared for both.

Now the pending crisis. There was a law passed to kill all Jews—this was genocide. The laws of the Persians once made couldn't be revoked.

Esther was a Jewish orphan who had been adopted by her uncle Mordecai. She knew nothing about the Persian culture. What chance did she have in becoming a successful queen of the Persian king? Nil. But she risked her life and went to see the king after being persuaded by her uncle Mordecai. Even his queen couldn't see the king without an invitation; she would have risked her life. You can understand her reluctance to speak to the king when Mordecai urged her to act.

> For if you keep silent at this time, relief and deliverance will rise for the Jews from another place, but you and your father's house will perish. And who knows whether you have not come to the kingdom for such a time as this?" Then Esther told them to reply to Mordecai, "Go, gather all the Jews to be found in Susa, and hold a fast on my behalf, and do not eat or drink for three days, night or day. I and my young women will also fast as you do. Then I will go to the king, though it is against the law, and if I perish, I perish." (Esther 4:14–16 ESV)

Strategic Positioning

Key Phrase

This has to be one of the most important texts you'll read about strategic positioning. Mordecai told Esther God had promoted

Before God promotes you to your wealthy place, He will take you through some tests involving your character and competence.

her to avert the annihilation of His people. If the king hadn't had a midnight crisis, there would have been no beauty contest. God used that opportunity to open the door for her.

Many people run from crises or problems because they want God's promotion and perks but not His problems (Esther 8:17, 10:3). Instead of trying to escape from a crisis, understand that God has strategically positioned you in a place of privilege, power, and prosperity to avert a wipeout of your clan, company, church, or country.

We're here because of a crisis or to avert a crisis; this is why we must be well schooled in how to handle crises. We cannot afford to hold our peace. Our anointing will get us on location when the time is right. If there's a crisis looming in your clan, company, church, and so on, don't panic! It could be a sign that God is getting ready to say to you, "Friend, come up higher."

Trademark Six: Promotion to your wealthy place by stewardship

Stewardship simply means the management of resources, but I'd like to push the envelope just a little. First, promotion by stewardship dictates that before God promotes you to your wealthy place, He will take you through some tests involving your character and competence. God will not promote those He has not tested. This is true of all the Bible characters.

Just for a refresher, Joseph was first steward over his father's house before he became steward over Potiphar's house, and he was in the

256

prison house before he became Mr. President of the Egypt. Notice the progression. Before he became king, he was proven in the wilderness. He learned humility as a servant and would have laid down his life for a single sheep. He proved faithfulness in caring for sheep before he became king of Israel.

Second, promotion by stewardship teaches us that if we cannot cherish small things, God won't trust us with things of greater value. If we cannot cherish a dollar, He won't trust us with a hundred much less a thousand more.

Third, promotion by stewardship dictates that we do our best all the time. Whatever your work is, make sure you perform with excellence even when you think no one is watching—that's because God is. If you do your best consistently, He'll say, "Friend, come up higher."

> One who is faithful in a very little is also faithful in much, and one who is dishonest in a very little is also dishonest in much. If then you have not been faithful in the unrighteous wealth, who will entrust to you the true riches? And if you have not been faithful in that which is another's, who will give you that which is your own? (Luke 16:10–12 ESV)

Trademark Seven: Promotion to your wealthy place by prophetic pronouncement

As a pastor, I'm saddened by how much the prophetic office is being abused these days by so-called prophets. Everybody is walking in the prophetic these days, but I'm happy that the prophetic is very much alive today. God will use genuine prophets to speak over your life and give you a glimpse of your destiny. Throughout Scripture, God gave His children a glimpse of their future through prophetic pronouncements, and these come in three parts.

- God will use a genuine prophet to give you a glimpse of what He will do in your life.
- God will use a genuine prophet to give you a glimpse of how He will do it.
- God will use a genuine prophet to give you a glimpse of when He will do it.

God commonly uses prophets to confirm what He has given you a glimpse of. Every prophecy must be in sync with what God has placed in your heart. God won't use someone to tell you to do something you despise. A true prophecy will energize you to climb the ladder of God's purpose. You might be overwhelmed, but you won't be entirely shocked by genuine prophetic pronouncements on your life. This was true of all the Bible characters when God gave them a foretaste of the mountaintop. Any opportunity or call that doesn't energize you, that compromises your integrity, or that moves you from the mountaintop of your prophetic destiny must be resolutely questioned.

Here are examples of what a prophetic pronouncement looks like. Sometimes, it was directly from God, and other times, it was conveyed via a prophet. First, God gave Abraham a glimpse of his wealthy place when He appeared and spoke these words into his spirit.

> Lift up your eyes and look from the place where you are, northward and southward and eastward and westward, for all the land that you see I will give to you and to your offspring forever. (Genesis 13:15 ESV)

God gave Joseph a glimpse of his future through dreams.

> Then he dreamed another dream and told it to his brothers and said, "Behold, I have dreamed another dream. Behold, the sun, the moon, and eleven stars were bowing down to me." But when he told it to his father and to his brothers, his father rebuked him and said to him, "What is this dream that you have dreamed? Shall I and your mother and your brothers indeed come to bow ourselves to the ground before you?" (Genesis 37:9–10 ESV)

Moses gave Israel a glimpse of their wealthy place numerous occasions.

> The LORD will command the blessing on you in your barns and in all that you undertake. And he will bless you in the land that the LORD your God is giving you. The LORD will establish you as a people holy to himself, as he has sworn to you, if you keep the commandments of the LORD your God and walk in his ways.
>
> And all the peoples of the earth shall see that you are called by the name of the LORD, and they shall be afraid of you. And the LORD will make you abound in prosperity, in the fruit of your womb and in the fruit of your livestock and in the fruit of your ground, within the land that the LORD swore to your fathers to give you.
>
> The LORD will open to you his good treasury, the heavens, to give the rain to your land in its season and to bless all the work of your hands. And you shall lend to many nations, but you shall not borrow. And the LORD will make you the head and not the tail, and you shall only go up and not down, if you obey the commandments of the LORD your God, which I command you today, being careful to do them, and if you do not turn aside

from any of the words that I command you today, to the right hand or to the left, to go after other gods to serve them. (Deuteronomy 28:8–14 ESV)

Fast forward to chapter 33; you're sitting at the bedside of Moses listening to his dying words, prophetic pronouncements on the tribes of Israel.

The eternal God is your refuge, and underneath are the everlasting arms. He will drive out your enemies before you, saying, "Destroy them!" So Israel will live in safety; Jacob will dwell secure in a land of grain and new wine, where the heavens drop dew. Blessed are you, Israel! Who is like you, a people saved by the LORD? He is your shield and helper and your glorious sword. Your enemies will cower before you, and you will tread on their heights. (Deuteronomy 33:27–29 NIV)

A Sense of Belonging at the Top

Notice I didn't say a sense of entitlement at the top but a sense of belonging; that's a big difference. At the top of this wealth ladder is treasure, value, power, prestige, prosperity, and sophistication. And the question is. How badly do you want to reach the top?

Eagles possess a sense of belonging at the top, and they refuse to nest anywhere else. That is how you have to think and behave. Have you ever visited a progressive company and imagined yourself right up there with those big executives? You had a sense of belonging, not entitlement, at the top. Have you ever visited a gated community and you feel you belong there but your friends say, "Take me back to the ghetto. I don't belong here"? The sense of belonging at the top—of the company, of the industry, of the school board and so on—is God's idea for your life. To get there, you must put yourself through these extra disciplines and steps that most people aren't

prepared to take. Continue
to work on your skills as the
Scriptures challenge us on
many occasions.

Key Phrase

*A promotion is not a promotion if it moves
you away from God's prophetic destiny for
your life.*

A man's gift maketh
room for him, and bringeth him before great men.
(Proverbs 18:16 KJV)

Do yourself a favor and learn all you can; then
remember what you learn and you will prosper
(Proverbs 19:8 GNB)

See someone skilled in their work? They will serve
before kings; they will not serve before officials of low
rank. (Proverbs 22:29 NIV)

Stay True to Your Anointing

Knowing when to say yes and when say no is the key to success.
Prosperity means being everything God wants you to be, having
God's blessing on your life, and using the talents and the anointing
He has given you. God guarantees you'll have more than you need. An
interesting story in the Bible sheds light on this.

Once upon a time the trees went out to choose a king
for themselves. They said to the olive tree, "Be our
king." The olive tree answered, "In order to govern
you, I would have to stop producing my oil, which is
used to honor gods and human beings."

Then the trees said to the fig tree, "You come and
be our king." But the fig tree answered, "In order to
govern you, I would have to stop producing my good
sweet fruit." So the trees then said to the grapevine,
"You come and be our king." But the vine answered,

261

'In order to govern you, I would have to stop producing my wine that makes gods and human beings happy.'

So then all the trees said to the thorn bush, "You come and be our king." The thorn bush answered, "If you really want to make me your king, then come and take shelter in my shade. If you don't, fire will blaze out of my thorny branches and burn up the cedars of Lebanon." (Judges 9:7–15 GNB)

The trees worthy to reign for their inherent brilliance declined the offer. They chose rather to stay true to what God had anointed them to do even though it was not a position of power. Recognize what you've been anointed to do in life in spite of opportunities to become king. A promotion is not a promotion if it moves you away from God's prophetic destiny for your life. The trees understood this concept. Saying yes means having the courage to say no to something else.

Final Word

Your anointing will take you to the top of the coperate ladder but won't keep you there. You must work on the eleven other skills mentioned in the previous chapter. Your anointing must work in sync with all those steps if you want to be unstoppable. You'll soon notice how your life begins to soar. You'll walk out of the darkness of debt into the wealthy place of light, and you'll have whatever you want, you will live where you want to live, you will drive what you want to drive, you will go where you want to go, and you will give what you want to give.

Friends, I trust I have challenged you to move up higher. The bottom of the economic ladder is crowded, but there's plenty of room at the top.

My Personal Wealthy Notes

Section VII

My Wealthy Place
Psalm 66:12

Chapter 16

What to Do with the Wealth God Gave You

Here is what I have found out: the best thing we can do is
eat and drink and enjoy what we have worked for during
the short life that God has given us; this is our fate.
If God gives us wealth and property ... lets us enjoy them, we should be
grateful and enjoy what we have worked for. It is a gift from God.
—Ecclesiastes 5:18–19 GNB

God Wants You to Enjoy Your Wealth

Learn to live your life with style. Unfortunately, many people have beautiful things but derive little or no enjoyment from them. They live in the best places and drive the best cars. They possess all the bling the eyes could desire, but they are unhappy with themselves.

Just don't learn how to earn well; also make sure you learn how to live well. Be sophisticated. Enjoy the arts and culture, concerts and plays. Fill your relationships with love, laughter, and romance. Go dancing, dining, and traveling to where you've always dreamed to go. Cruise the Caribbean. Sip a coffee in an outdoor café in Paris. Shop at Harrods in London and Saks Fifth Avenue in New York. You get the picture. I'm talking about developing a taste for the best and developing the means to achieve it.

The billionaire, John Davison Rockefeller said, "The only question with wealth is what you do with it?" He also said, "It is wrong to assume that men

Key Phrase

Happiness is not an amount or an account; it's an act and an art. Happiness is something you fashion regardless of the amount.

of immense wealth are always happy."*(quatiotionbook.com)* Reread this passage from Ecclesiastes.

> If God gives us wealth and property … lets us enjoy them, we should be grateful and enjoy what we have worked for. It is a gift from God. (Ecclesiastes 5:19 GNB)

Living Well at the Top

Living well at the top means being spiritually fulfilled by daily deepening your relationship with God; this is summit living. Unfortunately, no amount of money can buy you happiness. In my former, poverty-stricken life, I remember thinking, If I just had m*ore money, I'd be happy*, but I know better now.

If you tend to be miserable and mean, more money won't cure that; it's just going to magnify more of the same. That's because happiness is not an amount or an account; it's an act and an art. Happiness is something you fashion regardless of the amount. No matter how much you earn, you can still live your life in style.

It's Not the Amount that Counts

"It's not the amount that counts but what you do with that amount." I'm sure you heard that before. I was brought up by my poor grandparents; we could hardly make ends meet. But if you had come to our house, you would have believed we were wealthy. We hardly had any furniture, but we took great care of the little we had.

My grandmother kept us and the house very clean and tidy. Not much food, but the table was always set for dinner. I had one dress suit for church: a shirt, a pair of navy-blue slacks, and worn-out shoes with holes in the bottom. I wore this outfit to church every Sunday. I was clean as a whistle, and my shoes were shined. I can still hear my grandfather saying as we walked the three miles to church, "Boy, take your hands out your pockets and swing your arms."

I had a front-row seat with my grandparents in church every Sunday morning. Boy, you should have seen my slacks. I quickly outgrew the darn things; they stopped about six inches above my ankles. You'd think I was preparing for the next flood. That's what I call living in style on nothing. My grandparents taught us substance over style.

What to Do with Your Wealth

The way that you spend your money says a lot about your personal philosophy, your attitude, and your values. In 2006, *Forbes* ranked the late Helen Robson Kemper Walton, wife of Walmart and Sam's Club founder Sam Walton, twenty-first among the world's richest people. She said, "It's not what you gather, but what you scatter that tells what kind of life you have lived." She's so right—money speaks and reveals what's going on in your head, your decision-making process, and your ability to weigh and perceive. What does the way you handle money reveal about you? Below are five things we can do with our money as it relates to our lifestyles.

Five Things You Can Do with Money

1. **Support yourself and share it**

   The earnings of the godly enhance their lives, but evil people squander their money on sin. (Proverbs 10:16 NLT)

2. **Save and sow (invest) it**

The wise man saves for the future, but the foolish man spends whatever he gets. (Proverbs 21:20 LB)

The servant who got five bags went quickly to invest the money. Those five bags of money earned five more. (Matthew 25:16 ERV)

3. **Spend it**

And there was a woman who had had a discharge of blood for twelve years, and though she had spent all her living on physicians, she could not be healed by anyone. (Luke 8:43 ESV)

4. **Squander it**

Not long after that, the younger son got together all he had, set off for a distant country and there squandered his wealth in wild living. (Luke 15:13 NIV)

5. **Lose it**

Here is a terrible thing that I have seen in this world: people save up their money for a time when they may need it, and then lose it all in some bad deal and end up with nothing left to pass on to their children. (Ecclesiastes 5:13–14 GNB)

We touched on some of these in chapter 8, "Wiping Out the Number-One Enemy of Wealth," so we'll devote this chapter to saving money. If you master that art, you won't squander your wealth.

First Things First

Learn to live on 70 percent of your net income. Hello? You still there? You heard me right. Learn to live off 70 percent of your net income because you're going to do some very special things with the other 30 percent; this is the most practical financial principle to build wealth, yet many people find it the most difficult to follow. I can hear you screaming, "I can't live on 70 percent! I'm too poor. I don't earn enough." No, you're not too poor. Notice I said *learn* this discipline at whatever your income level is. And by the way, most of us don't really have an income problem; we have a spending problem.

Key Phrase

Money speaks and reveals what's going on in your head, your decision making process, and your ability to weigh and perceive.

I've talked to many low-income people who went from being broke to being blessed by practicing this 70/30 principle. They learned to be content and spend conservatively. They used up what they had, or wore it out, or let it last. Paul wrote about this.

> I know what it is to be in need and what it is to have more than enough. I have learned this secret, so that anywhere, at any time, I am content, whether I am full or hungry, whether I have too much or too little. (Philippians 4:12 GNB)

I promise you, once you've walked the 70/30 road, you'll never walk another road again. You'll never be persuaded by others' philosophies again.

Let's talk about what you do with the other 30 percent. I call this the Mercedes- Benz Model.

The Mercedes-Benz Model: A Financial Concept

I love those cars simply for their elegance. The S-class sedan is my car of choice. When I grow up, I'd like to invest in one. The car is just elegant in everything it does. It's strong, powerful, and majestic. It stands out in the crowd because it stands above it. The Mercedes Benz is

Key Phrase

Most of us don't really have an income problem; we have a spending problem.

instantly recognizable for its design. Picture yourself in the driver's seat. Look around. Check out the cabin, a celebration of time-honored handcraftsmanship. It's intricate, intimate, and impeccable. Virtually every surface is richly upholstered, precisely tailored, and swathed in sweeping spans of wood. Everything about this machine is designed to soothe and stimulate the senses. Touch-start the engine. Sniff the double-filtered, ionized cabin air infused by an innovative aroma-therapy system. (By the way, that's all standard.)

Rest your arm on the heated armrests. And if you wish, the seats can offer you a "hot stone" massage at the touch of a button. Fasten your seatbelt, engage the accelerator, and hit the freeway. You'll instantly notice how the S500 reads the road and bypasses the bumps.

As you slip through the wind with ease, take a look in the center of the steering wheel or on the top of the hood and see the Mercedes-Benz logo, a three-point star that represents its dominion of the land, sea, and air. The logo has become synonymous with class and speed. I'll use this logo as a metaphor about a financial life lived in style and class.

Of the 30 percent, set aside 10 percent for tithing and donations. This is capital you plow back into the kingdom of God. Allocate 10 percent to proprietorship, capital you manage. Allocate the last 10 percent to savings or investments. We'll talk about tithing in the next chapter; in this one, we'll discuss the second and third 10 percent. Keep your seatbelt fastened!

Financial Model Based on the Mercedes-Benz Logo

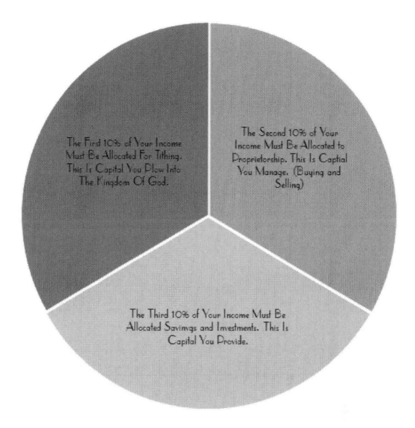

The First 10% of Your Income Must Be Allocated For Tithing. This Is Capital You Plow Into The Kingdom Of God.

The Second 10% of Your Income Must Be Allocated to Proprietorship. This Is Capital You Manage. (Buying and Selling)

The Third 10% of Your Income Must Be Allocated Savings and Investments. This Is Capital You Provide.

The Second 10 Percent: Proprietorship and Capital You Manage

One of the cornerstones of a capitalist economy is that it allows for private owners to profit from the goods and services they provide. This is also known as the free-market system—capital in the hands of the people that requires unregulated supply and demand with little or no government interference. What a contrast to communism! Communists think people are too stupid to entrust them with money. I love capitalism—money in the hands of ordinary people. Isn't that an exciting idea?

Here's what I love about that concept. Everyone can engage in, invent, invest in, trade, and produce whatever he or she wants and sell it at whatever price the market will bear. These decisions are determined by the laws of supply and demand. If there's no demand for a service or product, the producer won't profit, but if the demand is high, so will the profits be.

Key Phrase

So buy something and sell it for a profit.
Write something and sell it for a profit.
Build something and sell it for a profit.
Design something and sell it for a profit.
Grow something and sell it for a profit.

Does that remind you of the widow with the little jar of oil? This is the key to economic power, wealth, and greatness. Find out what the consumer wants and provide it.

So buy something and sell it for a profit. Write something and sell it for a profit. Build something and sell it for a profit. Design something and sell it for a profit. Grow something and sell it for a profit. Cook something and sell it at a profit. Bake something and sell it at a profit. Refurbish something and flip it at a profit. If you're a homeowner, invest in your home by remodeling it, improving your landscape, and enhancing its curb appeal and you can add thousands to its value.

We should all engage in some form of commerce even if it's just part-time. Use 10 percent of your income to create a product or service and take it to the marketplace. Service to many leads to greatness; that's what Solomon had in mind when he said,

> Help others, and you will gain more for yourself. (Proverbs 11:25 ERV)

Money in the hands of geniuses like you has built this incredible world economy. We have the schools, the tools, the markets, and the seasons to make us wealthy. The riches are there for the taking; the only thing we need is the will.

I hear about people turning pennies into fortunes in this free market, so why not you? Keep searching for opportunities until you find

Key Phrase

I hear about people turning pennies into fortunes in this free market, so why not you?

one that lights your fire. When you do, take full advantage of it.

The Third 10 Percent: The Capital You Provide

This is money you save. You're probably in the living room of your house with a mortgage. You probably own a business financed by a bank. You probably work for a company. You probably have the use of a computer, iPod, iPad, or an iPhone. Guess where the money came from? Answer: capital that people like you and me save in banks, which lend it out. We call this capital because some projects need more money than one person can provide. I prefer to call it an investment instead of a savings account because you get interest on the money you have saved. So when we speak of capital you provide, I'm talking about the 10 percent you save in a savings or investment account.

The more money you save, the more opportunities you create for other people and vice versa. It's society's way of assisting others. Not only are you helping others when you save, you're also securing your own financial future.

Saving: A Spiritual Standard

I can hear you screaming, "I'm not earning enough to save!" According to Scripture, saving for the future is a spiritual principle, a choice, a discipline. If you're not saving, could it be because you're not managing your finances well? Do you have that spending problem rather than a savings problem?

> The wise man saves for the future, but the foolish man spends whatever he gets. (Proverbs 21:20 LB)

You can save at any level of income if you think of it terms of only 10¢ of every $1 you make. This won't be easy. I know things are tight

all over, you haven't had a raise in nearly a decade, and it's difficult to save money (which is why you should consider taking your skills somewhere else). This is why I say it's a discipline.

I lived in the poor camp for a considerable time until I discovered that financial peace of mind isn't based on how much I made but on how much I spent. You need to start saving regardless of the difficulty. If you don't, you'll have to work all your life. What you set aside from each paycheck will earn interest. Saving makes your money work for you when you're no longer able to work.

The Four A's of Savings

Keep these four A's of saving in mind.

Amount

This is probably the most important of all the A's. The more money you save, the more interest you'll earn. If you haven't done so yet, set up an automatic debit to move money directly into your saving account on payday. If you don't, it's unlikely you'll ever save any money. One of the good things with direct debit is that you make the decision to do only once; otherwise, you'll have to make the decision to save every time you get paid.

Accounts

Not only is the amount you save important, the type of your savings is also critically important. Establish a good relationship with your banker and learn about the best accounts for your money. Ask to move your money into high-interest accounts. And take full advantage of all your employer's contributions to 401(k), HSA, IRA, and ROTH accounts.

Key Phrase

If you haven't done so yet, set up an automatic debit to move money directly into your saving account on payday. If you don't, it's unlikely you'll ever save any money.

Asset Allocation

Investing in stocks is one of the greatest wealth creators of the American economic system, but make sure you're well informed before you invest in stocks. If you decide to go this path, depending on your age, go for the long-term gain instead of get-rich-quick investments; they aren't for the faint of heart.

Age

It takes time to build wealth. I can tell you how you can get to your wealthy place, but I can't speed up the process, and neither can you. Don't try to get rich too quickly. Many people are willing to sign up for something that promises untold wealth overnight with very little effort. These get-rich-quick rich schemes work but only for the people who run them.

> Wealth gained hastily will dwindle, but whoever gathers little by little will increase it. (Proverbs 13:11 GNB)

> Plan carefully and you will have plenty; if you act too quickly, you will never have enough. (Proverbs 21:5 GNB)

The sooner you start saving, the better off you'll be in the future. Let's say you start saving when you're in your twenties; by the time you're in your fifties, you'll have enough money to do what you want instead of having to make do with what you have.

What if I'm a Late Starter?

Even if you're a late starter, don't sweat it! It's okay to fall behind on your savings schedule as long as you plan to get back on track. You might have to wait until you're in your fifties before college bills and mortgages are paid off. But you'll be surprised how quickly you can get back on track and still build enough wealth to build a financial wall around you and your family.

Key Phrase

Wealth gained hastily will dwindle, but whoever gathers little by little will increase it.

—Proverbs 13:11 GNB

Lessons from the Ant

Yes, the ant. Almost everyone I know has had some trouble with ants at some point in their lives. Someone I know has to deal with these critters at least once a month just to keep them from taking over his home. Have you ever wondered why God put these little creatures in our lives? They're mentioned twice in the Bible.

> You lazy people, you should watch what the ants do and learn from them. Ants have no ruler, no boss, and no leader. But in the summer, ants gather all of their food and save it. So when winter comes, there is plenty to eat. You lazy people, how long are you going to lie there? When will you get up? (Proverbs 6:6–9 ERV)

> Four things on earth are small, but they are exceedingly wise: the ants are a people not strong, yet they provide their food in the summer. (Proverbs 30:24–25 ERV)

God put them in our lives so we could learn from them. I love acronyms, so let's call this one ANTS.

A: Ants Anticipate Emergencies

Ants are smart; they know life won't always be the same. According to the text, they anticipate summer during the winter and winter during the summer; they think long-term; they think boom during a bust and bust during a boom and plan accordingly.Be smart like the ants. Think about tomorrow not just in terms of potential problems but also in terms of potential prosperity. Life and business are like the changing seasons, and seasons are predictable: spring follows winter, and day follow night, so we can plan for that rather than be discouraged when they change. If you understand, anticipate, and cooperate with what God is doing in your life and with your faith, you'll be operating from a position of great strength.

One of the ways to anticipate change is to learn how to play the "What if?" game.

- What if I lost my job?
- What if there's another recession?
- What if I become ill and can't work?
- What if my stocks suddenly take a turn for the worse?
- What if I were no longer needed?
- What if property prices decline?

I'm not encouraging you to engage in negative thinking here but to plan ahead and not be self-indulgent so you're prepared for whatever season comes next just as the ants do.

N: Ants Never Quit

Ants are probably the most diligent creatures I've ever come across. When they meet an obstacle, they negotiate a way over, around, or through it. If that doesn't work, they'll summon help. And if that doesn't work, they'll tunnel their way under whatever's in their way. They stick to their important plan: collecting food during the summer.

Be just as consistent and preserving in your march to your financial goals. Even if you've made some poor financial decisions in the past, don't allow that to freeze you. Learn from the ants; figure out ways to

Key Phrase

Take charge of your today, your future, your health and wealth, your happiness and retirement. Don't wait for someone to motivate you; you're perfectly capable of motivating yourself to turn your pennies into big bucks.

---

negotiate your way around, over, through, or underneath your obstacles by yourself or with help. Whatever you do, don't quit. Remind yourself to think summer when it's winter and boom during a bust.

What do ants do during the harsh winter? They dig a hole and dive in, and they say to themselves, *This won't last forever.* And come the first hot day, they crawl out. That's the attitude you must have. Even if you are in a harsh financial situation, be of good courage; it won't last forever. Think summer; you'll be richly rewarded if you do.

T: Ants Take Charge of Their Lives

> Ants have no ruler, no boss, and no leader. But in the summer, ants gather all of their food and save it. (Proverbs 6:7–8 ERV)

Ants are self-motivated creatures that work without oversight or government, no CEOs or managers. They work independently at group goals. You can take full responsibility for your life. Be the CEO of your life. Take charge of your today, your future, your health and wealth, your happiness and retirement. Don't wait for someone to motivate you; you're perfectly capable of motivating yourself to turn your pennies into big bucks.

S: Ants Save for the Future

> But in the summer, ants gather all of their food and save it. So when winter comes, there is plenty to eat. (Proverbs 6:8 ERV)

They gather food but don't eat it all; they save some. Too many folks aren't saving for their futures. Don't allow yourself to become one of them.

Final Word

Congratulations are in order if you're diligently saving for the future; come the next winter, you'll have plenty to eat.

My Personal Wealthy Place Notes

My Wealthy Place

Psalm 66:12

Chapter 17

Honoring God with Your Wealth— The Premise of Tithing

Honor the LORD with your wealth and with the firstfruits
of all your produce; then your barns will be filled with
plenty, and your vats will be bursting with wine.
—Proverbs 3:9–10 ESV

In this chapter, I address the first 10 percent you should invest in the kingdom of God, your tithe. This subject warrants a chapter by itself. As we discuss honoring God with our wealth, I want you to note how specific God was about tithing; He left nothing to chance. He told us about the proportion, purpose, place, practice, premise, and promise of tithing. Due to the controversial nature of the subject, I'll limit my personal views on the matter and allow the Bible to do all the speaking. I'll simply offer propositions and supporting passages from God's Word.

The Biblical Perspective on Tithing and Offering

According to the Bible, *tithe* simply means the tenth part. In essence, this means investing a tenth of your net income in God, who gave it to you in the first place. Your offering is anything you freely give in addition to your tithe. The word *offering* was first mentioned

in Genesis 4, when Cain and
Abel brought their freewill
offerings to the Lord.

> And in process of
> time it came to pass,
> that Cain brought
> of the fruit of the
> ground an offering unto the LORD. And Abel, he
> also brought of the firstlings of his flock and of the fat
> thereof. And the LORD had respect unto Abel and to
> his offering. (Genesis 4:4 KJV)

The Biblical Precedent for Tithing

The word *tithe* was first mentioned in Genesis 4, when Abram paid 10 percent of the spoils of war to Melchizedek, the king of Salem. Chedorlaomer, the king of Elam, and his allied forces ransacked Sodom and took all its possessions and people, including Lot, Abram's nephew, into captivity.

In time, one captive escaped and told Abram of the situation. Abram assembled 318 of his servants, defeated king Chedorlaomer, and recovered the captives (including Lot), the goods, and the treasure. Upon his return, Chedorlaomer and Melchizedek thanked Abram for a job well done.

> He (Melchizedek) was priest of God Most High, and
> he blessed Abram, saying, "Blessed be Abram by God
> Most High, Creator of heaven and earth. And praise
> be to God Most High, who delivered your enemies
> into your hand." Then Abram gave him a tenth of
> everything. (Genesis 14:19–20 NIV)

Melchizedek was no ordinary man; he was a type of Christ. It was the custom among ancient nations to pay tithes of the spoils of war to the object of their worship. Abram was honoring that age-old tradition

when he gave a tithe to
Melchizedek. Abram wasn't
a natural-born warrior, but
through God's help, he
became a triumphant warrior,

Key Phrase

*Your offering is anything you freely give in
addition to your tithe.*

and he paid tithes to show his gratitude to God for his victory. What
was he teaching us? That our tithing is intrinsically connected with
our deliverance.

The Second Voluntary Act of Tithing

The second person who tithed was Jacob. On the run from his
brother after Jacob stole his birthright, Jacob had an encounter with
God. He dreamed about a ladder that reached to heaven. He saw
angels of God ascending and descending it. He erected an altar and
made a vow.

> If God will be with me and will watch over me on this
> journey I am taking and will give me food to eat and clothes
> to wear so that I return safely to my father's household,
> then the LORD will be my God and this stone that I have
> set up as a pillar will be God's house, and of all that you
> give me I will give you a tenth. (Genesis 28:20–22 NIV)

Jacob made a fivefold commitment to God.

First: Partnership

If God will be with me,

Second: Protection

and will keep me in this way that I go,

Third: Prosperity

and will give me bread to eat, and raiment to put on,

Fourth: Peace

so that I come again to my father's house in peace,

Fifth: Proprietor

then Jehovah shall be my God.

In essence, Jacob said, "God, if you give me these five things I resolved, I will to return to your house and give you back a tenth of all you have blessed me with."

Abram and Jacob started the voluntary act of tithing before it was introduced to humanity in general and ratified by the Jesus Christ after the Law. And despite the controversies concerning tithing, it's well documented in Scripture that tithing was widely practiced 430 years before the lawgiver Moses.

Other Examples of Tithing

Levi practiced tithing through Abraham.

> One might even say that Levi himself, who receives tithes, paid tithes through Abraham. (Hebrews 7:9 ESV)

Hezekiah and Israel practiced tithing.

> People all around the country heard about this command. So the Israelites gave the first part of their harvest of grain, grapes, oil, honey, and all the things they grew in their fields. They brought one-tenth of all these many things. The men of Israel and Judah living in the towns of Judah also brought one-tenth of their

cattle and sheep. They also brought one-tenth of the things that were put in a special place that was only for the LORD their God. They brought all these things and put them in piles. (2 Chronicles 31:5–5 ERV)

Nehemiah practiced tithing.

Then all Judah brought the tithe of the grain, wine, and oil into the storehouses. (Nehemiah 13:12 ESV)

Even the hypocrites practiced tithing during Jesus' day.

Woe to you, scribes and Pharisees, hypocrites! For you tithe mint and dill and cumin, and have neglected the weightier matters of the law: justice and mercy and faithfulness. These you ought to have done, without neglecting the others. (Matthew 23:23 ESV)

From these few examples, we can conclude tithing was widely practiced in the Old and New Testament days. There were no substitute programs for tithing among New Testament believers.

The Biblical Propositions of Tithing

Let's examine at least fifteen biblical propositions for honoring God with our wealth. Regardless of the disputes on the matter, no one has disputed the blessing of tithing.

Proposition One

We should honor God with our wealth by giving back to Him the first 10 percent of our incomes because God commanded it.

A tithe of everything from the land, whether grain from the soil or fruit from the trees, belongs to the LORD; it is holy to the LORD. (Leviticus 27:30 NIV)

> Bring the full tithe into the storehouse, that there may
> be food in my house. And thereby put me to the test,
> says the LORD of hosts, if I will not open the windows
> of heaven for you and pour down for you a blessing
> until there is no more need. (Malachi 3:10 ESV)

Tithes belong to the Lord. Period. He said 10 percent; we can use the rest. Think about it this way—God said 10 percent. He could have said 90 percent, but He didn't; we can keep 90 percent. We shouldn't tithe and give because a preacher tells us to or because we feel pressured or forced. We should tithe for the simple reason that God *commanded* it.

Proposition Two

We should honor God with our titles because Jesus Christ commended tithing.

> Woe unto you, scribes and Pharisees, hypocrites! For
> ye pay tithe of mint and anise and cummin, and have
> omitted the weightier matters of the law, judgment,
> mercy, and faith: these ought ye to have done, and not
> to leave the other undone. (Matthew 23:23 NIV)

> "Teacher, we know that you are an honest man. You are
> not afraid of what others think about you. All people
> are the same to you. And you teach the truth about
> God's way. Tell us, is it right to pay taxes to Caesar?
> Should we pay them or not?" But Jesus knew that these
> men were really trying to trick him. He said, "Why are
> you trying to catch me saying something wrong? Bring
> me a silver coin. Let me see it." They gave Jesus a coin
> and he asked, "Whose picture is on the coin? And
> whose name is written on it?" They answered, "It is
> Caesar's picture and Caesar's name." Then Jesus said to
> them, "Give to Caesar what belongs to Caesar, and give

to God what belongs to God." The men were amazed
at what Jesus said. (Mark 12:14–17 ERV)

Two things most people despise paying are taxes and tithes;
hence, the reason for the question posed to Jesus by His critics. "Tell
us, is it right to pay taxes to Caesar?" Tribute (taxes) was demanded by
Caesar to fund his government and the army to defend the Israelites
from their enemies. God also demands His subjects give to Him the
things that are His. These include all spiritual matters such as worship
and obedience and of course funding for the kingdom of God. The
mature person understands the purpose and benefit of taxes and
tithing. Take taxes for example; they're levied in almost every country
of the world by governmental bodies to pay for many services

- roads and bridges
- foreign embassies
- immigration control
- commercial deals with other countries
- security and protection—police, firefighters and so on
- government employees, not to mention those nice people at
  the taxes offices
- public schools
- social and medical benefits
- the military

We'll all agree we pay too much taxes, and depending on our political
views, we'll argue that taxation is unfair and the government should
spend our money better, but do taxes help us? The principle of taxes is
biblical. State and church provide valuable services to the community
and equally deserve to be funded.

Can you imagine what would become of our country and churches if everyone evaded taxation and tithing? We shouldn't complain about

Key Phrase

God doesn't want our money! It's never about the money but what it represents—us.

lack of services if we're against tithing and taxation. I understand the benefit of taxes and tithing and have come to terms with them.

Proposition Three

We should honor God with our wealth because tithing confirms that God has first place in our lives. God doesn't want our money! It's never about the money but what it represents—us. He's interested in us and His place in our lives. That's why He didn't ask for leftovers but the first 10 percent.

> The purpose of tithing is to teach you to always put
> God first place in your life. (Deuteronomy 14:23 LB)

It's important to understand this about tithing: if you're not a tither, it means God is not first in your life. Regardless of the controversies surrounding tithing, it's a biblical principle, and it's important to know why you should tithe. How do you know when you have passed from childhood into adulthood? Answer: The moment you become a consistent tither and giver.

Tithing is never meant to be merely about raising dollars; it's to raise spiritual disciples. God uses tithing as a yardstick by which He measures the depth of our spiritual maturity. This is why we cannot separate tithing from all the other spiritual disciplines such as prayers and growing in grace and knowledge. God expects us to excel in the area of giving as we do in all other aspects of our Christian life.

> But since you excel in everything—in faith, in speech,
> in knowledge, in complete earnestness and in the love
> we have kindled in you—see that you also excel in this
> grace of giving. (2 Corinthians 8:7 NIV)

Proposition Four

We should honor God with our tithes because doing so reminds us that everything we possess comes from Him.

I used to get an attitude with my money; I didn't understand the principle of stewardship and giving to God what was truly His in the first place. Throughout the Bible, God went through extra pains to constantly remind His children of this basic truth.

> The earth is the LORD's and the fullness thereof, the
> world and those who dwell therein, for he has founded
> it upon the seas and established it upon the rivers.
> (Psalm 24:1–2 ESV)

> Everything comes from the Lord. All things were made
> because of him and will return to him. Praise the Lord
> forever! Amen. (Romans 11:36 CEV)

> Greatness, power, glory, victory, and honor belong to
> you, because everything in heaven and on earth belongs
> to you! The kingdom belongs to you, LORD! You are the
> head, the Ruler over everything. Riches and honor come
> from you. You rule everything. You have the power and
> strength in your hand! And in your hand is the power
> to make anyone great and powerful! Now, our God, we
> thank you, and we praise your glorious name! All these
> things didn't come from me and my people. All these
> things come from you. We are only giving back to you
> things that came from you. (1 Chronicles 29:11–14 ERV)

> Yet my people and I cannot really give you anything, because everything is a gift from you, and we have only given back what is yours already. (1 Chronicles 29:14 GNB)

Why should we begrudge God 10 percent when everything actually belongs to Him? If it weren't for Him, there would be no life, land, seed, strength, and income. Zilch! How kind and generous He is with us, and we are stewards of His bounty. Everything comes from God; if we understand that, our giving will take on a new meaning.

Proposition Five

We should honor God with our tithes because that communicates our gratitude to Him for his blessings.

> What shall I render unto the LORD for all his benefits toward me? (Psalm 116:12 KJV)

You should never tithe with the idea of getting anything back but because God has given to you so bountifully.

> Every man shall give as he is able, according to the blessing of the LORD thy God which he hath given thee. (Deuteronomy 16:17 KJV)

Giving is a statement of gratitude: "I thank you, Lord, for taking care of me in the past, and just as you took care of me in the past, you will bless me so I can live debt free and on 90 percent of my income."

Proposition Six

We should honor God with our tithes because if we don't, we're stealing from Him. We're robbing the Lord!

> Will a man rob God? Yet ye have robbed me. But ye say,
> wherein have we robbed thee? In tithes and offerings.
> (Malachi 3:8 KJV)

Everyone condemns stealing, but by not tithing, you're stealing. Tithes are sanctified, holy money set apart for the Lord (see Leviticus 27:30). How would you feel if someone were to steal from you? Not good. Would you give anything to that person? Don't expect God to bless you if you're withholding your tithes and offerings from Him.

Think about how foolish it is to rob God. He knows everything about you. He's aware of what you have; He gave it to you in the first place. So if you rob from God, you're robbing yourself of His blessings. By trying to cheat God, you're cheating yourself.

Proposition Seven

We should honor the Lord with our tithes because that gives Him a chance to bless us in return.

When we open your heart and pocketbook to God, He will open the windows of heaven to us.

> Bring ye all the tithes into the storehouse, that there may
> be meat in mine house, and prove me now herewith, saith
> the LORD of hosts, if I will not open you the windows of
> heaven, and pour you out a blessing, that there shall not
> be room enough to receive it. (Malachi 3:10 KJV)

God said, "I dare you to put me to the test by bringing me the full tithe and see if I will not bless you in return." What I love about this verse is that we get to choose how much God blesses us in return. When God asks us to tithe, it's not because He wants to take from us but because He wants to give more to us.

294

One gives freely, yet grows all the richer; another withholds what he should give, and only suffers want. (Proverbs 11:24 ESV)

Key Phrase

If you rob from God, you're robbing yourself of His blessings. By trying to cheat God, you're cheating yourself.

Be generous, and you will be prosperous. Help others, and you will be helped. (Proverbs 11:25 GNB)

Honor the LORD by giving him your money and the first part of all your crops. Then you will have more grain and grapes than you will ever need. (Proverbs 3:9–10 CEV)

The success of your financial future is directly tied to our being obedient to God's law of tithing and giving. Obedience brings God's blessings, and disobedience brings God's curses.

Proposition Eight

We should honor God with our tithes as a protective covering over every area of our lives—career, work, finances—you name it, it's covered.

I will rebuke the devourer for you, so that it will not destroy the fruits of your soil, and your vine in the field shall not fail to bear, says the LORD of hosts. (Malachi 3:11 ESV)

If you want God's protection, you must be willing to pay His price. Don't be like most people who want God's perks but aren't willing to pay God's price.

295

Proposition Nine

We should honor God with our tithes because that makes us more like Christ.

The Christian life is all about giving.

Key Phrase

When you give, you're saying, "God, I want to be just like you—a giver!" You cannot be a genuine follower of Jesus Christ and not be a giver.

> For God so loved the world that he gave his one and only Son, that whoever believes in him shall not perish but have eternal life. (John 3:16 NIV)

God is a giver. Giving is grounded in our heavenly Father's nature. The plan of redemption is built on giving and receiving. You can sum up the plan of redemption in one word: *give!* God wants us to become as generous as He is, so He asks us give. So when you give, you're saying, "God, I want to be just like you—a giver!" You cannot be a genuine follower of Jesus Christ and not be a giver.

Proposition Ten

Consistently honoring the Lord with our tithes teaches us to control our desires for material things.

We're naturally selfish and greedy, so God requires we put Him first by paying to Him the first part of our income. In this sense, our tithing becomes an antidote to selfishness, greed, and materialism.

> Honor the Lord by giving him the first part of all your income, and He will fill your barns with wheat and barley and overflow your wine vats with the finest wines. (Proverbs 3:9–10 LB)

Whenever you deny yourself material things and honor God with the proceeds, you're saying, "God, you're more important to me than material things. I love you, not them."

Give this command to those who are rich with the things of this world. Tell them not to be proud. Tell them to

Key Phrase

We're naturally selfish and greedy, so God requires we put Him first by paying to Him the first part of our income. In this sense, our tithing becomes an antidote to selfishness, greed, and materialism.

hope in God, not their money. Money cannot be trusted, but God takes care of us richly. He gives us everything to enjoy. Tell those who are rich to do good-to be rich in good works. And tell them they should be happy to give and ready to share. By doing this, they will be saving up a treasure for themselves. And that treasure will be a strong foundation on which their future life will be built. They will be able to have the life that is true life. (1 Timothy 6:17–19 ERV)

Proposition Eleven

When we honor God with our tithes, we celebrate and worship Him. Tithing is an act of worship. It's fine to give to charitable causes, friends, and family, but those aren't acts of worship. Have you ever wondered why the Scripture require that tithing be collected during the worship service?

On the first day of every week, set aside some of what you have earned and give it as an offering. The amount depends on how much the Lord has helped you earn. (2 Corinthians 8:7b–8 LB)

Worship and giving go together. Thousands of years ago during the Feast of Weeks, God commanded Israel to celebrate Him during their worship.

> Celebrate the Festival of Weeks to the LORD your God by giving a freewill offering in proportion to the blessings the LORD your God has given you. (Deuteronomy 16:10 NIV)

The time of giving should not be the dullest but the most exciting part of the worship service.

Proposition Twelve

We should honor God with our tithes because that draws us closer to God.

Jesus augmented this point.

> For where your treasure is, there your heart will be also. (Matthew 6:21 NIV)

Proposition Thirteen

We should honor the Lord with our wealth by tithing because we didn't carry anything into this world and won't carry anything out.

I don't know if the following story is true, but the story is that on his deathbed, Alexander the Great summoned his generals and told them his three wishes.

> The best doctors should carry my coffin. The wealth that I have accumulated should be scattered along my procession to the cemetery. My hands should be let loose so they hang outside my coffin for all to see.

One general asked Alexander to explain his unusual requests.

I want the best doctors to carry my coffin to demonstrate that in the face of death, even the best doctors in the world have no power to heal. I want the road

Key Phrase

When you open your heart, your pocketbook, and bank account to the Lord, He will open the windows of heaven to you.

---

to be covered with my treasures so that everybody sees that material wealth acquired on earth will stay on earth. I want my hands to swing in the wind so that people understand that we come to this world empty handed and we leave this world empty handed.

I bet that the great man was familiar with this quote from the Bible.

We brought nothing into the world, and we cannot take anything out of the world. (1 Timothy 6:7 ESV)

Allow me to give you my interpretation of the above verse: you cannot take your wealth with you, but you can send it ahead by investing it in getting people into heaven.

Proposition Fourteen

When we honor the Lord with our tithes, we're constructing our faith in God.

By sacrificing the things we need for ourselves, we learn to rely on the Lord. Tithing is a faith-building exercise.

"Bring the whole tithe into the storehouse, that there may be food in my house. Test me in this," says the LORD Almighty, "and see if I will not throw open the floodgates of heaven and pour out so much blessing that there will not be room enough to store it." (Malachi 3:10 NIV)

God said we were to bring the whole tithe, not a portion of it, and he said, "I dare you to tithe and see if I'm real." God said the windows of heaven would be opened to us and we would experience more supernatural blessings that we could store.

Final Word

Tithing is a faith-building exercise; regular tithing will sustain us during difficult economic times. It's an insurance policy that guarantees continued wealth and prosperity. I've experienced the blessings of tithing. If you have doubted the blessings of tithing, I encourage you to accept the Lord's challenge. When you open your heart, your pocketbook, and bank account to the Lord, He will open the windows of heaven to you.

My Personal Wealthy Place Notes

_____

_____

_____

_____

_____

_____

_____

_____

_____

_____

_____

_____

_____

_____

_____

_____

_____

_____

_____

_____

_____

_____

_____

_____

_____

_____

_____

_____

My Wealthy Place

Psalm 66:12

Chapter 18

Honoring God with Your Wealth—
The Practice of Tithing

But thou shalt remember the LORD thy God: for it is he that
giveth thee power to get wealth that he may establish his covenant
which he sware unto thy fathers, as it is this day.
—Deuteronomy 8:18 KJV

S cripture teaches that tithing and offerings were disbursed by
the church to establish God's covenant on earth. The purpose
of wealth is to promote the gospel; establish churches, schools, and
health centers; start new businesses; create jobs; and promote the well-
being of humanity. John Davison Rockefeller, an America business
magnate and philanthropist, cofounded the Standard Oil Company.
He wrote,

> God gave me my money. I believe the power to make
> money is a gift from God to be developed and used
> to the best of our ability for the good of mankind.
> Having been endowed with the gift I possess, I believe
> it is my duty to make money and still more money
> and to use the money I make for good of my fellow
> man according to the dictates of my conscience.
> *(quotationbook.com)*

The Promulgation of Tithes

Let's look at some biblical examples of how tithing was collected and distributed. First, tithing was used to support the Levities, who led worship and assisted the priests in the tent of meetings (another name for church). The Levites were compensated for their work.

> I give to the Levites all the tithes in Israel as their inheritance in return for the work they do while serving at the tent of meeting. (Numbers 18:21–24 NIV)

Second, tithes supported the high priests, who received a portion of the Levites' tithes.

> In this way you also will present an offering to the LORD from all the tithes you receive from the Israelites. From these tithes you must give the LORD's portion to Aaron the Priest. (Numbers 18:28 NIV)

A smart arrangement. Old and New Testament ministers were supported by tithes, and the principle of supporting ministries with tithing and giving still exists under the priesthood of Jesus Christ.

The apostle Paul said God had ordained that those who devoted their time to the gospel should be supported by the gospel. You can read all about this in 1 Corinthians 9, but examine a few verses from the chapter.

> Who serves as a soldier at his own expense? Who plants a vineyard without eating any of its fruit? Or who tends a flock without getting some of the milk? (1 Corinthians 9:7 ESV)

Soldiers, farmers, and shepherds obviously deserved support; Paul appealed to the Law of Moses by stating that those who devoted their lives to ministry were to be supported by it.

> Do I say these things on human authority? Does not the Law say the same? For it is written in the Law of Moses, "You shall not muzzle an ox when it treads out the grain." Is it for oxen that God is concerned? Does he not certainly speak for our sake? It was written for our sake, because the plowman should plow in hope and the thresher thresh in hope of sharing in the crop. (1 Corinthians 9:8–11 ESV)

Finally, in regard to the Jewish provision for the maintenance of the priests, Paul makes reference to the Levitical system in the affirmative.

> Don't you know that those who serve in the temple get their food from the temple, and that those who serve at the altar share in what is offered on the altar? (Then he drives home his point.) In the same way, the Lord has commanded that those who preach the gospel should receive their living from the gospel. (1 Corinthians 9:13–14 NIV)

Folks, I'm acutely aware so many ministers have abused this privilege. Paul himself did not take advantage of this right so the gospel wouldn't be blamed. He nonetheless maintained it was common practice that those who devoted their time to the gospel should be supported by it.

Third, tithes were collected every three years for the support of the poor and needy.

> At the end of every three years, bring all the tithes of that year's produce and store it in your towns, so that the Levites (who have no allotment or inheritance of their own). And the foreigners, the fatherless and the widows who live in your towns may come and eat and be satisfied, and so that the LORD your God may bless you in all the work of your hands. (Deuteronomy 14:28–29 NIV)

Fourth, tithes were collected for the maintenance of places of worship. Consider the building of the first worship center in the wilderness. It was state of the art—no expense spared. It was decked out with gold, silver, bronze, and other costly materials. God didn't perform a miracle to raise the money; rather, it was a requirement that His redeemed people provide the resources needed for such elaborate work.

> The LORD said to Moses, "Tell the Israelites to bring me an offering. You are to receive the offering for me from everyone whose heart prompts them to give. These are the offerings you are to receive from them: gold, silver and bronze; blue, purple and scarlet yarn and fine linen; goat hair; ram skins dyed red and another type of durable leather; acacia wood; olive oil for the light; spices for the anointing oil and for the fragrant incense; and onyx stones and other gems to be mounted on the ephod and breast piece. Then have them make a sanctuary for me, and I will dwell among them." (Exodus 25:1–8 NIV)

The Lord told Moses to accept offerings from the people for Him. The people were to bring of the best of their possessions to construct a sanctuary for Jehovah. Gold is the greatest and most precious item of value a person can possess; according to Scripture, gold symbolized the Lord—His personhood, righteousness, and mercy. Silver is a symbol of redemption, and bronze and copper symbolized the death of Christ. God was teaching His children not to bring Him their leftovers and their junk but their first and best.

We read about the people's remarkable response to Moses' appeal in chapter 36.

> So Bezalel, Oholiab and every skilled person to whom the LORD has given skill and ability to know how to carry out all the work of constructing the sanctuary are to do the work just as the LORD has commanded. Then Moses summoned Bezalel and Oholiab and every skilled person to whom the LORD had given ability and who was willing to come and do the work.
>
> They received from Moses all the offerings the Israelites had brought to carry out the work of constructing the sanctuary. And the people continued to bring freewill offerings morning after morning. So all the skilled workers who were doing all the work on the sanctuary left what they were doing and said to Moses, "The people are bringing more than enough for doing the work the LORD commanded to be done." Then Moses gave an order and they sent this word throughout the camp:
>
> "No man or woman is to make anything else as an offering for the sanctuary." And so the people were restrained from bringing more, because what they already had was more than enough to do all the work. (Exodus 36:1–7 NIV)

The people gave so much that they had to be restrained from further giving. I wish I were the senior pastor of that church! The church in the wilderness never had a financial need. We learn that the Lord had compelled the Egyptians to pay His redeemed people with interest for their four hundred years of slavery. The result was the Israelites went forth not as slaves but as wealthy people. God asked them to plow a portion of that into a sanctuary for Him.

The Bible clearly teaches the kingdom of God must be supported financially by the tithes and offerings of His people.

The Bible clearly teaches the kingdom of God must be supported financially by the tithes and offerings of His people.

Redemption Money

God also instructed Moses to collect redemption money from His people in remembrance of His mercy in sparing those whose lives were justly forfeit.

> Everyone who is num-bered in the census, from twenty years old and upward, shall give the LORD's offering. The rich shall not give more, and the poor shall not give less, than the half shekel, when you give the LORD's offering to make atonement for your lives. You shall take the atonement money from the people of Israel and shall give it for the service of the tent of meeting that it may bring the people of Israel to remembrance before the LORD, so as to make atonement for your lives. (Exodus 30:14–16 ESV)

Again, we see God asking for money not because He needed it but because of what it represented—us. The noticeable difference with this offering was both the rich and poor were required to pay the same amount. The implication here is that every redeemed soul is of equal value and precious in His sight. Because He designs equally the salvation of all, it was equally right the same sum should be paid by everyone.

The next point to notice here was that God stipulated the money be invested in the service of the tabernacle to reach other souls for the kingdom. What a great idea that was! Every time they gave, it reminded them of their own redemption. At the same time, they were getting other people into the kingdom. I cannot think of a better way to spend my money.

David's Offering for Solomon's Temple

Most times when we preach or talk about King David, we usually think about him being left out of the anointed line when Samuel came to anoint him or his affair with Bathsheba. We very seldom associate the psalmist with money. But do you know David raised the biggest offering of all times? When he needed to build the temple, he asked the people to give for its construction. We read in 1 Chronicles 29 that leaders, families, offices, and tribes gave for the temple an amount that today would be $40 million. That breaks all the records.

> They gave toward the work on the temple of God five thousand talents and ten thousand darics of gold, ten thousand talents of silver, eighteen thousand talents of bronze and a hundred thousand talents of iron. Anyone who had precious stones gave them to the treasury of the temple of the LORD in the custody of Jehiel the Gershonite. The people rejoiced at the willing response of their leaders, for they had given

freely and wholeheartedly to the LORD. David the king also rejoiced greatly. (1 Chronicles 29:7–9 NIV)

Joash's Offering

King Joash received an offering from the people to repair the Lord's house.

> And Joash said to the priests, All the silver from things dedicated to God, which is brought into the house of Jehovah, the silver from each man the silver of his valuation, all the silver that comes into any man's heart to bring to the house of Jehovah. (2 King 12:4 MKJV)

The king had a unique fundraising style.

> Jehoiada the priest took a chest and bored a hole in its lid. And he set it beside the altar, on the right side as one comes into the house of Jehovah. And the priests who kept the door put in it all the silver brought into the house of Jehovah. And it happened when they saw that much silver was in the chest, the king's scribe and the high priest came up.

> And they bound and counted the silver that was found in the house of Jehovah. And they gave the silver which was counted into the hands of those who did the work, those overseeing the house of Jehovah. And they laid it out to the carpenters and builders who worked on the house of Jehovah, and to masons and cutters of stone, and to buy timber and cut stone to repair the breaks of the house of Jehovah, and for all that went forth for the house, to repair it. (2 Kings 12: 9–12 MJKV)

Ezra's Offering

Ezra received an offering from the Jews returning from captivity in Babylon for the reconstruction of Solomon's temple.

And some of the chief of the fathers, when they came to the house of Jehovah at Jerusalem, offered freely for the house of God to set it up in its place. They gave according to their ability to the treasure of the work, sixty one thousand drachmas of gold, and five thousand minas of silver, and one hundred priest's garments. (Ezra 2:68–69 MJKV)

The New Testament Church

In New Testament times, tithes and offerings were collected for ministry.

Now, concerning what you wrote about the money to be raised to help God's people in Judea. You must do what I told the churches in Galatia to do. Every Sunday each of you must put aside some money, in proportion to what you have earned, and save it up, so that there will be no need to collect money when I come. (1 Corinthians 16:1–2 GNB)

Redeemed people have an obligation to plow a portion of their income back into the kingdom of God so they can reach more people for Christ. Many pastors and leaders are embarrassed to ask people to give toward the kingdom. I certainly lived in that camp for a long time, but I conquered that hang-up because there's no greater cause than raising money for the kingdom of God. We should never be embarrassed to raise money for that.

The Partnership

For we are laborers together with God: ye are God's husbandry, ye are God's building. (1 Corinthians 3:9 KJV)

We are God's coworkers. He doesn't want our money, but He wants His children to be partners with Him in building the kingdom of God. Hence, he asks us to give. What a tremendous privilege it is to be a co-investor in the kingdom business! There would be no sanctuary for our Lord to dwell unless the people of God were willing to contribute their tithes and offerings.

Final Word

Whenever you feel tempted not to give, think about what your tithes and offerings accomplish for the kingdom of God—the lives that are being changed, the marriages that are being saved, and the people who are being freed from all sorts of addictions. Healings and miracles take place daily.

I believe when we get to heaven, someone will walk over to us and say, "I'm here because of your financial investment." Giving is an investment for eternity. Giving is leaving a lasting legacy. That's what it's all about.

My Personal Wealthy Place Notes

My Wealthy Place

Psalm 66:12

Chapter 19

Honoring God with Your Wealth— The Principle of Blessing

Remember this: The one who plants few seeds will have a small harvest. But the one who plants a lot will have a big harvest. Each one of you should give what you have decided in your heart to give. You should not give if it makes you unhappy or if you feel forced to give. God loves those who are happy to give.
—2 Corinthians 9:6–7 ESV

In this chapter, I will deal with the right biblical attitude toward tithing and giving. I often hear people say, "God is by far more interested in your attitude toward tithing and giving rather than the amount." I don't believe that's true. God is interested in both. The amount matters; otherwise, God wouldn't have asked for 10 percent. That's specific.

If you want God's prosperity so you can enter your wealthy place, you must follow the biblical procedures for tithing. I present here seven attitudes God desires in regard to our tithing and giving, but first, let's talk about the place and the plan of tithing.

The Place of Tithing

"When and where should I pay my tithe?" is another question I'm often asked. According to the Bible, we should pay our tithe on the day we worship.

> On the first day of every week, set aside some of what
> you have earned and give it as an offering. This amount
> depends on how much the Lord has helped you earn.
> (1 Corinthians 16:2 LB)

To be practical, your tithes become due when you receive your paycheck, whether that's weekly, biweekly, or monthly. I prefer to pay my tithes on Sunday during the worship celebration as an act of worship. I love sowing money in the soil of the anointing. If that isn't possible for you, you can pay it at any time. Today, you can be sitting on a cruise ship and still pay your tithes. I don't think it matters much to God as long as you pay it as an act of worship.

"Where should I pay my tithes?" Answer: Malachi 3:10 (ESV) clearly states, "Bring your whole tithes to my storehouse," meaning the temple, the place where you're spiritually fed and worship, not your former church even if you still have ties with it. Let's handle some more questions.

Q. Should I tithe even if the church doesn't need my money?
A. Yes. No question. We should tithe for the simple reason that God commands us to.

Q. If I use my tithes to pay for special religious endeavors, television and radio ministries, missionary and other charitable activities, am I still tithing?
A. No. Use other monies for those purposes.

> Every tithe of the land, whether of the seed of the land
> or of the fruit of the trees, is the LORD's; it is holy to
> the LORD (Leviticus 27:30 ESV)

Q. What if I don't like the way the church disburses my tithes?

A. Good question. Your church is to manage the Lord's tithes in a responsible way for the ministry and the

Key Phrase

Tithe on whatever you want God to bless. If you want Him to bless you on your net, tithe on your net, and if you want Him to bless you on your gross, tithe on your gross.

kingdom of God. Your responsibility is over when you pay your tithes. The church is accountable to God, not you, for how it disburses the Lord's money.

Q. What If I use my tithes for something else but pay it back later?
A. Don't do that because it's never easy to repay. But if you have to borrow your tithes, that's not a sin. However, you are required to repay the tithes with interest just as if you had borrowed it from a bank. Here's the fine print.

> One tenth of all the produce of the land, whether grain or fruit, belongs to the LORD. If you wish to buy any of it back, you must pay the standard price plus an additional 20 percent. (Leviticus 27:30–31 GNB)

It's always better not to use your tithes for any other purpose. I got caught up in this practice a long time ago and ended up owing God so much that no matter what I did, I could never get caught up. So I filed for bankruptcy with heaven, and God placed me on a strict payment plan. I'm doing my best to stick with it, and my blessings are multiplying.

Perhaps you're in the same boat. You owe God so much that you'll never get caught up. Let me encourage you to file for bankruptcy or *'tithekruptcy'* if you will and start afresh today. To be a good tither, you simply have to plan it. We'll talk about this some more.

Q. Should I give my tithes based on my net or gross income?

A. Tithe on whatever you want God to bless. If you want Him to bless you on your net, tithe on your net, and if you want Him to bless you on your gross, tithe on your gross. The choice is yours. To get more, you must give more; tithing and offering is never about God taking from you; it's His way of getting things to you. As you excel in giving, learn not to tithe on how much you make but rather on how much you'd like to make. If you'd like to make $300 per week, tithe $30; I call this faith tithing.

Giving with the Right Attitude

> And they gave in a way that we did not expect: They gave themselves to the Lord and to us before they gave their money. This is what God wants. (2 Corinthians 8:5 ESV)

The key to giving with the right attitude is to first give yourself to the Lord. "They gave themselves to the Lord before they gave their money." God wants you before your money. When you do this with your life, all other forms of giving will become easy. After you give your person to Christ, it's much easier to give Him your purse.

First Attitude: Give Willingly

You should never give because you feel pressured to. The biblical requirement is to give from a willing heart. When God instructed Moses to collect an offering for the tabernacle, the privilege of giving was open to everyone, and He stressed that they should give from willing hearts.

And they received of Moses all the offering which the children of Israel had brought for the work of the service of the sanctuary, wherewith to make it. And they brought yet unto him freewill-offerings every morning. (Exodus 36:3 ASV)

When King David was raising the money for the temple, he also requested the people give with a willing heart.

Then the people rejoiced, for that they offered willingly, because with perfect heart they offered willingly to the LORD: and David the king also rejoiced with great joy. (1 Chronicles 29:9 KJV)

The apostle Paul taught that God would accept offerings only if they were made from a willing heart.

So I thought it necessary to urge the brothers to go on ahead to you and arrange in advance for the gift you have promised, so that it may be ready as a willing gift, not as an exaction. (2 Corinthians 9:5 ESV)

Each one must give as he has decided in his heart, not reluctantly or under compulsion, for God loves a cheerful giver. (2 Corinthians 9:7 ESV)

Your giving must be a matter of willingness, not wealth; otherwise, God won't accept it. If you want to be like Jesus, you'll have to learn to give willingly as He did.

Do as I did: The Son of Man did not come for people to serve him. He came to serve others and to give his life to save many people. (Matthew 20:28 ERV)

Second Attitude: Tithe and Give Joyfully

"I'm so caught up in my own pain and financial need that I can't think of helping others or even consider giving to a church right now. Being asked offends me." That's what some people's attitude is. If this is you, I encourage you to adjust your attitude. Do you know generous people are rarely sad or suffer from mental illness? Giving is a source of joy.

I'm saddened that most times, the lowest point in our service is offering time; it's anything but a joyous part of the service, but that's how our heavenly Father wants us to give.

> Let each man do according as he hath purposed in his heart: not grudgingly, or of necessity: for God loveth a cheerful giver. (2 Corinthians 9:7 ASV)

The next time you give, do so with a joyful heart.

Third Attitude: Give Generously

It feels great to be a generous giver. The happiest people are indeed the most giving people. The Bible says there's more joy in giving than receiving. Did you know that the word *miserable* comes from the word *miser?*

> I can assure you that they gave as much as they could, and even more than they could. Of their own free will they begged us and pleaded for the privilege of having a part in helping God's people in Judea. (2 Corinthians 8:3–4 GNB)

The believers were saying, "Please, we're begging you to take an offering; give us an opportunity to give." Wow! What a difference with our culture today.

Here's a classic from the Old Testament about the construction of the tabernacle in the wilderness. The people were invited to bring gifts and

Key Phrase

God gives extravagant blessings only to extravagant givers.

assist in the construction. Note their generosity. Earlier, we noted a spirit of generosity in the construction of the tabernacle in the wilderness (Exodus 36); the people had to be restrained from giving. Here we see the same pattern in the construction of Solomon's temple. Not only did the people give willingly, they gave generously. In the prayer of dedication, David acknowledged the people's generosity.

> But who am I, and who are my people that we should be able to give as generously as this? (1 Chronicles 29:14 NIV)

> O Lord our God, as for all this abundance that we have provided for the building you a temple for your Holy Name, it comes from your hand, and all of it belongs to you. (1 Chronicles 29:16 NIV)

The Extravagant Giver

King Solomon was probably the most extravagant giver of all times. Many people read only the verses in which God blessed Solomon with extraordinary wealth, but they've never read the preceding verses in which he's described as an extravagant giver.

> On one occasion he went to Gibeon to offer sacrifices because that was where the most famous altar was. He had offered hundreds of burnt offerings there in the past. (1 Kings 3:4 GNB)

The traditional gift offered by kings was one bull, but he offered way more than that. It was this kind of sacrificial giving that opened the door for God to bless Solomon tremendously. The Lord appeared to him and said, "Ask what you will and I will give it to you" because God gives extravagant blessings only to extravagant givers.

When you're generous, you're being like God. God so loved the world that He gave, and if you wish to be like Jesus, you have to develop the habit of generosity.

Fourth Attitude: Give Sacrificially

Giving sacrificially is an act of giving to a deity something precious or giving up something you want to keep or do something to help someone. This definition makes perfect sense because the main reason people don't give is because they aren't prepared to go without in order to give.

This is one of the most profound biblical stories concerning sacrificial giving.

> Jesus sat near the Temple collection box and watched as people put money into it. Many rich people put in a lot of money. Then a poor widow came and put in two very small copper coins, worth less than a penny. Jesus called his followers to him and said, "This poor widow put in only two small coins. But the truth is, she gave more than all those rich people. They have plenty, and they gave only what they did not need. This woman is very poor, but she gave all she had. It was money she needed to live on." (Mark 12:41–44 ESV)

This poor widow's financial resources were tight, yet when she gave her farthing, she gave more than all the rich folks did because she had given her all. My friend, that's sacrificially giving.

Note that Jesus didn't hand back her two farthings; His point was that no one was too poor to give. Even the widow had something to give, and because of her sacrificial giving, she was noticed by the

Master, her memory was immortalized, and her action and attitude has become a model and an inspiration for Christ's people through all time.

It's a myth when people say they can't give. Everyone can give something if he or she is willing. It's not about equal amounts but equal sacrifice. You cannot become like Jesus Christ if you don't give sacrificially as He did on the cross.

The Macedonians Christians

The apostle Paul used the Macedonians as an example of sacrificial giving. The Macedonians' giving was similar in nature to the widow's mite in that they were poor.

> Our friends, we want you to know what God's grace has accomplished in the churches in Macedonia. They have been severely tested by the troubles they went through; but their joy was so great that they were extremely generous in their giving, even though they are very poor. I can assure you that they gave as much as they could, and even more than they could. Of their own free will. (2 Corinthians 8:1–3 GNB)

The apostle Paul used the example of the Macedonians' sacrificially giving and challenged the Corinthians to do the same.

> But since you excel in everything—in faith, in speech, in knowledge, in complete earnestness and in the love we have kindled in you. See that you also excel in this grace of giving. I am not commanding you, but I want to test the sincerity of your love by comparing it with the earnestness of others. (2 Corinthians 8:7–8 NIV)

Everyone can give. By comparing these two group of believers, Paul made the point that even though the Corinthian believers were much wealthier than their Macedonian colleagues, the Macedonians gave extraordinarily more—beyond their ability. They increased their income or decreased their expenses or both. That's the way to give sacrificially.

Fifth Attitude: Give Thoughtfully and Thankfully

God doesn't want us to give impulsively. If we want God to bless us, we must learn to give thoughtfully and thankfully. Giving thoughtfully means planned giving. As is the case with everything else, we should plan for tithing.

> Every Sunday each of you must put aside some money, in proportion to what you have earned, and save it up, so that there will be no need to collect money when I come. (1 Corinthians 16:2 ESV)

We must also give thankfully, that is conscious of something we've received or are about to receive. Our gifts to God are in thanks for past, present, and future blessings. We learn to give thankfully by remembering two things: first, we remember the source of our blessings.

> And God, who supplies seed for the sower and bread to eat, will also supply you with all the seed you need and will make it grow and produce a rich harvest from your generosity. (2 Corinthians 9:10 GNB)

Second, we remember the guarantee.

> He will always make you rich enough to be generous at all times, so that many will thank God for your gifts which they receive from us. (2 Corinthians 9:11 GNB)

Sixth Attitude: Give by Reason or Revelation

This is another excellent way to give. Giving by reason means conducting an audit of your possessions and assets and calculating a reasonable amount to part with. This doesn't require any faith, and you certainly don't expect anything in return.

Giving by revelation means determining what you want to give by praying about it: "Lord, how much do you want me to give through me?" When you give by revelation, you're not asking, "How much can I give?" but "How much am I willing to trust God?"

Seventh Attitude: Give Expectantly

When you tithe and give consistently, you can expect God to bless you in return. Many people teach you should give without expecting anything in return from the Lord, but that's not in sync with biblical philosophy of reaping what you sow. Giving activates the receiving process; giving is God's way of blessing you.

> Give, and it shall be given to you, good measure pressed down and shaken together and running over, they shall give into your bosom. For with the same measure that you measure, it shall be measured to you again. (Luke 6:38 MKJV)

> Remember this: Whoever sows sparingly will also reap sparingly, and whoever sows generously will also reap generously. (2 Corinthians 9:6 NIV)

> One person gives freely, yet gains even more; another withholds unduly, but comes to poverty. A generous person will prosper; whoever refreshes others will be refreshed. (Proverbs 11:24–25 NIV)

> Generous people will be blessed, because they share their food with the poor. (Proverbs 22:9 ERV)

> Cast thy bread upon the waters: for thou shalt find it
> after many days. (Ecclesiastes 11:1 KJV)

How do you want to live? Sparingly or generously? You get to decide. Each time you sow your seed—give to the work of the Lord—do so in faith and expect to receive, take time to document your expected harvest, thank God for the expected harvest, and keep giving thanks until the harvest arrives. Giving expectantly also means giving on what you earn and on what you expect to earn. Here are four things you can expect when you give expectantly.

First, you can expect to grow spiritually in your walk with God. Anytime I give willingly, generously, cheerfully, thankfully, sacrificially, and expectantly to the Lord, I grow by leaps and bounds in Him. My faith, love, and hope in Lord become stronger. I dare you to try it. You'll grow from the experience of giving.

Second, you can expect to be harassed and hassled by Satan. You'll see different things happening to you. Satan will turn the heat up a notch on you. When God owns your heart, He also owns your money, and Satan will do all he can to keep you from doing that. Don't let him rob you of your blessing or hold you back from entering the wealthy place.

Third, you can expect a lot of joy. The happiest people in the world are givers; I've never seen a happy miser.

> Remember the words the Lord Jesus himself said,
> "There is more happiness in giving than in receiving."
> (Acts 20:35 GN)

Finally, and probably most important, you can expect to experience miracles. I had some personal miracles in my life as a result of tithing and giving—I mean financial miracles, healing miracles, salvation miracles, and debt-cancellation miracles. All kinds of miracles will happen to you too when you open your heart, pocketbook, and bank account to the Lord; He will open the windows of heaven to you. That's what He promised.

> Bring the full tithe into the storehouse, that there may be food in my house. And thereby put me to the test, says the LORD of hosts, if I will not open the windows of heaven for you and pour down for you a blessing until there is no more need. (Malachi 3:10 ESV)

Final Thoughts

Reader, it doesn't matter how much you give to the Lord, you can never *outgive* Him. Tithing is a fundamental law of God that's guaranteed to bless the tither. If you're not tithing and giving, you're being disobedient, and that will unleash the Master's anger and curses that will result in disappointments and despair.

Those who honor God by investing a specific portion of their income in the kingdom will be blessed with temporal and spiritual wealth. I've never known an exception to that. If you want to arrive at your wealthy place, you must embrace giving.

My Personal Wealthy Place Notes

_____

_____

_____

_____

_____

_____

_____

_____

_____

_____

_____

_____

_____

_____

_____

_____

_____

_____

_____

_____

_____

_____

_____

_____

_____

_____

_____

_____

_____

Section VIII

My Wealthy Place

Psalm 66:12

Chapter 20

If It's Going to Be, It's Up to Me!

Why are we sitting here waiting to die?
—2 Kings 7:3b ERV

Whata life-changing question! We all have to go at some time, but there's no good in sitting down and waiting for the bitter end. It's very seldom that opportunity will come knocking; you'll have to go looking for it.

In this chapter, I want to summarize what we've talked about and give you a call to action. It's my final appeal to you to get off your blessed assurance and commit yourself to a new journey.

Joshua said to a group of his complacent followers at Shiloh, a place of rest and complacency,

> How long are you going to wait before you go in
> and take the land that the LORD, the God of your
> ancestors, has given you? (Joshua 18:3 GNB)

Say to yourself, *The days of waiting are truly over, and it's time to get my life in high gear.* One of the cardinal laws of prosperity is not to be afraid in stepping out into new ventures and make the best of the opportunities you've been afforded to you. The brevity of life demands that you do. It's not that life is short; rather, we wait too long to get on with it.

331

> Teach us to number our days and recognize how few they are; help us to spend them as we should. (Psalm 90:12 LB)

If you're serious about entering your wealthy place, don't postpone your better future another day; start pursuing your dream today. The marketplace won't pay you for what you dream, desire, discuss, debate, or declare, only for what you do. John Ruskin said, "What we think, or what we know, or what we believe is, in the end, of little consequence. The only consequence is what we do." *The Success Principles, Jack Cranfield, (Harper Collins Publishers, 2007), 98*

That is true! It doesn't matter how good your thoughts, ideas, and intentions are; you won't be rewarded for them unless you translate them into action. Start taking steps toward becoming wealthy even if you don't have everything totally figured out; start moving now and recalibrate later.

The most challenging aspect of life is not accomplishing our goals but deciding what they should be. Furthermore, it's easier to accomplish big goals because small goals won't fire you up. Set yourself a big goal of becoming a millionaire.

Who Wants To Be A Millionaire?

Yes, set yourself a personal goal to become a millionaire! I write that without apology because there's a common belief that everyday people can't become millionaires. That's simply not true. If you apply the principles in this biblically based book, you can accumulate wealth beyond your wildest dream.

The millionaire club is not as exclusive as it seems. There are more than 10 million households in the United States with net worths of over a million. It's easier nowadays to run into a millionaire than a teacher. So set a personal goal of becoming a millionaire.

True Story

A true story from the Bible is my inspiration for this final chapter. I love the Bible, the best writing of all time and the best seller of all time.

The marketplace won't pay you for what you dream, desire, discuss, debate, or declare, only for what you do.

We've shared some life-changing stories from the Bible, an incredible book, and I guarantee you'll love the one I'm about to share.

The Four Lepers and the Will to Succeed

> There were four men sick with leprosy near the city gate. They said to each other, "Why are we sitting here waiting to die? There is no food in Samaria. If we go into the city, we will die there. If we stay here, we will also die. So let's go to the Aramean camp. If they let us live, we will live. If they kill us, we will just die." So that evening the four lepers went to the Aramean camp. When they came to the edge of the camp, no one was there! The Lord had caused the Aramean army to hear the sound of chariots, horses, and a large army. So the soldiers said to each other, "The king of Israel has hired the kings of the Hittites and Egyptians to come against us."
>
> The Arameans ran away early that evening. They left everything behind. They left their tents, horses, and donkeys and ran for their lives. When these lepers came to where the camp began, they went into one tent. They ate and drank. Then they carried silver, gold, and clothes out of the camp and hid them. Then they came back and entered another tent. They carried things out from this tent and went out and hid them. (2 Kings 7:3–8 ERV)

What an inspiring story! There comes a moment in every feel-good story when the protagonist, after being beaten down, impoverished, and forsaken, summons the courage to rise, confront the challenges, and change his or her life.

Key Phrase

Disgust with your current circumstance is the starting point for life change and success. With enough disgust, you can change anything you want to change.

God uses a predictable process to guide us from our dream to our destiny. I call them the twelve phases of faith. He does so because He wants us all to be successful, prosperous, and wealthy without apology. Say, "If it's to be, it's up to me!"

First Phase of Faith: Disgusted With Present Circumstances

Disgust with your current circumstance is the starting point for life change and success. With enough disgust, you can change anything you want to change. It was in the womb of disgust that the dream of a better life was birthed for these four lepers.

Consider their plight. The country was undergoing the worst economic recession ever. Their city was under siege and experiencing famine too awful to imagine; even the middle class was suffering.

Lepers were forbidden by law to live in cities; they were forced to make do outside the city walls. They lived on handouts tossed over the walls, but the famine stopped even that. Death stared them in the face. So they summoned the courage to ask, "Why are we sitting here waiting to die?"

What a life-changing day it can be when you finally bring yourself to say, "I've had enough of being beating down, poor, and broke." There's nothing like stating the truth. "You shall know the truth and the truth shall set you free."

Like these lepers, your wealth journey begins with you facing the reality of your circumstance. You need to know where you are financially

Key Phrase

For your circumstance to change, you have to take action. If you don't change, nothing will change for you.

among other things before you can decide where to go. "Why are we sitting here waiting to die" was an amazing statement of disgust from these lepers. This same principle applies to you if you want to become wealthy, sophisticated, and powerful. The prerequisite for becoming wealthy is disgust with your economic lack. Let that motivate you to change the situation without worrying if it's possible. At this stage, there are three important questions to ask yourself: *Is my life really how I want it to be? What do I want? What would I like to change?* Ask these questions about all the major areas of your life—physical, relational, health, business, spiritual, mental, educational, lifestyle, contacts, skills, passion, ambition, desire, willingness, and more. Cover all the major areas to assess where you are and where you want to be.

Don't just focus on the things you lack; that can paralyze you. You're already blessed. To be a success, you must think success. All the lepers had going for them was their "do it or die" attitude, and that might be all you need.

Wealthy people aren't necessarily the smartest or wisest people, but they have come to grips with where they were and where they wanted to be. They've been honest about their faults, weaknesses, inadequacies, and limitations, but then, they worked hard to overcome that. For your circumstance to change, you have to take action. If you don't change, nothing will change for you, but if you change, everything will change.

Second Phase of Faith: Declare Your Intentions Personally and Publicly

You must develop an unsettled conviction about wanting to become wealthy. You need to know exactly why you want to become wealthy. Once you've made that decision, clearly articulate your intention. Make a covenant, a resolution. The power of a vow is awesome, and it's particularly powerful if you put it in writing. Notice how specific the lepers were.

> Why should we wait here until we die? It's no use going into the city, because we would starve to death in there; but if we stay here, we'll die also. So let's go to the Syrian camp; the worst they can do is kill us, but maybe they will spare our lives. (2 Kings 7:3–4 KJV)

The lepers' purpose was to survive, an easily defined goal. You need to define clearly what you want because you can't achieve a vague goal—they have no pulling power. Be specific! The secret of the abundant life lies in a clearly defined purpose.

I'd like to build a financial wall around my family, give to good causes, and support my church and the hospital that healed me. Most important, I want to support the assignment the Lord has given me, and I'd like to invest in getting people into heaven. But all these require money. I want to make sure my goals line up with God's Word. Ask yourself, *Why do I want to become wealthy?* Then ask yourself, *Would God approve?*

Third Phase of Faith: Discover Wealth Promises in God's Word

Over seven thousand promises in the Bible are waiting to be claimed, and most of them relate to wealth. Everything you need from God comes with a promise from His Word, but you have to claim these wealth promises; they're checks just waiting to be cashed.

We've explored more than a thousand of God's promises in this book. I encourage you to review, read, and recite them until they're embedded in your spirit. What He has promised you He'll fulfill; if the Word said it, you can have it.

> The LORD your God will bless you in the land that he is giving you. Not one of your people will be poor if you obey him and carefully observe everything that I command you today. The LORD will bless you, as he has promised. You will lend money to many nations, but you will not have to borrow from any; you will have control over many nations, but no nation will have control over you. (Deuteronomy 15:4–6 GNB)

I'm not sure the four lepers heard Elisha's prophecy of economic recovery.

> Listen to what the LORD says! By this time tomorrow you will be able to buy in Samaria ten pounds of the best wheat or twenty pounds of barley for one piece of silver. (2 Kings 7:1 GNB)

But God must have planted a dream or hope in their spirit to act, because every great accomplishment first begins with a God-given dream. It's God's will for you to prosper, and when you saturate your soul with these promises, you'll gain confidence to move forward. So the question to ask is, "What promise can I claim from God's Word?" Don't worry about the how; simply allow yourself to be motivated by the greatness of your God. Keep reading the Bible's promises concerning wealth that will support your claim. Once you find a promise, stand on it. At this stage Ask yourself, *What promise can I claim?* Ready for the next step?

Fourth Phase of Faith: Determine the Pros, Cons, and the Payoff

Notice how the four lepers motivated themselves by talking about their vision. They discussed all their options. They weighed the pros and the cons. They said to each other,

> Why should we wait here until we die? It's no use going into the city, because we would starve to death in there; but if we stay here, we'll die also. So let's go to the Syrian camp; the worst they can do is kill us, but maybe they will spare our lives. (2 Kings 7:4 GNB)

They weren't sure of the outcome, but they didn't allow that to derail their plans or dreams. They played the "What if?" game, and so must you. "What will happen if we stay or step out?" That was a moment of truth. They reasoned they couldn't be worse off.

Maturity teaches us this: every venture, dream, goal, or pursuit comes with challenges. Things don't always go according to plan, so make sure to weigh all your options. There must be a moment of truth for you, and it's worth it to invest your time, money, energy, and reputation and let go of security. The Master asked,

> For which of you, intending to build a tower, does not sit down first and count the cost, whether he has enough to finish it? (Luke 14:28 NKJV)

It's also important to describe the payoff up-front. When you figure out what you want to do with your life, you'll be on a mission that will motivate you to keep going when you get discouraged. The reward motivated the four lepers to pursue their dream. The prize must be worth the price of your staying up late and getting up early. You need to know the payoff to avoid discouragement when things get challenging.

Ask yourself, *What's the reward in becoming wealthy? How will I feel when I get to my wealthy place? Is the price worth the promise?*

Fifth Phase of Faith: Diagnose the Problems

The lepers had big problems. They were impoverished, forced to live outside the city walls, and trying to live through a famine. Mission impossible. "They might kill us if we go," they said to each other.

> Now there were four men who were lepers at the entrance to the gate. (2 Kings 7:3 ESV)

Perhaps that passage was meant to highlight the fact that their condition could be a barrier to them from taking part in the promised abundance. In spite of the odds, they decided to do something even if they didn't know the outcome; they weren't paralyzed.

Critical to realizing your wealth ambition is an understanding of the emotional, intellectual, educational, relational, fear, indecision, timidity, and health barriers you face. The barriers confronting these four men were gigantic, but they weren't intimidated by them. Never let an impossible situation intimidate you; let it motivate you. Don't pray for fewer challenges because overcoming challenges is part of success.

Avoid Analysis Paralysis

Whatever the challenges are, avoid overanalyzing your situation. This is where many people give up. Indecision is often the result of too much thinking; challenges aren't going to get easier by overthinking them. Diagnose your barriers; don't over diagnose them. Trust the next steps to help you move forward. Ask yourself, *Why haven't I possessed the wealth God has promised me? What am I going to do about it?*

Sixth Phase of Faith: Develop a Plan

The challenge is to develop a plan that will help you overcome the barriers you've identified. A plan is a psychological necessity, a written picture of your journey toward your wealthy place. Without a plan, you're just playing around. The four lepers had to come up with a plan to overcome their challenges.

Key Phrase

A plan is a psychological necessity, a written picture of your journey toward your wealthy place. Without a plan, you're just playing around.

> So they arose at twilight to go to the camp of the Syrians. But when they came to the edge of the camp of the Syrians, behold, there was no one there. (2 Kings 7:5 ESV)

You'll agree their plan was ingenious and SMART: specific, measurable, attainable, realistic, and time sensitive—a masterpiece. You can come up with a SMART plan by answering these questions: Where do I want to be on the journey toward my wealthy place five years from now? How will I get there? What will I do to overcome the barriers?

To possess your wealthy place, start with your disgust with the present, declare your intentions, discover a promise from God's Word, describe the payoffs, diagnose the problems, and develop a plan.

Seventh Phase of Faith: Discipline Your Personality

Discipline is like a bridge that will take you from fantasy to reality. An undisciplined life leads only to the destruction of your dreams. This is a crucial step in possessing your wealthy place because nothing ever gets done without discipline.

These four lepers were great examples of discipline. They were disciplined in their decision; they didn't just talk a good talk—they translated it into action: they

The right time to act is when your dream is clear and your desire is strong. When the light turns green, do not wait, accelerate.

"arose and went." A plan is useless until you do something about it. The world is full of dreamers. For every ten of them, there's only one dream maker.

They were disciplined with their time. Some people say, "I'm waiting on the perfect condition." No such thing. "One of these days" will never arrive. You must have a starting point. Seize every opportunity to get on with your plan.

> If you wait for perfect conditions, you will never get anything done … Keep on sowing your seed, for you never know which will grow-perhaps it all will. (Ecclesiastes 11:4, 6 LB)

The Right Time to Act

"When's the right time to take action?" I'm often asked. I answer, "You don't need to be hasty if that's not required. If it can wait, let it wait, but you don't want to lose much valuable time either." If you wait too long, you can fall prey to what I call diminishing intent. Your desire, your feeling, your fire might be lost forever. Time management is a spiritual matter; time is God's greatest gift. If you kill time, you're committing suicide. Don't waste valuable time pondering—you'll end up poor. The wealthiest man ever, Solomon, warned,

> People who waste time will always be poor. (Proverbs 28:19 GNB)

Understanding Time Dimensions

The key to success is to understand time dimensions. Every successful person knows when to take

When highly successful people make a decision, they die by it. Be willing to die for your decision.

action, when and where to invest, when to buy and when not to buy, when to sell, and when not to sell. This doesn't mean they're always right. To be successful, you must be a master of timing and master at recognizing opportunities—a fine balance. The right time to act is when your dream is clear and your desire is strong. When the light turns green, do not wait, accelerate. Don't get stuck in analysis paralysis.

Die for Your Decisions

Once you know the direction God wants you to take, you must have the confidence to move ahead. Don't doubt what God has called you to do. Once you've set your goals, the devil will get you to start questioning it. *Is this really God's purpose for my life? What if I am incorrect? Do I really deserve this? Am I just being egotistical?*

Once you've started, don't look back. Many people are afraid to commit to anything. They begin one job, and when it gets tough, they switch to something else. They start attending the gym until that gets too hard. If you're not committed, you'll never finish anything. When highly successful people make a decision, they die by it. Be willing to die for your decision.

> The person who is right with me will live by trusting in me. But I will not be pleased with the one who turns back in fear. But we are not those who turn back and are lost. No, we are the people who have faith and are saved. (Hebrews 10:38–39 ERV)

The Jordon Crossing

God made a promise to Joshua and his followers that He would part the waters of the Jordon River and transition them to their promised destiny.

> Behold, the ark of the covenant of the Lord of all the earth passes over before you into Jordan. And now take yourselves twelve men out of the tribes of Israel, out of every tribe a man. And it shall be, as soon as the soles of the feet of the priests that carry the ark of Jehovah, the Lord of all the earth, shall rest in the waters of Jordan, the waters of Jordan shall be cut off from the waters that come down from above. And they shall stand all in a heap. And it happened, when the people moved from their tents to pass over Jordan, and as the priests carried the Ark of the Covenant before the people, and as those who bore the ark had come to Jordan.
>
> And the feet of the priests that bore the ark were dipped in the edge of the water (for Jordan overflows all its banks, all the time of harvest); that the waters which came down from above stopped and rose up all in a heap, very far from the city Adam that is beside Zaretan. And those that came down toward the sea of the plain, the Salt Sea, were completely cut off. And the people passed over across from Jericho. And the priests who bore the ark of the covenant of Jehovah stood firm on dry ground in the middle of Jordan. And all the Israelites passed over on dry ground, until all the people had passed completely over Jordan. (Joshua 3:12–17 MKJV)

This was a significant time for Joshua's advancing army. Joshua was a transitional leader. They had spent forty years on this side of the

Jordon with their parents. But then, they were standing on a brink of a major breakthrough to the wealthy place God had promised them.

God didn't translate the prophecy into promise until they took their first step into the river of impossibility. Jordon had overflowed its banks, but God said, "Step in," and as soon as the feet of the priest hit the water, it started backing up. You'll never know what opportunities will be opened to you until you step out in faith.

What is keeping you out of your wealthy place? Jordon can be interpreted as anything keeping you from your wealthy place, so confront and conquer it. Like Joshua's people, if you've been stuck into a rut for a long time, this could be your moment. Listen to the voice of God and step out in faith. Don't allow the torrent of life to intimidate you. Is what you're doing with your time moving you closer to your destiny or farther from it? Are you willing to die for your dream?

Eighth Phase of Faith: Deposit the Price

I meet people who want to become wealthy but only at others' expense or through get-rich-quick schemes. There's always a price to be paid if you intend to become wealthy. One of the most pitiful things I've seen is believers sitting in a corner and constantly distributing blame for their circumstances and waiting on others to do it for them or acquire for them. You can't get something for nothing in life. You can get out of debt, build savings, and become financially independent, but nobody else can make it happen for you. If it's going to be, it's up to you.

These four lepers risked their lives and stepped out in faith "If they spare our lives we shall live, and if they kill us, we shall but die." Don't you just love their do-it-or die attitude? I'd rather die attempting to achieve something and fail than never try at all.

Accumulating wealth requires a willingness to go where others have not gone, do what others won't do, become what others dare

344

not become, and attempt what most people say cannot be done. Ask yourself, *What am I willing to do? What will it cost me? Is it worth the cost?*

Ninth Phase of Faith: Depend on People

Many people don't believe this is step of faith, but I believe it is. It takes a great amount of faith to trust people, and you can't succeed on your own; you need your alliances. Success always involves other people. Expect people to help you. Big thinking always attracts big thinkers. These lepers didn't go it alone; they epitomized the importance of teamwork. Check off the plurality of their statements in the following narrative.

- And they said to one another,
- "Why are we sitting here until we die?
- Let us go over to the camp of the Syrians."
- So they arose at twilight to go to the camp of the Syrians.
- They went into a tent and ate and drank, and they carried off silver and gold and clothing and went and hid them.
- Then they came back and entered another tent and carried off things from it and went and hid them.
- Then they said to one another …

Without people, your dream will die prematurely. Those who are successful have employed the right support system into their lives. The lone-wolf way is never the best approach to life and wealth. It is the talents, gifts, ideas, and counsel of other people that make us complete. King Solomon talked about this many times.

> Two people are better than one. When two people work together, they get more work done. If one person falls, the other person can reach out to help. But those who

345

are alone when they fall have no one to help them.
(Ecclesiastes 4:9–10 ERV)

The ability to get along and work with people is one of the greatest wealth-creating skills you can possess. You will not acquire much in life until you master the art of getting along and working with people. My best advice is for you to find at least five people with goals similar to yours and meet with them once a month for support as part of your wealth strategy. You'll discover these folks can open doors for you that you can't open yourself.

But don't allow yourself to be a slave to people for the rest of your life when they open a door for you. Others are conduits through whom blessings flow, but God is the source, not them. They might open the door, but your skills and calling keep it open. Treat your colleagues as professional associates, not life partners or spouses. If you have to separate, it won't break your heart. Ask yourself, *Who can I ask for help? Is there a success group that I can join?*

Tenth Phase of Faith: Desire in Prayer

Many people have serious reservations about praying to be wealthy, but you should pray to be wealthy. What's the alternative? Praying to be poor?

I'm not sure the lepers prayed before they acted; the Bible doesn't say. But it must be for some special reason that their story is in the Word. On the other hand, when you consider their dire situation, they must have muttered a few words of prayer to the Lord. Prayer is the master key that unlocks every door to God's favor.

> Therefore I tell you, whatever you ask in prayer, believe that you have received it, and it will be yours. (Mark 11:24 ESV)

In that day you will ask nothing of me. Truly, truly, I say to you, whatever you ask of the Father in my name, he will give it to you. Until now you have asked nothing in my name. Ask, and you will receive, that your joy may be full. (John 16:23–24 ESV)

God has a financial plan for your success whether you believe it or not, but you must unearth it through prayer and work. He wants you to live differently from the world and be prosperous and wealthy. I believe we should pray about every area of our lives—our health life, our social life, our physical life, our educational life, our emotional life, and certainly our financial life. God is infinitely interested in that also.

We should make plans—counting on God to direct us. (Proverbs 16:9 LB)

The Purpose of Prayer

Prayer does two things; first, it expresses the depth of our desires and differentiates between our wishes and our whims. If it's worth getting wealthy, it's worth praying for. The second purpose of prayer is it demonstrates our dependence on God. Our prayers say, "God, I'm trusting you, I'm relying on your power to help me become successful. I cannot do it without your help. I can't become wealthy in my own strength and effort."

Do not be anxious about anything, but in everything by prayer and supplication with thanksgiving let your requests be made known to God. (Philippians 4:6 ESV)

Does the word *everything* cover praying about your wealth? Indeed it does.

The Prayer of Jabez

The story of Jabez has to be the greatest example and affirmation from the Word of God empowering us to pray for wealth.

> Jabez was more honorable than his brothers. His mother had named him Jabez, saying, "I gave birth to him in pain." Jabez cried out to the God of Israel, "Oh that you would bless me and enlarge my territory! Let your hand be with me, and keep me from harm so that I will be free from pain." And God granted his request. (1 Chronicles 4:9–10 NIV)

God granted Jabez his request for wealth and prospe-rity. Being wealthy can help other people and can bring glory to God, so it's legitimate to pray for wealth. If the Word of God says you can have it, you can. Don't be persuaded otherwise because everything is possible in the kingdom of God. Don't limit God in your petition.

Take the Limit off God-Do It or Die

God doesn't limit us and say, "This is all the wealth you can have." Rather, we limit God and ourselves and say, "This is all I'm allowed to have." Since it's okay to pray for wealth, let me challenge you to remove all limitations from your mind when you pray.

> With God's power working in us, he can do much, much more than anything we can ask or think of. To him be glory in the church and in Christ Jesus for all time, forever and ever. Amen. (Ephesians 3:20–21 ESV)

You can never ask for too much. If you're limited in your thinking, you'll limit God in your asking and receiving. You're the custodian of your lips; your life is the total of what you've prayed for. If it's worthwhile becoming wealthy, it's worth talking to God about it. So ask yourself, *Am I seriously praying about possessing my wealthy place?*

Eleventh Phase of Faith: Determine Your Purpose

Key Phrase

God doesn't limit us and say, "This is all the wealth you can have." Rather, we limit God and ourselves and say, "This is all I'm allowed to have."

Don't get sidetracked; fight to the finish. It's easy to start something, but it can be a challenge to finish it. It's easy to pick up a book or start a workout routine, but at times, it can be tough to finish those. Now that you're on the road to wealth, don't abandon the trip.

Beware of delays and difficulties. There will always be an interval between your putting a plan into action and completing it, but delay doesn't mean denial. And you'll face problems, but don't quit—don't let the critics and circumstances get you down.

> Let us not become weary in doing good, for at the proper time we will reap a harvest if we do not give up. (Galatians 6:9 NIV)

Satan's greatest tool against you will be your fear of failure. Base your goals and dreams on what you believe God can accomplish through you, not on what you think *you* can. Even if you don't achieve it, let it be inscribed on your tombstone, "At least I tried!"

Twelfth Phase of Faith: Deliverance and Discovery of the Promise

> And when these lepers came to the edge of the camp, they went into a tent and ate and drank, and they carried off silver and gold and clothing and went and hid them. (2 Kings 7:8 ESV)

The lepers expected to find just some food, but God surpassed their desires by providing them much more. Things will fall into place when you trust God, so don't become complacent. Do something today, do it every day, do it now.

Key Phrase

You'll never know what you're capable of or what you'll discover until you face the unknown, take the initiative, stretch your imagination, and step out in faith.

> And they rose up in the twilight, to go unto the camp of the Syrians: and when they were come to the uttermost part of the camp of Syria, behold, there was no man there. (2 Kings 7:5 KJV)

> Wherefore they arose and fled in the twilight, and left their tents, and their horses, and their asses, even the camp as it was, and fled for their life. (2 Kings 7:7 KJV)

Great rewards often require great risks. You'll never know what you're capable of or what you'll discover until you face the unknown, take the initiative, stretch your imagination, and step out in faith. I've learned from experience that there are some blessings you'll never realize until you begin to make bold moves.

Life is too short for pity parties and daydreaming. Show up for life because miracles are waiting to happen to you. Ask yourself, *What would I attempt to do for God if I knew I couldn't fail?*

Let Me Finish

Earlier, I told you my childhood story of how I did not meet my parents until I was in my teens. After I graduated from Bible College, I visited my parents in England. I was about twenty-two then. It was a dream come true for me. I met some great people and made lots of friends. And most important, I reconnected with my only sister and got to know my younger brother.

Due to a major life-changing experience, London became my home for twenty-three years. I loved London! It's one of those places you have to see before you die. Be sure to include it in your bucket list. Samuel Johnson once said, "The man who tires of London tires of life for there is in London all that life can afford." I spent three months under the same roof with my parents, but we really never talked about what we were all thinking—whether I was my father's child. At first, I didn't have an emotional connection with my parents, especially my father, who never showed me any love. I would do anything just to hear him say, "My son," but it was never to be. Perhaps he spent all his time assessing if I was his son, and I was certainly assessing if he was my father. This must have been very difficult for my mother; who knew what her thoughts were? She was most certainly assessing the interplay between us. Indeed, she was the only one with the right answers.

These were tense moments, but no one had the courage to bring up the subject at least in my presence. I overheard my mother and my "maybe" father having an argument one night, and I guess that is what it was all about.

After a series of life-changing events, including a failed marriage, (another book by itself), I moved on. After many moons, I relocated to the United States in 2004 after I met and married my beautiful wife, Shelia Blake. In 2009, my mother called to inform me of my "maybe" father's death. He was seventy-five. I attended the funeral but felt nothing. As far as I was concerned, my father had died the day I met him and we were just getting around to laying him to rest. Isn't that the case with many people? They died at age twenty-five, but we buried them age seventy-five. I guess my father died wondering if I was his son and I wondering if he was my father.

Fabrication

As far back as I can remember, I was told by some relatives that my father was not my real father. People would taunt me with, "Why did your parents take your sister and leave you on the island when you were only nine months old?" I'm telling you, they really messed up my mind! I grew up resenting and hating my mother for the seeming deception and dishonesty. I carried this pain and sense of abandonment with me throughout life. I would often find comfort in the Psalms: "When my mother and father forsake me the Lord will take me up into his arms." I carried this pain until I was fifty-four.

Heart Talk

I often talked to my wife about my personal pain and feelings of abandonment and not having the courage to speak to my mother about it. However, in October 2015, my mother came to spend some time with us in the United States. One morning when I was in my office working on this book, my mother walked in. "Good morning, son!"

"Good morning, Mom! How was your night?"

"Very well. Can we talk?"

"Sure! What would you like to talk about?"

"My life!" she said, not making eye contact.

Mom is very smart but shy. She hates confrontations. I guess I inherited that gene from her. In the vainness of my imaginations, I was thinking she would confess what I had concluded, that my "maybe" father wasn't my real father and that the man I was told by a relative I resembled was my real father. But he as well had passed on.

But my mother poured out her heart to me, unrushed, and without the slightest worry about condemnation. This heart talk went on for approximately three hours. She told me of her highs and lows, from being a timid, unwise teenager to a smart seventy-six-year-old great-grandmother. Then we came to the moment I had been waiting for. "Cornie, I know you were told that your father was not your father, but he was, and I'm sorry it took so long to clarify this."

I really hadn't wanted to hear he was my father. I wanted her to tell me of another person who was alive so I could try to build a relationship with him. But it was never to be.

The most time my mother and I were able to spend together under the same roof was three months, and neither of us had had the courage to talk about the issues until it was too late for myself and my father. We simple succumbed to the lies and deceit and the fabricated story of negative relatives.

Maternity Moment

But this time, on the morning of October 2015, when my mother and I had the heart talk, everything changed for me; it was a born again moment. I told my wife, "Honey, my mother and I had a heart talk this morning, and for the first time in my life, at age fifty-four, I know what it feels like to have a mother."

Mr. Jack Canfield, cocreator of the *Chicken Soup for the Soul Series*, defines a heart talk this way.

> A Heart Talk is a very structured communication process in which ... deep level communication occur without the fear of condemnation, unsolicited advice, interruption, or being rushed. It is a powerful tool used to surface and release any unexpected emotions ... it is used to develop rapport, understanding, and intimacy.[5]

I guess that's what happened to both of us. We live in different countries, but we try to talk every day, and I'm praying she'll be around for a long time. I'm thrilled we were able to lay that matter to rest.

The Point

It hurts how we both allowed negative relatives to talk us out of fifty-four years of relationship with each other. I believed their lies about my parents. I don't believe that my mother ever convinced him that I was his child. I never will know what it feels like to hear him say, "My son" and what it means to say "Dad."

I say all that to make this simple but powerful point: if you're not careful, negative people can talk you out of your wealthy place. Wasn't that the case with Israel? Ten of the twelve who spied out the Promised Land talked them out of it with a fabricated story of the land.

> So they spread a false report among the Israelites about the land they had explored. They said, "That land doesn't even produce enough to feed the people who live there. Everyone we saw was very tall, and we even saw giants there, the descendants of Anak. We felt as small as grasshoppers, and that is how we must have looked to them." (Numbers 13:32–33 GNB)

Each of the spies repeated their dismal tidings with exaggerations to their tribes, and as the fabricated story spread swiftly through the tents, the mourning became universal, and they decided to form a pack and return to poverty.

> All night long the people cried out in distress. They complained against Moses and Aaron, and said, "It would have been better to die in Egypt or even here in the wilderness! Why is the LORD taking us into that land? We will be killed in battle, and our wives and children will be captured. Wouldn't it be better to go back to Egypt?" (Numbers 14:1–3 GNB)

This was very unfortunate; their wealthy place was within reach. God has so much in store for us; we should do our own research and not allow people to deprive us of it. I challenge you to reject the voices that are trying to talk you out of your desired wealthy place.

Don't Die in the Wilderness

> For the children of Israel walked forty years in the wilderness, till all the people that were men of war, which came out of Egypt, were consumed, because they obeyed not the voice of the LORD: unto whom the LORD sware that he would not shew them the land, which the LORD sware unto their fathers that he would give us, a land that floweth with milk and honey. (Joshua 5:6 KJV)

They died in the wilderness. They died in poverty. Don't let this be said of you. The wealthy place is promised to you as a gift from the Almighty.

God's desire for you is to live differently from the world. Hence, you must make His desire yours. Let others lead small lives. Stagnation, excuses, mediocrity, complaining, and complacency must not be your friends; they're enemies of wealth and success and must never be part of your vocabulary. Your wealthy place is there for the taking. I challenge you to heed the voice that says,

> The land we explored is an excellent land. If the LORD is pleased with us, he will take us there and give us that rich and fertile land. (Numbers 14:8 GNB)

> Let us go up at once and possess it. For we are well able to overcome it. (Numbers 13:30 MKJV)

Please say after me: *"If it's to going to be, it's up to me."*

My Personal Wealthy Place Notes

_____

_____

_____

_____

_____

_____

_____

_____

_____

_____

_____

_____

_____

_____

_____

_____

_____

_____

_____

_____

_____

_____

_____

_____

_____

_____

_____

_____

My Wealthy Place

Psalm 66:12

For Afters

Nobody Listens to Poor People

If the wise man is poor, he will be despised, and
what he says will not be appreciated.
—Ecclesiastes 9:16b NIV

W e've shared a great intellectual meal, and every good meal
should be followed by the perfect *afters*, the British name for
dessert. I hope you've left room for it because I have prepared for you
an incredibly decadent dessert. Let's linger at this intellectual table to
feed the mind with a few more sweet thoughts. Grab your intellectual
dessert spoon and dive in.

> There was a little city with few men in it, and a great
> king came against it and besieged it, building great
> siege works against it. But there was found in it a
> poor, wise man, and he by his wisdom delivered the
> city. Yet no one remembered that poor man. But I say
> that wisdom is better than might, though the poor
> man's wisdom is despised and his words are not heard.
> (Ecclesiastes 9:14–6 ESV)

This is a pretty neat story—a town besieged by a powerful king was
in a hopeless situation. Let's take the first bite of the story. First, a poor
but wise man devised a plan and saved the city from occupation and
destruction. Then the text asserts, "Yet no one remembered that poor

man." Someone else probably took credit for this man's wisdom. But the main reason why this poor man was forgotten was for the simple but sad reason that he was poor.

Next bite: notice that the text didn't say, "a poor wise man." Your poverty will always obscure your wisdom. Listen to me, if you are poor, the world will not listen to you.

Next bite: it doesn't matter how much wisdom you possess; if you don't possess wealth, your words will be lost to the wind. Money speaks, my friend. It's sad, but the world would rather pay thousands of dollars to listen to a rich man telling lies than a few hundred to listen to a poor man telling the truth.

If the church of Jesus Christ is poor, the world won't listen to its message. The text asserts, "The poor man's wisdom is despised and his words are not heard."

If you don't believe me, ask your bank for a multimillion-dollar loan you say you'll pay back by prayer and faith; they'd laugh. You better have some assets in the bank.

I believe the church should have the most attractive buildings, well-manicured lawns, and best commercials on TV and glossy flyers and brochures on display, but it all requires money. When it comes to spreading the gospel, finance should never be an issue for the body of Christ.

I don't believe the greatest lack in the body of Christ is a spiritual one. There are many faithful, Holy Spirit–filled people in the church, but our major problem is we are simply too poor, so our message isn't heard. We need money to establish the kingdom of God on earth.

So my friend, I hope you've been inspired and motivated to take advantage of all the wealth God has made available to you. However, in the unfortunate event I have failed to make my argument clear, as we linger at the table, I say the Almighty didn't intend for you to revel in self-pity and poverty or to scrape and beg for all your life. Such is not His grand design for your life. He came that you might have life in all its fullness.

Reader, poverty is evil, and wealth is a gift from God. I wish you prosperity. Let us recite the following doxology together as we leave the table.

The Doxology of Prosperity

> Beloved, I wish above all things that thou mayest prosper and be in health, even as thy soul prospereth. (3 John 1:2 KJV)

Your wealthy place is not out of reach.

My Final Wealthy Place Notes

Acknowledgement

My first thanks, as usual, goes to my heavenly Father for endowing me with the gift of writing.

Next, I'd like to say thanks to my wife, Pastor Shelia R. Blake, who shares her thoughts with me daily, helps sharpen my ideas, and most important, loaned me her personal and our relational time to work on this project.

Finally, I am grateful to my editorial team: Ms. Chinetta Henry, senior proofreader; Ms. Jeannette Campbell, proofreader; Mrs. Patrice Anderson, proofreader; Dr. Jennifer Nelson, proofreader; and Minister Shamus Gordon, critical reader and thinker.

About the Author

Bishop Cornelius Blake is a certified entrepreneur, wealth coach and the senior pastor of All Nations Life Development Christian Center in Port St. Lucie, Florida. It's one of the largest and culturally diverse churches in the area, which serves over twenty-five nationalities. He previously served as senior pastor and executive member of New Testament Assembly in the United Kingdom and as an accredited partnership lecturer for the University of Wales.

He gained secular qualifications in applied social studies from the University of Kent in Canterbury UK and received a diploma degree in social work. Before he was released to full-time ministry, he worked as a certified probation officer and care manager for an alcoholics agency in the UK. He is a certified wealth coach.

He received initial ministerial training from the Caribbean Pentecostal College in Mandeville, Jamaica, and bachelor's and master's degrees in ministry from Chesapeake Bible College & Seminary, USA.

He lives with his wife, Rev. Shelia Blake, in Florida, and they share four lovely daughters. He is also the renowned author of *Better Birthing Your Own Baby* and the popular *Sinduction*. He is a frequent host of TBN Treasure Coast and can be heard weekly on FM 89.9 Caribbean Gospel Train.

Other Books by Bishop Cornelius Blake

Better Birthing Your Own Baby **(Amazon.com)**

Are you pregnant with God's purpose? Are you ready to make it a reality? This book will help you do just that. This is a book for every person who senses the call of God for a bigger picture but is constrained by traditional thought processes. Employing the female reproductive system as an analogy, *Better Birthing Your Own Baby* maps out your ministry journey from conception to delivery.

Sinduction **(Amazon.com)**

Picture the scene with three main actors: Scrupulous, Simpleton, and Seductress. Scrupulous tells how Simpleton embarks on a thoughtless journey when quite unexpectedly he is met by the patrolling Seductress.

Bewitched by her evil eloquence, the pondering Simpleton sets out on a forbidden affair with her but soon learns that flirting with the sultry Seductress is not a joke, a prank, or a thrill.

In *Sinduction*, Cornelius Blake draws on all his expertise as a pastor and speaker to make you laugh, cry, and narrow your eyes, but most of all, think about the seriousness of your faith in Christ.

Notes

1   *The Success Principles*, Jack Canfield, 374.

2   Othnielle Blake (daughter).

3   *How Money Works*, Primercia, 12.

4   Bishop Wayne Malcolm, 23.

5   *The Success Principle*, 331–32.

Printed in Great
Britain
by Amazon